What Workers Want

What Workers Want

Richard B. Freeman
and Joel Rogers

ILR Press *an imprint of*

Cornell University Press *Ithaca and London*

Russell Sage Foundation *New York*

First published 1999 by Cornell University Press
First printing, Cornell Paperbacks, 1999

Printed in the United States of America

Library of Congress Cataloging-in-Publication Data
Freeman, Richard B. (Richard Barry), 1943–
What workers want / Richard B. Freeman & Joel Rogers.
   p.   cm.
Includes index.
ISBN 0-8014-3583-8 (cloth : alk. paper). — ISBN 0-8014-8563-0
(paper : alk. paper)
1. Job satisfaction — United States. 2. Employees — United States — Attitudes. I. Rogers, Joel, 1952–   . II. Title.
HF5549.5.J63F74 1999
331.2'095 — dc21   98-38848

Cornell University Press strives to use environmentally responsible suppliers and materials to the fullest extent possible in the publishing of its books. Such materials include vegetable-based, low-VOC inks and acid-free papers that are recycled, totally chlorine-free, or partly composed of nonwood fibers. Books that bear the logo of the FSC (Forest Stewardship Council) use paper taken from forests that have been inspected and certified as meeting the highest standards for environmental and social responsibility. For further information, visit our website at www.cornellpress.cornell.edu.

Cloth printing   10 9 8 7 6 5 4 3 2 1
Paperback printing   10 9 8 7 6 5 4 3 2 1

FSC FSC Trademark © 1996 Forest Stewardship Council A.C.
      SW-COC-098

To Jennifer Amadeo-Holl

and Alida Castillo-Freeman,

who did the work and kept

at least one of us sane

CONTENTS

List of Exhibits, ix

Acknowledgments, xiii

Chapter 1   Ask the People Who Live There, 1

Chapter 2   Finding Out What Workers Want, 15

Chapter 3   What Workers Want and Why They Don't Have It, 39

Chapter 4   How Workers Judge Unions, 65

Chapter 5   How Workers Judge Management, 90

Chapter 6   How Workers Judge Government Regulations, 117

Chapter 7   If Workers Could Choose, 140

Appendix A   Wave 1 of the WRPS: Structure and Methodology, 157

Appendix B   Wave 1 of the WRPS: Questionnaire, 159

Appendix C   Wave 2 of the WRPS: Structure and Methodology, 183

Appendix D   Wave 2 of the WRPS: Materials, 185

Appendix E   Wave 2 of the WRPS: Questionnaire, 190

Notes, 203

Index, 221

LIST OF EXHIBITS

Exhibit 2.1   The WRPS and its progeny: more than a survey, 37

Exhibit 3.1   Percentage of workers who are satisfied or dissatisfied with influence on workplace issues, 41

Exhibit 3.2   One-third of workers are dissatisfied, 44

Exhibit 3.3   Workers' loyalty and trust of their firm, 46

Exhibit 3.4   Percentage of workers with positive attitudes toward their jobs and firm, by satisfaction with influence on workplace decisions, 47

Exhibit 3.5   A big gap exists between the importance of wanting and having influence on workplace decisions, 48

Exhibit 3.6   Summated rating measures of how much influence workers want and have on workplace decisions (by groups of workers), 52

Exhibit 3.7   Some employees prefer individual voice; others prefer group voice, 55

Exhibit 3.8   Management cooperation perceived as essential, 57

Exhibit 3.9   Report card for managers, 61

Exhibit 4.1   Who wants unions? One-third of nonunion workers and almost all union members, 69

Exhibit 4.2   Percentage of workers who want unions (by characteristics of workers), 71

Exhibit 4.3   No simple explanation for why union members are more likely to vote union, 73

Exhibit 4.4   Union members are more likely to vote union than are former members with similar union experiences, 75

Exhibit 4.5   Percentage of union members satisfied with their union, 78

Exhibit 4.6   What do unions do for members?, 79

Exhibit 4.7   Percentage of union members satisfied with influence on local union and on workplace decisions, 80

Exhibit 4.8   Percentage of nonunion employees who want unions, 82

Exhibit 4.9   Predicting which nonunion employees would vote union, 84

Exhibit 4.10   Percentage of workers who want a strongly independent workplace organization (electing representatives and using arbitration to settle issues), 85

Exhibit 5.1   Modern human-resource policies are widespread, 92

Exhibit 5.2   Distribution of advanced human-resource practices, 96

Exhibit 5.3   Percentage of workers in the upper decile of firms with
               advanced human-resource practices, 98

Exhibit 5.4   Effective advanced human-resource practices and worker
               satisfaction go together, 99

Exhibit 5.5   The value of employee involvement (EI) to the firm, 104

Exhibit 5.6   Employee-involvement (EI) participants have more
               positive attitudes toward their work and
               management, 109

Exhibit 5.7   Employee involvement (EI) participation gives workers
               more influence on the job, 111

Exhibit 5.8   Representation/participation gap (by employee
               involvement [EI] status), 112

Exhibit 5.9   Employee involvement (EI) reduces workers' desire for an
               independent organization, 114

Exhibit 5.10   Unionized workers with employee involvement (EI) are
               more satisfied with their union, 115

Exhibit 6.1   Employees believe the law protects them when it
               doesn't, 119

Exhibit 6.2   Legal system produces many unsatisfied complainants
               compared with union and employer systems for solving
               problems, 125

Exhibit 6.3   Percentage of employees who go to the
               courts/agencies, 128

Exhibit 6.4   Workers want more legal protection, 130

Exhibit 6.5   Percentage of workers who say laws give too little
               protection to employees or put too few restrictions on
               management (by worker characteristics and workplace
               characteristics), 131

Exhibit 6.6   Workers' views of using arbitration to settle legal
               disputes, 134

Exhibit 6.7   The "ideal" arbitration system to settle employee disputes
               about legal rights, 136

Exhibit 6.8   Employees' views of workplace committees for workplace
               standards, 137

Exhibit 6.9   The "ideal" workplace committee system to enforce
               workplace standards, 139

Exhibit 7.1   Percentage of employees choosing attributes of an ideal
               organization, 142

Exhibit 7.2   Proportions of workers favoring a workplace organization
               with different degrees of independence from
               management, 147
Exhibit 7.3   Employee-management relations dominate workers' desire
               for independence of the employee organization, 149
Exhibit 7.4   Most workers want joint committees; more want unions
               than are unionized, 151
Exhibit 7.5   Percentage of workers who choose different ways to
               increase workers' say, 154

ACKNOWLEDGMENTS

In conducting the Worker Representation and Participation Study (WRPS) and writing this book, we had considerable help.

For the financing that made it possible, we thank the Russell Sage Foundation, the Joyce Foundation, the Alfred P. Sloan Foundation, and the Spencer Foundation.

For their counsel and patience in meeting our many requests or advice or data, we thank Paul Allaire, Marcella Berland, Elaine Bernard, Bruce Carswell, Joshua Cohen, Diane Colasanto, Phil Comstock, Dawn Crossland, John Dunlop, Sam Estreicher, Mike Farren, Larry Gold, Lydia des-Groseilliers, Larry Hugick, Susan Jessop, Jack Joyce, Michael Katz, Thomas Kochan, Susan Jessop, Randall MacDonald, Karyn Matchey, Angela McDermott, Nora Cate Schaeffer, Judy Scott, Barney Singer, Ernie Savoie, David Silberman, Elisabeth Smith, Andy Stern, Greg Tarpinian, Paula Voos, Ruy Teixeira, Joe Uehlein, Eric Wanner, Paul Weiler, Erik Olin Wright, and Cliff Zukin.

For extraordinary help throughout, special thanks to Diane Colasanto and the two people to whom we dedicate this book: Jennifer Amadeo-Holl and Alida Castillo-Freeman. Jennifer managed the process of developing the survey and producing the manuscript for the book. Alida did most of the actual data analysis relied on in the study, and is the master of the vagaries of the WRPS data set. They both worked long hours to help us complete this work. We are very grateful.

CHAPTER 1

Ask the People Who Live There

Do you like going to work? Do your firm's managers treat you and your coworkers fairly? Do you want to have a greater influence on the decisions that affect your job and workplace? If so, how do you think this would be best accomplished: By having more individual discussion with management? By electing a union to represent you? By being part of a worker committee that talks with management? By having more legal protection?

In the United States, more than in any other industrial democracy, how well you do in life depends on how you do in the job market and how your employer treats you and other workers. Americans spend more time at their workplaces than do the citizens of virtually any other developed country. The incomes and benefits from work determine living standards more than in other countries. Many benefits that governments universally guarantee citizens elsewhere — paid vacation, job training, and health insurance — are in the United States decided on at the workplace by employers. And the pay and conditions of work vary more across jobs in the United States than in other countries. Unions and collective bargaining, which require employers in particular fields of manufacture and service to comply with national standards, are relatively weak and limited. Only 10 percent of private-sector workers in the United States belong to unions, and collective-bargaining agreements are generally limited to unionized firms.[1] As a result, the difference between a "good" and a "bad" job in our labor system is greater than is the case for other countries. Our private employers have more authority in deciding how to treat their workers than do private employers in other advanced countries.

Despite the importance of jobs to American living standards and employer influence on the quality of jobs, however, the United States has not seriously examined the basic framework governing employee-employer relations in more than half a century. That framework was established in the 1930s and 1940s, when industrial factories with largely male workforces dominated the economy. The choice then was to encourage unionization and collective bargaining with management as the best way to deal with workplace governance. Today, the structure and demands of the economy are very different, unions are shadows of their former selves, and the law de facto reduces the chances of successful worker organization. Despite an outmoded labor system, however, America has not had a serious national discussion of how the workplace might be governed in the modern economy.[2]

Every few years or so, unions or management groups propose changes in our labor law, but usually these suggestions are limited to tinkering with the existing framework rather than fundamentally reforming it. In their weakened state, unions are suspicious of where an open-ended reform discussion might lead. Because business holds the upper hand over unions, it naturally prefers the present system, despite its inefficiencies. The reform discussions that typically result are classic inside-the-Beltway fights — deadly contested by the parties but generally ignored by the broader public. What is most striking about discussions of American labor policy is that those most affected by it—the workers themselves — are not even part of the discussion. This is indeed a strange situation — rather like having an election without bothering to count votes.

This book's goal is to move the discussion of the laws and rules that govern workplaces and the national debate on ways to improve that governance, so that it addresses what workers want, not what insiders want. The book arose from the fact that one of us (Richard Freeman) served on the Commission on the Future of Worker-Management Relations, a national body that the first Clinton administration appointed to consider some changes in labor law. Early on, the commission's hearings and discussion focused largely on what the insiders thought should be done in the area and seemed oblivious to what American workers might want. To bring the voice of the worker into the debate, we decided to undertake as objective and scientific a survey as we could of worker views toward how workplaces operated and how their workplaces might be improved. This book reports the findings of the Worker Representation and Participation Survey (WRPS).

We hope that the voice of American workers that emerges in *What Workers Want* will someday spur, and guide, a serious effort at reforming our national labor policy and developing the labor institutions and policies that fit modern workers and firms.

Some Background on the WRPS

The WRPS was an ambitious, sprawling project. We view it as the most extensive analysis of American worker attitudes toward workplace relationships and power in more than twenty years.[3] The study sought to determine the levels and kinds of representation and participation workers wanted within their firms; how workers rated existing institutions of workplace governance (for example, unions, management-led personnel policies, and government regulation) as satisfying their desires for representation and participation; and the types of reforms workers desired. It included managers but not top executives and many employees who did some supervision as part of their job.

The WRPS began with a set of focus groups with workers in similar occupations, followed by a half-hour national telephone survey of more than 2,400 workers. It concluded with a mail/telephone follow-up survey of some 800 of the original respondents. This follow-up survey probed earlier responses and gathered reactions to written information on potential labor-law reforms that had been provided in advance. Along the way, it entailed or spawned a number of related surveys, many national in their own right, that were undertaken to check or reproduce our results.[4] We have amassed a huge amount of data that should occupy researchers for some time to come.[5]

The WRPS was also a contentious project — contentious because labor relations are contentious and because, at least briefly, it appeared that our results might influence policy. The ways in which workers participate in a firm's decision-making — be it as individuals, through union representatives, or through other channels — are controversial because they involve the division of power at the workplace. Management and labor regularly argue over this division before Congress and administrative agencies. Certain phrases, code words, and jargon — right-to-work laws, company unions, striker replacement, teamwork, and even labor-law reform — evoke strong emotional reactions on both sides. Such reactions reflect dispute and tension at the ground floor, in the workplaces from which we drew our respondents to the survey. In such an atmosphere, finding out what American workers truly want by way of participation and representation on their job is difficult. Even assuming that we could get workers to talk to us about their jobs, we needed to be especially careful in phrasing our questions. All the usual issues that public-opinion researchers worry about — for instance, the wording of questions, the order in which they are asked, and the scaling of attitudes — could be critical in getting accurate answers.

The survey's potential influence on policy was through the Commission on the Future of Worker-Management Relations.[6] The commission was chaired by John Dunlop (the dean of American labor relations and, among many other things, a former secretary of labor) and was widely known as the "Dunlop Commission." He and other members of the commission welcomed our effort to bring workers' voices into the policy discussion. But both management and labor groups worried that the WRPS might yield findings inimical to their positions.

To navigate these tensions, we tried to ensure that the WRPS was not only fair and accurate but also perceived as such. We enlisted academic survey experts to serve as our informal advisors, and probably more important, we asked for the guidance of management and union representatives. Our operating premise was that only if both groups accepted the WRPS survey design as valid would it have much chance of accomplishing what we wanted: a respectful hearing of the views of American workers. How we worked with management and labor on the survey, and the lessons we learned from that experience, is a story in its own right. We hope to describe not just our findings but also the difficulty of bringing social science to bear in contested issues of public policy.

Basic Findings
So what did we learn? Here's the kind of say workers want in workplace decisions and the barriers they see to attaining it:

- American workers want more of a say/influence/representation/ participation/voice (call it what you will) at the workplace than they now have. We call the difference between the say that workers want and what they currently have the *representation/participation gap*. The gap varies among groups and across workplace issues, but it is ubiquitous.
- Employees want greater say both because they think it will directly improve the quality of their working lives and because they think it will make their firm more productive and successful (which also enhances their work lives over the long run).
- Employees want greater workplace participation as individuals and as part of a group as well. Generally, workers like the open-door policies, suggestion boxes, and other employer-based mechanisms that give them individual access to management. Indeed, on many issues they

prefer to deal with management individually. But on other issues, for example, workplace health and safety, pay and benefit plans — where problems affect workers as a group — , workers want to speak as a group. And here, as in general, workers believe that such collective voices will benefit the firm as well as them.

- Workers want *cooperative relations* with management. Approximately one-third of employees are displeased with how management treats workers, and many give management low scores in concern for employees, trustworthiness, and willingness to share power. But few workers believe that the long-run solution to these problems is institutionalized labor-management conflict. Rather, the vast majority think that a workplace organization can only be effective if it enjoys management participation and support. Employees want a positive relation with management, not a war.

- Workers want some measure of *independence and protection of that independence* in their dealings with management. Having cooperative relations with management does not mean saying "Yes, boss" to any employer wish; it entails some measure of joint decision-making. The ideal organizational form for this cooperation varies across different groups of workers. Union members want to maintain union representation, and many nonunion workers also favor a union. An even larger share of workers want some form of a labor-management committee that stops short of collective bargaining but in which they have some significant independence in selecting representatives and resolving disputes. Whereas most workers favor more government protection of employees, only a handful think it preferable to a workplace-based organization — an organization of the kind very few now have.

- Workers believe that *management resistance* is the primary reason they do not have their desired level of influence at the workplace. They give managers high marks for business competence but believe that most managements are unwilling to share power or permit much independence in worker decision-making. They know that management would fight them if they tried to form a union, and many believe that management opposes independent worker representatives even in advisory workplace committees.

Here's what workers think about the way current institutions of workplace governance and worker protection (unions, personnel policies, and government regulation) operate:

- Unionized workers strongly support their unions, and the vast majority would vote to retain them in an election for union representation. Members believe that local unions represent their interests well but are more skeptical of their national union, particularly when it comes to representing them in politics. Nonunion workers have a less positive view of unions, but about one-third would vote for a union if given the opportunity. Taking union and nonunion workers together, that translates to a private-sector unionization rate of 44 percent, or better than three times the rate of representation among those surveyed and almost five times the national private-sector unionization rate.[7]

- Workers generally welcome management-initiated employee involvement (EI) programs and other advanced human-resource policies, but most think that these programs do not go far enough in devolving authority to employees. Workers in companies with EI programs are more satisfied with their working lives and are less likely to want unions than other workers. But most participants in such programs believe that the programs would work better if management gave greater decision-making power to workers.

- Workers exaggerate their statutory rights at workplaces. They believe that almost anything that seems blatantly unfair is also illegal, when in fact national labor law allows many acts — for example, firing someone without any reason — that most would consider "unfair." Still, most workers seek greater government protection on the job, even while recognizing the burden this might place on the firm. More than one in twenty workers reported that they had brought complaints about their workplace to courts or regulatory agencies, and nearly one in ten said they had seriously thought of doing so. But workers are not particularly pleased with the legal system being the major forum for dealing with workplace problems: Most would prefer to resolve problems through workplace-based organizations or institutions and to have the option of using those organizations for more informal resolution of disputes.

Finally, workers are clear and consistent about the institutions or organizations they would like to see at their workplace:

- Most workers want an organization that is run jointly by employees and management, to which workers elect their own representatives and in which disputes between management and labor are resolved through independent arbitration rather than management discretion.

- The vast majority of workers want the option of resolving problems concerning legal rights at their workplace through arbitration, and most said that they would use such an alternative dispute-resolution system rather than going to court or an administrative agency. But workers do not want firms to be allowed to require that workers forgo their rights to legal redress in favor of company-instituted arbitration systems as a condition for employment. Most workers also favor supplementing current enforcement of labor laws and standards through workforce-based regulatory committees, which would have some power to enforce labor laws and standards.
- Given a choice between improving their position at the workplace through labor-management committees, unions, or other employee organizations that collectively bargained with management or increased government regulation, about 25 percent of workers would choose union or unionlike organizations, and about 15 percent would opt for more regulation. Some 60 percent would prefer labor-management committees, where workers would have varying degrees of independence from management, often including electing representatives and carrying disagreements with management to an outside arbitrator. Overall, 45 percent of employees want a strongly independent workplace organization (which only unions provide in the current system), 43 percent want an organization with more limited independence from management, and the remaining workers want a workplace in which management alone rules.

And here's what the managers had to say:

- Managers broadly confirm worker assessment of their unwillingness to share power. Many are anti-union. Many oppose programs that would keep them from making the final decisions about workplace governance.
- At the same time, much of management favors a more substantial employee voice in joint committees. Perhaps most striking, nearly one-half of managers said that they favored employees electing their own representatives to such committees.

That workers (and managers) have these views may be surprising to some and annoying to many. Managers might be irritated that workers give them such poor marks for sharing power, that the vast majority of workers want some independence from them, and that unions are so popular with their members. Or maybe they'd be angry that half of their colleagues seem to think a bit of democracy through employees electing people to advisory committees is a good thing. Unions, or those believing in old-fashioned class struggle, might be annoyed to learn that workers just don't think workplace organization is achievable without management acceptance, that they seek a cooperative relation with managers, and that they are vitally concerned about the health of their firms.

However you respond to the preceding findings, we hope that this book will convince you that workers have consistent views on, and strong desires for, a workplace-relations system quite different from what now exists. They want a more varied system of participation and representation with a more cooperative and equal relationship to management.

We believe that a system of labor relations consistent with these views is both desirable and feasible for America. We think it would certainly make workers happier, and would probably make firms more productive. But *What Workers Want* is not about arguing for that system; it is not about limning its institutional features or strategizing about how workers, unions, and firms might achieve it. Rather, and more simply, this book seeks to open the discussion by being as clear and accurate as possible on the worker aspirations that would provide its motivation and support.

Why Care about What Workers Want?

Why do we think that finding out what workers want is worth an entire research project and ultimately a book?

We did not ask this question when we began our research. It seemed obvious that in a capitalist democracy in which nearly everyone earns his or her living as a worker, finding out what workers wanted on the job was the sine qua non of developing good labor policies at the company or national level. But in the course of our work, critics and skeptics sometimes put "Why care?" questions to us.

Why care what employees want at the workplace when long-term jobs are a thing of the past? We'll call this the "death of the job" objection, in reference to a *Fortune* magazine story on the topic.[8]

Why care when employees who are dissatisfied with their workplace can always switch to another one? We'll call this the "take this job and shove it" objection, after the country and western song.

Why care about workplace governance at all when overall employment and income are booming in the United States as they were when we wrote this book? We'll call this the "it's the economy, stupid" objection, after the Clinton campaign theme.

And why care what ordinary workers want, when management and labor experts know better about how to design systems of workplace governance and labor laws? We'll call this the "father knows best" objection.

Implicit in these questions are strong views or beliefs about how American labor markets function, and the way in which public policy is and perhaps should be determined. Some of these views are simply wrong; others are inconsistent or, more kindly, not readily commensurate with our country's democratic ideals. But such views are definitely out there. So before presenting our findings about what workers want, we will now take a moment to respond to these objections to the very task we have set for ourselves.

Death of the Job?

Consider first the belief that workers now change jobs so frequently and are so minimally involved in firms that it is silly to look to them for concern or knowledge about ways to improve labor-management relations. This view imagines the firm as a nexus of short-term contracts between capital and skills, suppliers and purchasers. The firm is virtual, hiring contingent workers or consultants for specific projects for most activities. In such a world, workers flit like mayflies from one employer to another, and people lack the information, interest, or standing to provide instruction on workplace governance.

This story has both a critical version and a celebratory one. The critical version stresses the rise in contingent work and subcontractor relations, in which workers lose fringe benefits and protection of some labor laws. The celebratory one exalts independent professionals working at home on short-term contracts — the epitome of the medieval artisan. Common to both versions is the conviction that managers and workers simply do not spend enough time together to develop valid expectations of one another. The romantic equivalent would be leading a life of bar-hopping, one-night stands, and short-term dating rather than entering a permanent relationship.

Despite the popularity of this spot-market view of the U.S. job market, it is wrong. Contingent work and subcontracting have certainly become more important. Temporary help agencies are among the fastest-growing firms. Management consultants, who often hire young professionals for short-term intensive work, are another growth area. Some especially prominent and talented workers — professional athletes under free agency, for example, or recording stars shopping for new labels, or CEO turnaround artists — make bundles under short-term contracts in which their unique skills command unique compensation. Today a Red Sox, tomorrow a Brewer, and next week a Yankee.

These situations are not the norm in the United States, however, nor are they likely to become so in the foreseeable future. Contrary to the claim that the job is dead, the typical American employee still works for the same company for many years (as the staff at *Fortune* themselves undoubtedly do) and thus has good reason to care about how his or her firm performs and how it handles its workplace relations.[9] Respondents to the WPRS reported, on average, that they had been with their current employer for 7.6 years. On standard statistical assumptions, their job tenure — the time they stay with one employer — will average twice as long, or about fifteen years.[10]

Also, the link between an employee and a firm, moreover, is not just a function of time but of the position that the worker holds in the firm and the firm's reliance on that individual. Take the case of supervision, certainly an important firm function. To a striking degree, American firms spread supervisory tasks widely in the workforce. Some 15 percent of WRPS respondents identified themselves as managers, engaged in supervision more or less full time; 31 percent of nonmanagerial employees reported that they supervised other workers as part of their job. Weighting these as shares of our respondent groups, 41 percent of American workers engage in some supervisory activity. At the very least, these are not casual or contingent workers but a critical part of the firm's stock of human capital.

Consistent with these facts, better than 60 percent of WRPS respondents describe their current job as long term or as an opportunity for advancement in the same company. Only 15 percent view their job as part of a career or profession that will probably take them to different companies. But even these workers, who might best fit the spot-market view of virtual corporations, are concerned about how their workplace functions. They might be with the firm only a few years, but those years can be critical in their acquiring the skills needed to advance in their career. And how the firm treats them even during limited periods can still make their lives enjoyable or miserable.

The remaining quarter or so of employees describe their job as something that they will probably leave — a short-term or noncareer position. Nearly one-half of these workers were eighteen to twenty-four years of age;

most were in wholesale/retail trade; most made $200 or less a week. They are in the early search phase of their work lives, or are part of the low-skilled group who have, in recent years, suffered the worst wage losses in the U.S. job market.

Still, it is possible that while the spot-market description of firm relations is wrong, the lack of attachment to firms that it predicts might be right. Perhaps even workers who are with a firm for many years don't give a damn about how it's doing. But this is not so. More than one-half of non-managerial employees describe themselves as having a lot of loyalty to their company, compared with 15 percent who say they have only a little loyalty or no loyalty at all.[11] An even larger portion of managerial employees have a lot of loyalty to the firm, as do employees with greater tenure. To be sure, employees report greater loyalty to their immediate supervisors and to fellow employees than to the firm itself; managers also report greater loyalty to their supervisors and to the people who work for them than to the firm. But overall, the majority of workers report that they have a lot of loyalty to the firm itself.

In short, employees have good reasons to be concerned about workplace governance, and top management has good reason to know those concerns. The two groups are going to be living together, and depending on each other, for quite a while.

Take This Job and Shove It

If the spot-market view of American labor is fundamentally misleading, so, too, is the easy-exit view. This view contends that the labor market is like a consumption market: an environment in which employees can switch companies as costlessly as consumers switch the supermarket where they buy groceries. If the job market were like a supermarket, a worker unhappy at a given workplace could readily move on to the next employer. If his or her current employer was able to determine what it was doing wrong — a big "if" when workers leave[12] — the firm would presumably change, or face the consequences of a shortfall of workers and lost productivity, market share, profitability, and so on.

For most workers, however, telling the employer to "take this job and shove it" is easier said than done. While the United States has one of the most mobile workforces in the world, most workers, as we've just seen, stay with the same employer for a long time. Most workers have invested a lot in their job. It's easy to quit if you are in a low-paying job; you probably won't lose much, and you might end up in a better job. It's easy to quit if you are an unattached young professional or craftsperson whose skills are salable and who has no family concerns in changing location. But it's not so easy when your career is tied to a particular firm and you have bills to pay, kids to raise, or a spouse or partner working in the same locale. Given the relatively low social safety net and employer provision of many benefits at work, workers cannot afford to leave jobs lightly. Leave your job and you lose your health insurance and, if you are not vested, your pension rights. Voluntary quitters are not eligible for unemployment benefits. In the United States, more so than in other advanced capitalist nations, income depends on the particular job one has: Easy exit is not an option for most workers.

For most American employees, then, the opportunity for improving their position is not exit but voice — staying in the employment relationship and communicating or bargaining individually or collectively for desired changes.[13] The analogy with a personal relationship is clear. When you have a problem with your spouse or partner, you can take the easy-exit option and split, or you can stay and talk about the problem and bargain over a solution. Whenever the benefits of a mutual relationship exceed the uncertain benefits of breaking that relationship, it is better to talk and improve the relationship than to break up and start anew.[14] The same holds true for employee-firm relations at the workplace, where the possibility for discussion and change depend critically on worker voice and bargaining power. When both workers and management have some say in decision-making, each group has an incentive to be forthcoming about their problems and preferences, rendering discussion valuable. By contrast, when all the power at a workplace resides with one side, it is often better to keep information to oneself: Why give management facts that it might use for its benefit but not for yours?[15]

It's the Economy, Stupid

The "Why care?" question we have heard most frequently concerns the overall performance of the U.S. economy. Why worry about employee concerns about workplace relations when the national income and employment aggregates look so favorable? (At this writing, low unemployment, rapid employment growth, and low inflation has created the best aggregate economy in fifty years, according to the chairman of the Federal Reserve.) Isn't the economy's overall performance more important in how the average American will fare than what goes on at a particular workplace? Won't any change in U.S. labor relations risk upsetting the economy that is doing well for everyone?

If the economy were doing well for everyone, we might agree with this objection. As important as the quality of work and workplace relations are to employee self-esteem and well-being, full employment and rising incomes are arguably the more important guarantor of living standards. So if the benefits of American economic growth went more or less equitably to all employees, or if changing workplace relations in the ways workers want would upend the economy, perhaps we should not care what workers want in the form of representation and participation at their place of employment.

But the fact is that American workers are not getting their fair share of our economy's benefits. For most American workers, real hourly pay has stagnated or declined for more than a generation, whereas in other advanced countries workers' earnings have risen during that same period.[16] The level of income inequality in the United States has skyrocketed, making the country's economy the most unequal in the developed world. For example, data from the Organization for Economic Cooperation and Development (OECD) show that the top 10 percent of U.S. workers earn 5.6 times as much as the bottom 10 percent. By contrast, the top 10 percent of workers in the European Union or Japan earn, respectively, 2.1 and 2.4 times as much.[17] The United States is, by this simple measure, almost three time more unequal than the world's other great centers of capitalism.

Full-time workers near the bottom of the American wage structure are particularly badly off compared with their peers in the European Union or Japan. American poverty rates are the highest in the developed world, and while the number of professional, managerial, and technical jobs has increased greatly, so, too, has the number of low-paying jobs with no benefits. It is shameful that "prisoner" is just about the fastest-growing "occupation" in the United States, the "trade" of more than 2 percent of American men.

Consider that from 1979 to 1996, peak to peak in the business cycle, U.S. gross domestic product (GDP) increased some $2.5 trillion in real (1996) terms — a gain in average family income of $6,360. But almost two-thirds of that gain went to the top 5 percent of families, whose income rose more than $72,000 on average, and virtually all the rest of the gain went to other families in the top two-fifths of the distribution. As a result, average income of families in the bottom 60 percent of the income distribution was actually lower in 1996 than in 1979. Rather than falling with economic growth, poverty actually increased. The "rising tide lifts all boats" effect of economic growth — the belief that growth benefits all and reduces poverty — ceased to work in the past two decades.[18] It lifted the yachts but sank the dinghies.

No one knows precisely why this happened. Some people blame increased trade with Third World countries. Some people blame technological change. Some blame immigration. But surely workplace relations and the ability of workers to influence decisions at their firm are a major part of the story. Far from being a reason not to worry about workplace relations, recent U.S. economic performance gives every reason to look at those relations closely, in the hope that they might help us to alleviate the one big flaw in our economic performance: the concentration of the gains of growth among the very few.

Father Knows Best

Finally, we come to the "father knows best" view, the idea that matters of workplace governance are best left to the "experts" — be they of the management, union, government, or academic variety — and that there is little to be learned from nonexpert workers. You mean you don't know what a Section 8(a)(3) violation is? Don't tell me how you want your workplace changed! You say you don't know what the Seventh Circuit said about sexual harassment claims last week? How dare you think you've got something to say about the dilemmas faced by working women! Leave it to the experts; they're the ones who know what they're talking about.

We respect expertise. Indeed, we count ourselves among the experts. Which leads us to reject the "father knows best" view more or less completely. As researchers in labor relations, we know that the expert does not in fact know best. The employment relation is dense, rich, and particular. It involves human beings, not arcane law arguments or abstract economic models. Experts can usefully remind everyone that we're operating under a different economy from the one we had in the 1930s — a different economy with different people in it. But even the greatest expert in the world cannot say what that implies for Harry or Juan or Mary's workplace without listening pretty closely to those workers themselves. Experts on workers should heed the wisdom Dr. Spock, the baby specialist, who told worried young mothers: "I don't know your baby nearly as well as you do." Workers know their workplace a lot better than any expert does.

So for those who'd really like to know how to improve the American workplace, we can confidently recommend this: Ask the people who live there! This is what we did in the WRPS. *What Workers Want* tells you what we found.

CHAPTER 2

Finding Out What Workers Want

So, how do researchers determine the kinds of changes a hundred million American workers would like to see in hundreds of thousands of workplaces?

One way, attractive to certain academics, is to sit in an office and ponder what some theory of capitalism tells us workers want. Marxists thought they knew what workers wanted: the destruction of capitalism and the creation of socialist heaven. Some competitive-market theorists think they know what workers want: what they now have, for otherwise the workers would switch jobs until they found the employer that provided the desired workplace arrangements.

Another way, attractive to journalists, is to interview a few selected people. Lunch-pail Lou. Manager Mary. Programmer Pete. With more time, one can mimic Studs Terkel, author of the best-selling oral history *Working*, and interview in depth a few dozen employees around the country.[1] Or one can do what former university president John Coleman did in the 1970s: leave your normal profession and try different jobs in which you interact with coworkers.

A third way, attractive to politicians, is to hire a polling firm to add a one-line question or two to their standard battery: "Are you satisfied with your job?" or "Who do you think can better deal with labor issues, the president or Congress?" Hire a consultant to interpret the results: "And so, boss, what you should be saying on TV tonight is A, because the opposition's vulnerability is B. Here's the wedge issue for our side, and the best sound bite to raise it."

All of these approaches have some value, but had we followed any of them we trust that you would not have accepted our results as anything approaching a systematic and objective representation of the views of American workers. And for our part, we wouldn't have had the chutzpah to ask you to. General theories of labor markets or class struggle can be elegant and exciting, but they often prove vacuous or misleading when it comes to understanding actual workplace practice (again, "father" does not know best, in part because he just doesn't have the details). Intense discussions with small groups of workers can be instructive as to how people are thinking, but such anecdotal evidence is unlikely to represent the views of the broader population of workers. And standard opinion polls, while useful for lobbying, in attack ads, and for gaining some sense of people's everyday anxieties, usually call for snap reactions more than considered judgments. Answers may be sensitive to question wording and sequence and might change when people have more information or time to think about the issues.

Our goal for the Worker Representation and Participation Survey (WRPS) was more ambitious. We wanted it to represent, accurately, the views of the whole of the workforce. We wanted it to capture attitudes on a wide range of workplace issues: human-resource and personnel practices, different modes of representation and participation, legal regulation and alternative means of enforcing the law. And we wanted to allow respondents to reflect on their answers and digest and respond to new information. To bring the American worker's voice into the nation's labor-policy debate, the WRPS, we knew, would require scientific validity beyond your run-of-the-mill opinion poll. On the dynamics of workplace power, it had to be the "mother of all workplace surveys."

As already noted, however, we had to be especially careful because labor policy is an area of such bitter dispute and because our survey threatened to have consequence. In addition to being squeaky clean academically, we needed to involve the protagonists of labor policy in the survey design. In standard academic studies, one worries about scientific critiques. Professor X might question sample design; Professor Y might worry about the sequencing of questions; Professor X^2 might wonder why we did not ask about her pet problem; and Professor Y^2 might criticize us for not using his favorite high-powered statistical technique to analyze the data. Criticism is the name of the game in seminars and classrooms throughout the country, and well it should be. Knowing that other researchers will look for flaws in your work pushes every researcher toward greater rigor and care. But the WRPS risked criticism of a different kind as well: politically motivated attacks where unions or management disagreed with the findings. Their concerns rest mainly with whether the views presented go against those of the AFL-CIO Executive Council, the Business Roundtable, the National Association of Manufacturers, the National Federation of Independent

Business, the Chamber of Commerce, or a host of other groups. If they do, the findings have to be wrong — or at least attacked as if they were wrong.

What to do?

We proceeded with care. Our initial scheme was simple. We would convene focus groups around the country to discuss workplace issues. Based on what we learned from these groups, we would develop a questionnaire and survey a representative sample of employees. To find out how these workers viewed proposed policy reforms, we thought we might produce a short instructional video (one of us wanted to be a Hollywood producer, if only for a day) that would explain these reforms and give examples of how they might work. We'd distribute the video to our sample, employees would watch it on their home VCRs, and then we'd ask them what they thought. Finally, to make sure we interpreted responses properly, we planned to hold focus-group meetings after the survey to discuss our conclusions.

We asked a number of experts in survey research to help us plan the survey, and we interviewed several survey research firms that would administer the project. Some were allied with Democrats and labor, others with Republicans and business. Some were less attentive than we wanted to the difficulties of getting at the data we sought. After a number of these meetings, we finally settled on Diane Colasanto and Princeton Survey Research Associates. In addition to being tireless, and smart, Diane and PSRA were politically neutral in a way many polling firms are not. She also seemed genuinely interested in the project's objective, not just in the fee our foundation supporters could provide. And, as if to clinch the deal, she was a former academic who had researched and taught survey design, and was thus fully current on the sometimes arcane methodological concerns that troubled us. Unlike many pollsters, she actually knew Professors X and X^2 — even the supercritical Professor Y^2.

Focus Groups

Setting up focus groups sounds simple. You invite some people to meet somewhere to talk about something you want to learn about. You give them coffee or soda and sandwiches and cookies, and you listen to what they have to say. Afterward you review a tape or transcript of the session, and *presto!* you now know what America thinks about a particular issue. If you are a politician of a certain type, you get an extra dividend: After deep deliberation, you finally know what you yourself think about that issue!

But it's not quite that easy. Many decisions in organizing a focus group can affect what people say and what you learn from them. The first decision is to determine the composition of the group itself. Should it include a heterogeneous collection of workers, whose variety reflects the working population as a whole? Or should it consist of a more homogeneous collection defined along the lines of common race, sex, occupation, age, or whatever? This decision is important not only because variation in the group can affect the questions that the researcher can pursue in depth but also because the group's composition can affect what participants had to say. Women and minorities often speak less in a group that mixes sexes or races than in one that does not. Blue-collar workers might talk differently in the presence of professionals or managers than in their absence. Young workers might feel uneasy criticizing seniority rules in the presence of older workers. And so on.

In addition to deciding who's in the group, issues about how to guide the discussion in useful ways also need to be resolved. It's important that everyone in a focus group gets a chance to talk, but some people are more comfortable speaking, and they often speak much more than others. Unless the group discussion is sufficiently focused, and the group facilitator sufficiently disciplined and forceful, the meeting can degenerate into the dictatorship of the blabbermouth. But there is also a danger that the group facilitator might exert too much influence on how discussion proceeds, inducing responses rather than letting them arise naturally. For instance, if we thought that workers were particularly upset about how firms regard issues of workplace safety, we could instruct the focus-group leader to ask bluntly, "Who's upset about safety?" Or we could allow the focus-group leader to talk generally about issues that make people happy and unhappy at workplaces and hope the safety issue arises by itself.

Yet another issue is how to deal with situations when the group is confused about the facts. Ought the facilitator to introduce expert knowledge about the information in question, or should he or she let the workers' confusion run its course? In the case of workplace safety, what should one do if everyone in the group agrees that the United States has the best workplace safety record in the world, when in fact its record ranks poorly among those of advanced countries? Or what if everyone in the group thinks that half of the U.S. workforce is unionized, or that American labor laws provide certain protections when in fact they do not? If you do not intervene, the discussion may give an accurate picture of how people view matters at a particular moment but not what they would think if provided the evidence necessary to make an informed decision. If you intervene by correcting misconceptions, you risk putting one or two facts before the group, but not the full spectrum of evidence on an issue.

To prepare for our focus groups, one of us attended a meeting of employees organized by a pro-union research group in New York City. These employees were divided by gender: Women met separately from men. Listening to the discussion behind a one-way mirror (standard practice in focus-group research) taught us two things in developing the WRPS focus groups.

The first lesson was that sex and race are less important in talking about one's job than is occupation. Gender might matter in many areas of discourse, but when it came to workplace issues, the major variation in attitudes among these people was by occupation rather than by demographic characteristic. Female blue-collar workers had similar concerns to male blue-collar workers. Female professionals and managers had similar concerns to male professionals and managers. Blue-collar workers were interested in unions; white-collar workers were not. The only demographic factor that mattered considerably was that blacks in all fields of work favored unions more than whites.

The second lesson was that whereas employees know a lot about their workplace, their knowledge tails off quickly on issues and people related to the Washington labor scene. Consider the following exchange at a session with women workers in New York City:

> Focus-Group Leader: "Can anyone here name a living American union leader?
> *Dead silence.*
> Women Worker 1: "There's that Puerto Rican man who leads the hospital workers, but I don't know his name."[2]
> Focus group leader: "Anyone else?"
> *Dead silence.*
> Focus Group Leader: "Well, has anyone heard of Lane Kirkland?" (the then-head of the AFL-CIO, nominally the nation's most prominent trade union leader).
> Woman Worker 2: E-laine Kirkland? I know her. That's the fat lady who did the grapefruit diet on Oprah Winfrey last week."

Unbelievable?

Believe it. In highly unionized New York City, workers, including union members, hadn't a clue about the man who was the longest-presiding leader of the AFL-CIO since Samuel Gompers spoke oodles about the presence of American labor leadership in the public. It told us to direct the WRPS at the issues employees faced at their workplace, about which they had direct knowledge, and to stay away from references to Washington policy debates. If we were to find out how workers felt about potential alternative dispute-resolution systems or possible changes in the National Labor Relations Act (the Wagner Act of 1935), we would have to provide information about how those specifics would affect their working lives. Reflecting this, the WRPS contains a lot of "How are you/your employer doing at your workplace?" questions and very few "How are employers or employees in America doing?" questions.

For our focus groups, we assembled workers by occupation and varied the regions of the country from which they were drawn. The occupations covered were (1) less skilled workers in small firms (participants included a cashier, a cook, a waiter, a porter, a roofer, and an automotive service worker), (2) less skilled service workers in large firms (a cable technician, a janitor, a deli clerk, a cocktail waitress, and a truck driver), (3) manufacturing workers (a machinist, a tool designer, a pipe fitter, a metal polisher, a warehouse worker, and a forklift operator), (4) low- to mid-level office workers (a financial database analyst, a customer sales representative, a bookkeeper, and an insurance underwriter), (5) knowledge workers (a defense analyst, a computer software engineer, a medical technologist, and a computer programmer and technical writer), and (6) middle managers (from firms ranging from steel manufacturers to health-care providers to retail and computer support services). We held two groups in each of the following locations: Charlotte, North Carolina (Groups 2 and 4); Pittsburgh (Groups 3 and 6); and San Diego (Groups 1 and 5). These groups discussed workplace issues in February of 1994, while we watched from behind the one-way mirrors.

What the Focus Groups Said

It is standard practice in focus-group analysis for the professional firm that conducts the meetings to review the outcomes and offer a summary interpretation of what the people said. This qualitative assessment is based both on particularly memorable or insightful comments and on a general sense of how the meetings went. Princeton Survey Research Associates summarized the comments and meetings as follows:

- Focus-group participants were eager to talk about conditions in the workplace and their relationship with management. (This was good news for us, as interest in talking about these issues was critical to doing a lengthy telephone survey on them.)
- Workers pleased with their employer cited a responsive boss and policies and practices that eased communication with management and gave workers some say in the firm's decisions. (This began to tell us what workers were looking for.)
- Most participants believed that companies undervalued worker input and effort and expressed some distrust of management, and many complained that management was not communicating well with them about what was happening at the workplace. (This told us that issues of voice and representation, on which the WRPS was to probe, were indeed important to workers.)
- Many workers viewed new forms of worker representation or participation suspiciously. (This alerted us to the problem of getting workers to assess alternative institutions — a point that labor and management representatives reinforced strongly.)
- Workers recognized and accepted that the reason companies exist is to make a profit, and that bottom-line considerations must dominate management decisions. (This told us that regardless of the changes workers wanted in their participation in the firm's decision-making, they understood that these changes needed to fit into competitive business operations.)

Beyond the points highlighted by PSRA, however, what most impressed us was the wide variation in each group in the quality of labor-management relations that employees experienced. In nearly every group, one or two workers would tell a glowing story about good relations between workers and management at their workplace. Maybe there was an employee-involvement (EI) program that was working well or a management that empowered workers to make important decisions, or that did something else that showed that managers viewed workers as a company asset. Other employees would look at them and sigh: "You're really lucky. I've got nothing like that where I am." At which point someone would invariably say, "Why is that? Why such a difference?" To which nobody had an answer, except "That's just the way it is."

From these discussions, we drew three conclusions that played a major role in developing our national survey.

The first conclusion was that any labor policy or practice must allow for the substantial diversity in the American workforce and in the concerns workers had about their jobs.

Blue-collar workers had different specific worries from those of white-collar workers. Factory workers were troubled about safety conditions and job security, and recognized that the market dictated some trade-offs between them. "We know there are violations of OSHA [Occupational Safety and Health Administration] regulations, but if the union demanded change, it might just put the company out of business," said one factory worker in our Pittsburgh meeting. White-collar employees worried more about job security and opportunities for advancement. "The new CEO says he's more geared toward employees," commented one, "but in this last lay-off he was looking for people over fifty. Those were the people he wanted to get rid of. So everybody over fifty basically was gone, which makes you think about what will happen after you put in the time." Knowledge employees generally had a sense that their skills gave them some employment security, although not security at a particular job. A defense analyst in San Diego ruefully reported his previous boss once making this credible threat: "Do any of you want to leave? Go ahead, we can replace you in five minutes." But many of these workers could get a job fairly quickly.

The least-skilled, though, were something else entirely. Here job insecurity, and consciousness of being expendable, combined to produce a sort of despairing anger. In focus groups that we found difficult to observe, these employees felt lucky to have a job; they seemed afraid to think about it much and beaten down by the job market. A food service worker in Charlotte complained of feeling "walked on":

I'm the welcome mat. I must have welcome printed on my forehead or something, because I get the crap jobs to do, and I'm the one that gets — I mean, I've been through three stores in the past year, and they just all treat me bad. [My present employer] thinks their employees are expendable. . . . And I'm the type of person, I've taken too much crap for too long, and I ain't gonna shut up no more; I'm gonna stand up exactly for what I believe in, and on that day he told me that . . . I said, "I don't agree with you," and I said, "If that's the way you think, you can kiss my butt, and I'll leave." But I'm still there.

A custodial worker commented, "[In] every job, mostly every job I've had, management always felt like there's too many people out there that need jobs for us to have to put with you, you know, put up with you. Well, you either do what we say, or we'll let you go and it wouldn't be hard to fill it in, you know."

In short, the focus groups gave real faces and voices to the inequality of the U.S. earnings distribution that we described in Chapter 1 — the division of our society into the "haves" and the "have-nots." Inequality shows up not simply in earnings but also in the way people look at their jobs, their employers, and the way they interact with their employers.

Second, although most employees are committed to their firm and want to contribute more to their workplace than they are doing, there is discontent about how firms run workplaces that surfaces when employees start talking about specific issues and problems. In the first few minutes of general discussion, most people said that their workplace was OK: "I have no real complaints. I'm pretty satisfied." But when the discussion moved to specific issues — for instance, independence on the job, communication with management, and safety — people began raising problems. Employees have a clear notion of what constitutes a good employer, and many found their firm falling short of this notion. Many workers said their firm had an EI program, total quality management, teams or quality circles, or whatever label management had chosen, and they welcomed these initiatives. But a few thought the programs a complete hoax, and most felt the programs failed to live up to their promise. As participants got more comfortable with the discussion, they volunteered all sorts of problems. This is how our Charlotte focus group ended:

Moderator: "I'm done. I've covered everything I need to cover. . . . Is there anything else you want to tell me?"
Participant 1: "Oh, yeah, a couple little stories in . . . " *(laughter)*
Participant 2: "I've realized how much I mistrust my employer, and I don't think about that on a regular basis."
Participant 3: "That's true."
Participant 4: "And that's depressing."
Participant 1: "It's like wearing blinders."
Participant 3: "Yeah."
Participant 5: "Because in the beginning I was like 'my company's perfect.'"
Moderator: "Well, you did say that in the beginning."

Participant 1: "But I think you now realize there's some things that . . . "
Participant 5: *(interrupting)* "Yeah"
Participant 4: "It's not our life."
Participant 1: "But you can't have a life . . . "
Participant 4: *(interrupting)* "Without it."

That people changed their tone in talking about workplace problems as the focus groups proceeded confirmed our unease with standard job satisfaction questions that fail to probe attitudes about workplace specifics. For our survey to work, we would require much more time and attention from respondents than the standard opinion poll.

Third, after reflection or discussion, we found that employees can specify the type of representation or participation they want at the workplace. The focus group of white-collar employees in Charlotte was again the most striking. The discussion started with several employees making a clear statement about workplace representation, along the following lines: "We're southerners. We don't like unions [the image of a fat balding union leader with a mustache seemed to float in the air, not Norma Rae], so let's not talk about them." "Fine, let's not talk about unions," said the focus-group leader. "Is everything fine at your workplace, or do you have problems you wish you could address with management?"

These employees went on to raise a host of problems regarding their say in their job and how their firm was run. "We wouldn't dare go to management on these issues by ourselves." "Why not?" "They'd label us troublemakers." "So, what should you do?" "Elect someone to take our concerns to management. But the spokesperson would have to say he had no problems and was just telling management what others thought, or else his career would be endangered . . . on second thought, maybe it would be safer and less disruptive to hire an outsider, though there might be other problems with that."

Shades of a trade union!

Other focus-group discussions, however, went in different directions. The knowledge workers in San Diego did not want any collective solution to their problems. And the least skilled seemed to be too beaten down to imagine that they could improve their lot. If we hadn't fully appreciated it before, this brought home to us the fact that for a country and workforce as heterogeneous as ours, no single design for workplace representation or participation was likely to be effective nationwide. One shoe of a single style and size would never fit the diverse feet of the American workforce.

Double-Checking, Moving On

Some weeks later, we wondered whether we and PSRA had drawn the right broad conclusions from the discussions. Could it be that we heard what we expected or wanted to hear or paid too much attention to the most articulate at the exclusion of the soft-spoken? To check our conclusions, we hired two students to watch videotapes of the focus groups and to code the responses of employees along various dimensions. This gave us a quantitative measure of what people said to complement PSRA and our qualitative reading of the results. The student coding told us that the professional focus-group report and our impressions were on target. People had areas of discontent. They wanted more say at their workplace. They differed, along occupational and educational lines, on the issues that concerned them most. And they had some ideas, albeit vague ones, about the changes that might resolve their job problems and improve their working lives.

Of course, the comments of sixty-odd employees in six focus groups is scarcely representative of the American workforce. But the point of holding focus-group meetings was not to reach any general conclusions but to shape our inquiry. The groups gave us a better sense of (1) the sorts of issues that seemed to concern a large number of employees and (2) the ways that people talked about those issues. They also gave us a sense of the difficulties of getting answers to problems at the workplace right away, and thus the need for conducting fairly lengthy interviews with workers and for posing probing questions on specific issues. And the focus groups told us which issues were more or less susceptible to easy answers, and thus which questions should be asked as close-ended (whereby the interviewer asks the respondent to give one of a specified set of alternatives) or open-ended (whereby respondents answer in their own way, and the interviewer transcribes what they say and codes it later).

So, equipped with what we had learned, we proceeded to draft our national telephone survey. This included numerous questions on current workplace practices and numerous questions on possible reforms.

Hold It!

Our next step was to ask the business and labor advisors we had recruited but hadn't yet met with as a group to review our survey and general project design. Again, we wished to include them early on so as to get the benefit of their wisdom and to minimize possible future objections. At this early point in the process, we thought we had matters pretty well in hand. The focus-group results were instructive and verified. We had an excellent pollster working with us. The kinds of questions we needed to ask were pretty clear, and we were confident that we knew how to ask them.

At a meeting in Washington, D.C., we presented our plan of action. In the room were people on opposing sides of what some might call "the great class war" — employers and business lobbyists, trade union presidents and staff. Many of those on one side knew those on the other; they'd been fighting on Capitol Hill for years. Going into the meeting, our principal concern was that it would descend to aimless wrangling. How could we keep the two sides focused on improving the survey rather than arguing with each other?

The meeting went in an utterly different direction. It wasn't business and labor arguing against each other; it was business and labor united against the way we planned to find out what changes workers might want:

Business Lobbyist: "That will never work. There are so many problems with what you want to do that I don't know where to begin. For starters, you can't show a video of how laws or rules will work at the workplace and ask people to judge them, and get anything I'd believe. Who's going to play the manager — a fat balding guy with a mustache?"

Union President: "I agree. You can't do that. Who's going to play the union organizer — a fat balding guy with a mustache? You'll never get people's real views. They'll go for whoever looks like Robert Redford."

Employer: "You've got to be careful about how you give information to people. It's easy to get the answers you want. . . . I know." *(ha, ha)*

Union Lobbyist: "Lots of workers will be scared to answer your survey. How do they know this isn't a company scheme to find out who might favor a union?"

Business and Labor in Unison: "It's OK to ask people about their workplace and relations with management, but you cannot ask them to think about policy reforms. You can't ask hypotheticals about what to do. Leave changes in labor law to us."

It was ugly. Instead of gaining the backing for the WRPS we expected from the meeting, it looked as if we'd become pin cushions for labor and management representatives. Business and labor lobbyists, divided on almost everything, agreed that we shouldn't be doing what we were. What did a couple of pointy-headed academics know about workplaces or labor problems anyhow? Leave it to the Beltway crowd.

Time to regroup.

Redesigning the WRPS

People calmed down after the meeting, and when it became clear that we were determined to proceed and would respond to their criticisms, they helped — at first a little, and then a lot. Over the next few months, we had innumerable conversations with business and union representatives, and with their own survey experts. "Don't just criticize us," we kept saying. "Help us make this work! Show us the surveys you've done, and tell us what questions you found worked and what questions didn't give useful information."

Many did, revealing confidential internal surveys they had conducted of employees or union members. Some of the surveys conducted by firms were revealing. One showed that many middle managers and professionals at a major company utterly distrusted the top management, leading us to wonder if the CEO had a bodyguard, or had read the survey himself before handing it over to us. A leading manufacturing firm directed the consultant who designed their internal surveys to review every one of our questions — again and again it seemed (but with definite improvements in question wording through the process). A top-level staffmember at the AFL-CIO helped to coordinate the union oversight of what we did. He also reviewed every draft of the survey (we eventually got to seventeen different complete drafts) and called us regularly with comments.

In short, business and labor got into the spirit of the enterprise. Business pollsters warned us against wordings of questions sure to evoke exaggerated pro-business responses. The AFL-CIO staffer and union pollsters corrected question wording likely to exaggerate pro-union response. And throughout, we checked in with our outside academic experts, who warned us about many other problems.

The improvements made in the WRPS were substantial. Originally, we had designed the survey to deal almost exclusively with workplace representation without thinking much about how management viewed their own participatory human-resource practices. The "P" in the WRPS, and the module of questions focused on EI programs, reflect the suggestions of management representatives. One question, suggested to us by a union-organizing director, came to play a major role in our analysis:

You know what I would really like you to show? Show that when workers think about organization, what they most worry about is how business will react. We hear all the time that workers don't want unions because unions aren't offering them what they want, or aren't offering enough variety, or whatever. That's BS. It's what management does, and their power to act, and workers sensitivity to that, that really determines worker choice. What else explains the difference between public-sector and private-sector organization? The workers aren't that different. The only thing that's different is management and how it acts.

Good point. So we devised a question to probe whether in their desire for representation or participation workers were more sensitive to management behavior than to the characteristics of a worker organization. Specifically, we asked if workers would rather have a weak employee organization with which management cooperated at their workplace, or a stronger organization with which management did not cooperate. As we shall see, the answers to this question made some union activists livid.

But it was not only on broad issues that management and labor representatives helped form the survey. Virtually every WRPS question benefited, in one way or another, from somebody's criticism. Meanwhile, Diane Colasanto brought us up to speed on modern survey technique. To deal with the possibility that question wording or placement might bias responses, we became enthusiastic practitioners of "split questions" and "alternative sequencing." With split questions the researcher asks different parts of the sample the same basic thing, but in different ways. With alternative sequencing, the researcher puts questions in a different order to different respondents; this allows you to track the effect of the survey itself on respondents. To make the most efficient use of our time with respondents, we also posed numerous "skip questions"; these enabled us to pursue issues that were a particular concern to some members of the sample without boring those for whom the issues had no concern. If someone said they were in a union or an active participant in EI programs, we'd ask a series of additional questions; if they said they weren't, we'd skip down to the next appropriate question. Computer-assisted telephone interviewing, which we used, makes it easy to do this, as the ordering of questions is programmed on a computer and appears on the screen as the interview is conducted. This permits interviewers to take a single general survey instrument and tailor its questions to particular respondents: Different questions can be asked in different ways, or different people can be asked different questions.

By summer's end we had something that everyone thought was scientifically defensible, good, and possibly dangerous — just what we wanted! We pretested the redesigned survey among a large group of respondents to learn (1) how long it took people to answer the questions and (2) which questions people found troubling, boring, or tending to lead them toward certain conclusions. The most important thing we learned from the pretest was that respondents seemed interested. If asked, people like to talk about their work: perhaps not as much as they like to talk about their kids, or the latest scandal in Washington, or the hottest television show or sports event, but enough to stay on a telephone for nearly half an hour answering serious questions.

Oh, and we also chucked the video idea — to the disappointment of one fat balding actor with a mustache. So now we were just about ready to go into the field — that is, to get on the phones and ask folks about their workplace.

What to Do about Managers?

One in every ten or eleven American employees works as a manager, and many more employees are supervisors of some form or other. Because managers are workers, it is reasonable to ask them many of the questions that one asks other workers. But some questions that apply to nonmanagerial workers are irrelevant or peculiar to managers. The problem that management faces when employees seek to form a union, for example, is not whether to join the union but whether to try to convince employees not to join, and how hard to try. In nonunion firms, management decides, more or less unilaterally, how much authority to give to EI committees, how to discipline workers who are not living up to expectation, how to treat grievances, and other vital labor-relations matters. It made little sense to ask management to judge management activity in these and other areas.

Given this situation, we decided to exclude managers from some questions, just as we excluded nonunion employees from questions about how their union functioned or excluded employees who said their firm did not have an EI program from questions about how that program operated. But Erik Wright, an academic colleague of a leftist bent (some might call him the last living American Marxist), reviewed our survey design and came up with a better idea. Why not rephrase the questions to get management's perspective? Ask them if they would oppose an employee effort to unionize and why, how they feel about dealing with workers individually as opposed to in a group, and so on.

This would let us compare management and employee views of the same issue as seen from their differing positions within the firm. A capital notion! We would be able to report on how managers felt about issues as employees and also as managers. Ensuing chapters exploit this feature of the WRPS.

If You Could Choose . . .

Our meetings with business and labor representatives led us to develop a new strategy for trying to determine the workplace reforms employees wanted. But we still felt employees were capable of assessing how alternative reforms would function at their workplace and that their views had as much or more validity as those of Washington power groups. But how could we discover what reforms employees might want when they had no experience with those reforms?

The problem of getting people to express their true views to a hypothetical situation is a classic one in survey research. Everything depends, of course, on how the situation is described. Consider, for example, whether people think it is fair or unfair for a landlord to raise the rent on a longstanding, elderly widowed tenants in a rent-stabilized apartment. If the background is described as "City taxes and maintenance costs have risen, so the landlord raised the rent," a large share of people will judge the rent hike to be fair. But if it's described as "The real estate market tightened, the neighborhood was gentrifying, and the landlord saw an opportunity to squeeze old tenants out," then obviously that share will decline. If it's described as "Some drug dealers said they wanted the apartment to conduct business and offered to double the rent" it would drop to close to zero.

To avoid having the context determine answers, one needs either questions that give as neutral a context as possible or split questions to reflect different contexts. Because the disagreement about workplace issues is considerable, even the most careful survey design risks inadvertently leading the respondent in one or another direction on hypothetical questions. Moreover, there is the danger that this bias could color answers to succeeding questions.

Our solution was threefold.

First, we asked how respondents viewed particular reforms or institutional choices at the end, not the beginning, of questioning. In this way, even if we inadvertently phrased these questions in leading ways, we ensured that these questions would not bias responses to other questions in the same area.

Second, when we tried to infer worker preferences about possible new labor institutions or reforms, we usually asked the respondents to choose among narrowly focused attributes of those institutions, rather than inviting respondents to choose between comprehensive institutional schemes. So, for example, in asking about a hypothetical "workplace organization," we separately asked about how employee participants in the organization might be chosen, what the powers of the organization would be, how disputes within it would be settled, and so on. The typical form of these questions was "If it was your decision alone and everyone went along with it, would you prefer Attribute A or Attribute B (for example, "an organization with access to confidential company information or one without that access," "an organization of just similar employees or everyone in your plant," "an organization funded by workers alone or one jointly funded by management")?" By focusing on attributes and dealing with them precisely — and always referencing the respondents own workplace, not Capitol Hill — we could tease out preferences for new institutional forms without the fear of straying too far into never-never land, even if we couldn't specify those forms themselves.

Third, as we shall detail momentarily, when we did ask participants to consider specific reforms, we gave them a short write-up on them. These descriptions made arguments for and against the reform, as blandly and symmetrically as we could. We then asked respondents how, on reflection, they thought that reform would or would not work — again and always, at *their* workplace.

Wave 1 of the WRPS: The Big National Survey

Wave 1 of the WRPS was a national telephone survey of about 2,400 employees in private-sector establishments of twenty-five or more employees. Excluded from the survey were top managers, the self-employed, owners or relatives of owners of firms, public-sector workers, and employees in small firms. We excluded these various groups because we believed that they would have different problems and might prefer different institutional solutions from those of employees in larger, private-sector firms. You can't really ask the self-employed about relations with their employer, nor can you sensibly ask employees in a firm with three to four workers about EI committees. Although we thus cannot report on the attitudes of some workers, we covered the vast majority of the U.S. workforce. The population from which our sample draws covered approximately 75 percent of all private-sector workers — some 70 million workers at the time of the survey.

The sample size of 2,400 was also roughly double the standard national opinion survey. We chose this size because we wanted to test different wording or sequencing of questions (which we would ask of only part of the sample) and to assure ourselves of a substantial number of employees in select groups, such as unions or EI committees. The survey averaged twenty-six minutes, which pressed the outer bounds of conventional telephone surveys. (A copy of the Wave 1 questionnaire is contained in Appendix B.)

The survey was conducted in mid-September to mid-October of 1994. We had a high response rate[3] and a lower-than-feared cut-off rate from people terminating the interview part-way through. We evaluated only completed questionnaires. The demographics — age, race, sex, education, location, and so on — were nationally representative for the target population. The estimated sampling error on the responses of the entire group was very low — plus or minus 2 percent.

Verifying the Scaling

We did have one last scare, however. Shortly after we went into the field with our main design, our principal advisor from the AFL-CIO called up, very upset. He had made many suggestions. We had followed some of them but had also rejected some, and one of the ones we had rejected he thought was crucial to getting an accurate result. It involved a technical issue on which he (and, we presumed, AFL-CIO survey experts) disagreed with the decision of our survey firm, PSRA: the scaling of certain variables. The convention used through most of the WRPS was to scale responses using a four-point scale: (4) very, (3) somewhat, (2) not too, and (1) not at all. For example, we ask, "Would you say you are very satisfied, somewhat satisfied, not too satisfied, or not at all satisfied with your say in training?"

Our friend at the AFL-CIO had problems with this. First, if we were to do a four-point scale, he preferred a division that treated satisfaction and dissatisfaction equally. For example, he wanted to ask, "Would you say you are very satisfied, somewhat satisfied, somewhat dissatisfied, or very dissatisfied with . . . ?" Second, he wanted the WRPS to use more five-point scales, with a neutral position marked clearly between satisfaction and dissatisfaction to give respondents the option of saying that they were neither satisfied nor dissatisfied.

The motivation for both criticisms was the fear that our wording and structure biased responses toward reported satisfaction. He argued that the answers "not too satisfied" and "not at all satisfied" are less meaningful than "somewhat dissatisfied" and "very dissatisfied." Fewer people would choose them, and the largely nonunion U.S. workforce would look more satisfied with workplace arrangements than it truly was. Failure to allow respondents to take a neutral position, combined with general reluctance to admit dissatisfaction, would have the same result. "You're setting us up for a survey that will just show happy workers!" he yelled at us on the phone.

We believed that he was wrong. Once they got to talking, employees in our focus group were outspoken in their views. PSRA found four-point scales superior to five-point ones: They take less time and force people to come down on one side or the other of an issue rather than waffling in the middle (say, giving a "3" value to most questions). This is why we had rejected his suggestion of alternatives when he had made it earlier, but less vociferously than he was making it now. But our promise to the business and labor groups was that we would respond to their criticisms. What could we do? Was there a scientific way to determine who was right?

It was too late to alter the WRPS, but we found out that we could add questions to a national weekly "omnibus survey" (so-called because polling companies conduct these surveys weekly with an omnibus of questions, submitted by various clients). We could ask respondents the same questions we had asked on our own survey, but we would scale half the responses our way and half the way our critic at the AFL-CIO wanted. This would be expensive and risky. If he was right, parts of the main survey would be invalid, but we had to respond to any criticism for the results to be beyond reproach.

We dipped into a dwindling budget and bought some questions on a national omnibus to test the alternative wording, and to see what people would do if permitted a neutral response. This omnibus supplement was conducted in two waves in November 1994. It expanded our sample by an additional 1,100 workers. And what a relief! The results from different scaling were not noticeably different. If anything, asking questions the way our critic wanted produced more satisfied responses than our own — the opposite of the effect he had predicted.

Wave 2 of the WRPS: The Follow-Up

Even though our survey was long and detailed, we still wondered whether respondents might have answered some questions differently if they possessed additional information or could reflect longer on a particular issue. And we wanted to do one thing that our business and labor critics had advised us against — ask employees to judge specific feasible policy reforms.

We devised an inexpensive way to accomplish this goal: We conducted a follow-up survey of some of the participants of the national telephone survey. At the end of the Wave 1 questionnaire, we asked survey participants if they would be willing to read written descriptions of possible changes in national labor policies, to think about those proposals, and then to give their opinion of these changes. Although respondents had already talked with us for half an hour, a sizable proportion said they would look at additional materials.

And so, with preliminary results from Wave 1 in hand but not yet announced to the world, we set about Wave 2. In November we mailed written descriptions of three policy proposals to a sample of respondents who said that they would be willing to look at such material and talk to us again. A few weeks later we telephoned these respondents to get their reactions to the policy proposals and to ask a few other questions. We received responses from some 800 persons. The follow-up sample did not differ noticeably in its demographic or economic characteristics from our initial sample and was large enough to qualify as an independent national poll in its own right. (The materials for this sample are also included in Appendix D.)

Unique to the U.S. Private Sector or General?

You'd think this would be the end of "the mother of all workplace surveys." But mothers have kids, even mother surveys.

Any survey can speak with confidence only about the population from which the sample was drawn during the period of sampling. We wanted the WRPS to be more than a snapshot. We wanted it to capture the fundamental attitudes of employees in the U.S. private sector as the country approached the twenty-first century — what in grandiose moments we sometimes called "the deep structure" (whatever that means) of employee feelings about their workplace. Had we done that? Or did the responses simply reflect feelings in the particular setting of the U.S. job market in the mid-1990s?

One possibility, in particular, troubled us. One of our major findings was that, in response to the question about worker preferences for a strong labor organization or management cooperation, employees preferred a cooperative management. They were, to put it bluntly, the antithesis of Karl Marx's vision of a class in conflict with capitalism. We wondered if this reflected labor's weakness in the 1990s rather than deep-seated employee attitudes. If unions were stronger and wages growing for normal workers as well as for CEOs, maybe the desire to cooperate would diminish and workers would be more militant. The standard measure of labor militancy — the incidence of strikes — certainly varies over time and over the business cycle. Maybe our snapshot was limited in time or place. We could see Marx's ghost rising from his grave in London's Highgate Cemetery, denouncing us for mistaking ephemeral attitudes for genuine class unconsciousness.

One way to probe whether our findings represented workers in general, or were unique to American private-sector workers in a particular period, would be to compare the responses of workers in our own survey who faced different job markets. We could ascertain whether union workers had different attitudes from nonunion workers, whether those workers who believed they could easily find a comparable job at similar pay had the same attitudes as those who said they would have trouble if they lost their job, and so forth. The smaller the variation in attitudes among these groups, the more likely it would be that we had identified some universal attitudes rather than time/place contingent attitudes. (We make such comparisons in the ensuing chapters.)

Another way to try to probe would be to compare the responses of U.S. private-sector employees to the responses of private-sector employees in another country with a stronger labor movement. The obvious other country for the United States is Canada. With a labor-relations system that is in many ways very similar to that of the United States, Canada has a private-sector union density that is about twice as high as the United States'; its laws are much more protective of workers, and its business community historically has been less fiercely opposed to unionism than has American business. Why not take our survey (en Français pour les Quebecais) and see how Canadians responded? Because so much of the work had been done, the expenses would be modest, and we would be able to respond to Marx's ghost. In November 1995, we conducted the Canadian WRPS, which covered 1,000 Canadian workers, making it the largest such survey conducted up to that time in Canada.

Yet another way to test whether our results held generally would be to look at public-sector American workers. While unions are weak and declining in the private sector, they have been strong and stable in the public sector. In 1995, about 40 percent of public-sector workers were organized. If we could ask public-sector workers similar questions to those we had asked private-sector workers, we would have a good contrast. The problem was that identifying public-sector employees through a national survey is very expensive. Because about only 10 percent of the workforce is in the public sector, the number of calls necessary to obtain a nationally representative sample is large, and we had very little budget left. But, luckily for us, the Clinton administration had appointed a panel on public-sector labor-management relations with the ungainly name of The Secretary of Labor's Task Force on Excellence in State and Local Government through Labor-Management Cooperation.[4] After listening to our early findings from the WRPS, the task force asked if we could replicate our study with public-sector employees. Yes, we said, but only if they could provide a good sample of employees. The sample they provided was imperfect: membership lists of unionized public-sector workers and a sample of largely nonunion public-sector workers in one southern state. While this was hardly ideal, we decided to proceed: We figured that even an assessment by only some public-sector employees would be useful. If their views agreed with those of the private-sector employees on our main survey, we could tell Karl's ghost to go back to the grave, although maybe not too loudly. In any case, in November 1995 we conducted a survey of the public-sector.

Enough? For us, yes, but a British management group that read our study decided that they wanted to find out how workers in the United Kingdom felt about their jobs. This management group commissioned two Oxford experts to develop a British version, which gave us another country of comparison. At this writing, parts of the WRPS are also being replicated in Japan and Australia (but fortunately not by us).

Here we do not report on the "children" of the basic WRPS. We simply note that Canadian private-sector workers express much the same attitudes as American private-sector workers, that U.S. public-sector workers differ only modestly from private-sector workers,[5] but that British workers seem less cooperative and more aggressive in their attitudes toward management than either Americans or Canadians. Nothing in these follow-up surveys leads us to question our findings about private-sector U.S. workers.

The Final WRPS Design

As you can see, the WRPS on which this book is based consists of much more than a single survey or opinion poll. We ended up with a four-part

EXHIBIT 2.1. The WRPS and its progeny: more than a survey.

The WRPS

Focus groups
  One-and-a-half-hour discussions with 56 workers in six occupational groups;
  designed to give us a better sense of the general workplace concerns and
  appropriate language for asking about them.
Wave 1
  Twenty-six-minute national survey of 2,308 employees; extensive use of
  split questions and alternative sequencing to minimize bias.
Wave 2
  Fifteen-minute follow-up survey of 801 respondents to Wave 1 questionnaire
  who had also read mailed fact sheets on workplace alternatives; designed
  to probe initial responses and to allow respondents to consider alternative
  policies described by fact sheets.
Omnibus
  Ten-minute survey of 1,000 respondents, designed to test the WRPS's four-
  point scaling questions against five-point alternatives.

The follow-ups

Canadian survey
  Twenty-six-minute combination of questions from Waves 1 and 2,
  administered to 1,100 respondents; designed to see which U.S. employee
  responses reflect specifics of the U.S. private sector and which generalize
  to private-sector workers in a closely related economy.
Public-sector survey
  Twenty-five-minute survey of 1,002 unionized and nonunionized public-
  sector employees; designed to see which private-sector U.S. responses
  reflect specifics of that sector and which generalize to public-sector workers
  in the same economy.
British survey
  Twenty-five-minute survey of 1,000 private-sector employees; designed to
  illuminate the "new employment contract" between workers and firms,
  using many questions from Waves 1 and 2 of the WRPS.

study, with each part designed either to add additional knowledge or to test
the reliability of other parts, and three additional surveys that probe the
universality of the results' specificity (see Exhibit 2.1). We took care to
establish the study's authority by basing question design on what employees said in focus groups; by using split questions and sequencing questions
differently; by taking criticisms seriously; by using a follow-up survey to
push the survey instrument to its limit; and by comparing the results with
responses abroad, and in the very different climate of public-sector
employment.

We have shared some of the nitty-gritty details of our survey design for two reasons. First, we hope to convince you that the findings reported in *What Workers Want* are as valid as we could make them and, more likely than not, correctly capture the attitudes of American workers. We cannot conceive of the nation dealing with its workplace problems without responding to these attitudes. Second, we want to make it clear that social-science surveys do not appear by magic from some survey organization or government agency but in fact are designed as scientific tools by fallible folk who seek answers to important social problems.

Does all of our effort and safeguards mean we got it right? Social science is not laboratory science, a discipline in which you vary the variable or parameter of interest while controlling (mostly) everything else. People are not quarks. They can and do change. Social movements arise suddenly. We think we got it right. We wouldn't have written this book if we didn't think so. It's undoubtedly more "right" for America in a period of high inequality and labor quiescence than for all time, but we would be surprised if most of the attitudes we report will change all that much in the foreseeable future.

CHAPTER 3

What Workers Want and Why They Don't Have It

Shortly after we completed the Worker Representation and Participation Survey (WRPS), we rushed our top-line findings to business and labor groups and to the Clinton Administration's Commission on the Future of Worker-Management Relations. Some plaudits and some brickbats came back. Union representatives who had hoped our study would support the AFL-CIO line on all issues took offense at the finding that workers wanted cooperation over a strong organization and that most workers wanted joint committees at their workplace. Press reports that played up these results irritated them to no end. The Republican victory in the 1994 congressional elections made business representatives mellow about our finding that workers wanted greater input in workplace decisions and that many nonunion workers wanted unions, for they knew they could prevent any changes in labor legislation inimical to their interests. One lobbyist told us cheerfully that labor policy would be set by his lobbying firm, which represented the bosses of the world, not by any commission or survey, so who cared what we found workers wanted?

In Washington, what matters is the immediate. If something is not on this week's policy talking points or this session's legislative calendar, who cares? From this perspective, the capsule summary in Chapter 1 suffices to tell the story of the WRPS. Our desire to capture the "deep structure" of worker attitudes toward employee relations and to demonstrate that workers could contribute to improving labor relations were looked on as the mad rantings of ivory-tower pinheads.

But a capsule summary of the "mother of all workplace surveys" did not satisfy us, nor, we venture, will it satisfy you. By its nature, a summary can neither give the details that underlie our interpretation of the evidence nor document the variation in attitudes toward the workplace among the diverse American people. Nor can it examine the reasons why some workers are dissatisfied with their influence on workplace decisions and want new arrangements at their workplace while others are happy with their situation.

In this chapter we examine how workers' desire for more say at the workplace depends on the characteristics of workers and their workplaces. We provide a brief narrative to help you put our findings into a broader perspective. We address objections that we imagine the critical reader might have to our interpretation of the survey, much as we would respond to objections in an academic seminar.[1]

Workers Want More Influence

The WRPS shows as conclusively as any survey can that the vast majority of employees want more involvement and greater say in company decisions affecting their workplace. This finding is not grounded in a single question — "Do you want more say or not?" — but in a battery of questions that poke and probe at such desires.[2] We poked and probed at the desire for influence because every other part of our study hinges on this issue.

One way to determine whether workers want more influence on workplace decisions is to ask if they are satisfied with their say on the job. But employees might answer such questions without carefully considering their situation. In our focus-group discussions, people often expressed critical attitudes as they considered their workplace concerns in greater depth than they had at the outset. It is easy to reply, "I'm satisfied, sort of," to a stand-alone question, without giving it much thought. It is harder to give such a cursory response after talking for a while about various aspects of the workplace.

We used a split-sample design to deal with this potential problem. In two spots in the survey, we asked, "Overall, how satisfied are you with the influence you have in company decisions that affect your job or work life?" For half the respondents we asked it *before* we asked workers to discuss particular workplace decisions; for the other half we asked it *after* a battery of questions about particular workplace issues. We hypothesized that the *after* group would be more critical than the *before* group about the amount of influence they had at the workplace.

Exhibit 3.1 shows that this was indeed the case.[3] In the *before* sample, 28 percent of employees reported that they were "very satisfied" with their influence on the job, whereas 19 percent said that they were "not too satis-

EXHIBIT 3.1. Percentage of workers who are satisfied or dissatisfied with their influence on workplace issues.

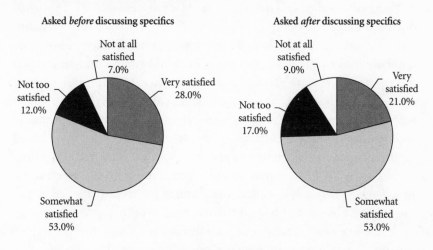

Asked *before* discussing specifics

Not at all satisfied 7.0%
Very satisfied 28.0%
Not too satisfied 12.0%
Somewhat satisfied 53.0%

Asked *after* discussing specifics

Not at all satisfied 9.0%
Very satisfied 21.0%
Not too satisfied 17.0%
Somewhat satisfied 53.0%

Percentage of workers who want more influence at workplaces

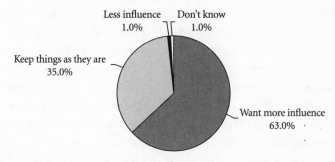

Less influence 1.0%
Don't know 1.0%
Keep things as they are 35.0%
Want more influence 63.0%

Note: Pie-chart portions must add to 100 percent, so some numbers have been rounded up.

Source: Based on these WRPS questions: (Wave 1.14_1,2,3,4) "Overall, how satisfied are you with the influence you have in company decisions that affect your job or work life?" (satisfied, somewhat satisfied, not too satisfied, not satisfied at all); (W1.14b) "If it were your decision alone, and everyone went along with it, would you generally like to have more influence in these areas, less influence, or would you want to keep things the ways they are now?"

fied" or "not at all satisfied," a 9-point difference in favor of greater satisfaction. In the *after* sample, 21 percent of employees said that they were "very satisfied" with their influence on the job, whereas 26 percent were "not too satisfied" or "not at all satisfied," a 5-point difference in the opposite direction. The most plausible interpretation of this 14-point swing is that workers gave a more accurate and less perfunctory response after discussing workplace specifics.

Using yet another split design, we asked employees with whom we had discussed particular workplace decisions, "If it were your decision alone, and everyone went along with it, would you generally like to have more influence in these areas, less influence, or would you want to keep things the way they are now?" This puts the "Are you satisfied?" issue into the more dynamic terms of changing workplace conditions. It offers a way to judge whether workers who are "somewhat satisfied" want some change in their situation. Nearly two-thirds of the workers reported that they wanted more influence, compared with 35 percent who were content to keep things as they are and 1 percent who actually desired less influence (see Exhibit 3.1). The workers who wanted more influence were better educated, worked more hours, and had greater tenure than other workers.[4]

Do these results offer any news, or is this just social science reporting the obvious? Surely most people want more influence on decisions affecting their job, as influence is likely to improve their work lives. If we asked people if they want more money, they would all say, "Yes. Big deal."

To address this objection, we asked about the benefits that workers would get from greater influence at the workplace. Eighty-seven percent of workers told us that employees would enjoy their jobs more if more decisions about production and operations were made by employees, instead of by managers. But that was not the only benefit workers saw as flowing from having greater influence on workplace decisions. Three-fourths said that their company would be stronger against its competitors and 79 percent said that the quality of products or services would improve if employees made more decisions about production and operations. In addition, most employees thought that if employees had more say in how workplace problems were addressed at their company, those problems would be solved more effectively.[5]

Still, you might wonder if workers are simply giving self-serving answers. Say your spouse claims that if he or she made more household decisions, everything would run more smoothly, but what might actually happen is you ending up doing more of the dirty work. If this was the case, managers should have told us that giving workers a greater say in decision-making would be harmful to the firm and make problem-solving less rather than more efficient. To the contrary. Fifty-eight percent of managers agreed with workers that workplace problems would be more effectively solved at their company if employees collectively had more say. If the workers and managers are right, the bottom line for companies is better performance.[6]

Many managers have, moreover, acted on their belief that empowering workers can improve the firm's effectiveness. More than half of the workers in the WRPS are employed by firms with some sort of employee-involvement (EI) program, and one-third participated in that program. But, as we shall see in Chapter 5, most EI participants believe that the programs would be more effective if employees collectively had more say in how the programs were run. And most managers of such programs agree that even when firms try hard, they do not give employees enough authority in decision-making.

The Discontented Third

On the average day, what best describes your feelings about going to work? Would you say you usually look forward to it, or wish you didn't have to go, or don't care one way or the other?

Overall, how would you rate relations between employees and management at your company/organization? Would you say they are "excellent," "good," "only fair," or "poor"?

To see whether worker desire for greater say reflects a general malaise with how management treats workers in the United States or is a stand-alone problem, we asked the preceding two questions. We found that, on average, two-thirds of workers were reasonably satisfied with their work lives, but that the other one-third were dissatisfied, and their dissatisfaction was closely linked to their lack of influence on the job.

Exhibit 3.2 shows the responses that constitute the "discontented third." The first pie chart shows that 25 percent of respondents wished that they didn't have to go to work, while 9 percent said they didn't care one way or another. Together these figures imply that about one-third of the workforce are not eager to do their job. The proportion dissatisfied is particularly high among workers in the lower part of the earnings distribution — that is, among the less educated, black workers, and manufacturing workers[7] — as compared with workers in stronger positions in the job market. In this sense, inequality in job satisfaction mirrors the inequality in the earnings distribution. But then 28 percent of college graduates and 39 percent of workers with some college education also wished they didn't have

EXHIBIT 3.2. One-third of workers are dissatisfied.

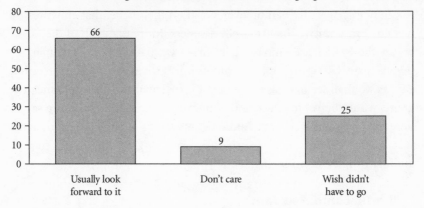

Percentage of workers who do not look forward to going to work

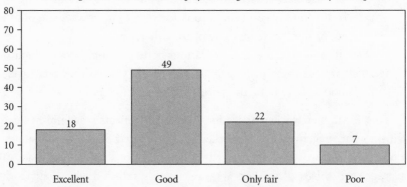

Percentage of workers who rate employee management relations as only fair or poor

Source: Based on these WRPS questions: (W1.8) "On an average day, what best describes your feelings about going to work? Would you say you usually look forward to it, wish you didn't have to go, don't care one way or the other"; (W1.10b) "Overall, how would you rate relations between employees and management at your company/organization? Would you say they are excellent, good, only fair, or poor?"

to go to work or didn't care one way or the other, and 30 percent of white men also placed themselves in this boat.

A similar pattern is found in employee ratings of employee-management relations. Eighteen percent of workers rate relations between employees and management at their company as being excellent, and nearly one-half label them as good; more than one in five, however, rate labor relations as only fair, and one in fourteen rate them as poor. Cumulating the "fair" and "poor" responses gives us, again, our discontented third. Discontent with labor-management relations is not, moreover, a case of workers thinking "the grass is always greener on the other side." Fifty-one percent of our respondents viewed labor-management relations at their firm as about the same as in other places, and 38 percent thought they were better than average. Only 9 percent thought their company's labor relations were worse than average.

Discontent with labor-management relations shows up in how workers see trust and loyalty at workplaces.

> How much loyalty would you say you feel toward the company/organization where you work — "a lot," "some," "only a little," or "no loyalty at all"?
>
> How much do you trust your company/organization to keep its promises to you and other employees — "a lot," "somewhat," "only a little," or "not at all"?

Exhibit 3.3 shows that considerably more workers feel "a lot" of loyalty to their firm than trust their firm "a lot" to carry out its promises to them and to other employees. Approximately two-fifths trust their company somewhat, while one-fifth trust it only a little or not at all. At the individual level, one-third of workers reported a greater amount of loyalty than trust, compared with 10 percent who said they trusted their firm more than they felt loyalty to it.[8] Again the discontented third.

Discontent and Lack of Say

To what extent, if at all, is discontent with jobs and labor-management relations linked to dissatisfaction with influence on workplace decisions?

Extraordinarily so, according to the data summarized in Exhibit 3.4. This exhibit shows how workers with different degrees of satisfaction with their say on decisions responded to other questions about their attitude toward their workplace: whether they look forward to going to work, their rating of employee-management relations, and their trust in their firm. The linkages between satisfaction with influence and these other attitudes is strong. Workers satisfied with their say look forward to going to work, report excellent employee/management relations, and trust their firm. By contrast, workers dissatisfied with their say in workplace decisions disproportionately do not look forward to work; they report fair or poor labor management relations and distrust their employers.

EXHIBIT 3.3. Workers' loyalty and trust of their firm.

Percentage of workers feeling loyalty to their firm

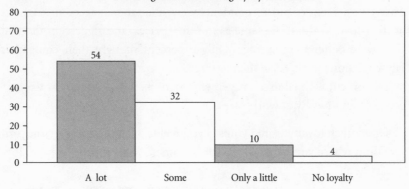

Percentage of workers who trust their firm to keep its promises

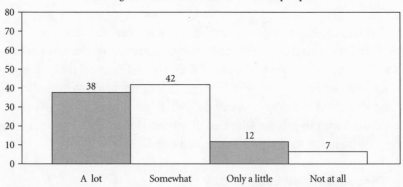

Source: Based on these WRPS questions: (W1.9C) "How much loyalty would you say you feel toward the company/organization you work for as a whole?" (a lot, some, only a little, no loyalty at all); (W1.10a) "In general, how much do you trust your company/ organization to keep its promises to you and other employees?" (a lot, somewhat, only a little, not at all).

By organizing the data to show how worker discontent differs by satisfaction or dissatisfaction with say, we do not mean to imply that dissatisfaction with say is the primary cause of discontent. Our data show correlation, not causality. We could just as easily have organized the cross-tabulations the other way around: We could have documented that workers distrustful of their employer, who rate labor relations as poor, who do not enjoy going to work, or who give management a low grade in concern for employees are exceptionally dissatisfied with their say at the work-

EXHIBIT 3.4. Percentage of workers with positive attitudes toward their jobs and firm, by satisfaction with influence on workplace decisions.

	Satisfaction with influence on workplace decisions			
	Very	Somewhat	Not too	Not at all
Looking forward to work				
Usually look forward to work	85	69	46	32
Wish didn't have to go	10	21	43	59
Trusting firm to keep promises				
A lot	65	36	14	8
Little or none	4	16	40	65
Rating employee/management relations				
Excellent	39	15	5	0
Poor/fair	10	27	56	80

Note: We do not adjust for the effect of asking the overall satisfaction question both before and after.
Source: Based on WRPS questions given in Exhibit 3.2 and 3.3 cross-tabulated with (W1.14_1,2,3,4): "Overall, how satisfied are you with the influence you have in company decisions that affect your job or work life?"

place.[9] The key point is that dissatisfaction with say at the workplace is not a trivial issue: It is intrinsically tied to how workers feel about other aspects of their jobs and employers.

The Influence Gap

Very well, you say, a chunk of American workers are unhappy with their influence on workplace decisions and are concomitantly dissatisfied with working life overall. But in your organization, or in any other one for that matter, no one gives people influence in an abstract sense. People have a say in particular decisions by conferring with management in those areas, or by sitting on committees that deal with specific problems, and so on.

Exhibit 3.5 shows worker attitudes toward influence on the job in eight different areas of workplace decision-making. Column 1 records the proportion of workers who said that having influence in a particular area was very important to them. The proportion of workers reporting that it is very important to have influence on decisions varies considerably among items. Over three-quarters of workers (76 percent) said it was very important to have influence on how to do their job and organize their work, while only

EXHIBIT 3.5. A big gap exists between the importance of wanting and having influence on workplace decisions.

	Wanting influence	Having Influence	Average gap	Individual gap
	Percentage of workers for whom it is very important to have a lot of influence	Percentage of workers who said they had a lot of direct influence and involvement	Difference between the columns "wanting influence" and "having influence"	Percentage of workers with less involvement than they want
Deciding what kinds of *benefits* are offered to employees	60	6	54	83
Deciding how much of a *raise* in pay the people in your work group should get	41	6	35	76
Deciding what *training* is needed for people in your work group or department	62	29	33	53
Deciding how to work with new *equipment or software*, if that's ever been needed	52	28	24	46

Setting *goals* for your work group or department	55	32	43
Setting *safety* standards and practices	55	35	45
Deciding *how* to do your job and organize the work	76	57	31
Setting work *schedules*, including breaks, overtime and time off	42	30	47
Average	55	28	53

Source: Based on these WRPS questions: "How much direct involvement and influence do *you* have in (W1.12aa and 12ba) Deciding *how* to do your job and organize the work? (W1.12ab and 12bb) Deciding what *training* is needed for people in your work group or department? (W1.12ac and 12bc) Setting work *schedules*, including breaks, overtime, and time off? (W1.12ad and 12bd) Deciding how much of a *raise* in pay the people in your work group should get? (W1.12ae and 12be) Setting *goals* for your work group or department? (W1.12af and 12bf) Deciding how to work with new *equipment or software*, if that's ever been needed? (W1.12ag and bg) Setting *safety* standards and practices?" (W1.12ah and 12bh) Deciding what kind of *benefits* are offered to employees? (a lot, some, only a little, no direct involvement at all); (W1.13a) "Suppose you *could* have a *lot* of influence in all these areas at work — regardless of whether you do now or not. As I read each area again, please tell me how important it would be to you to have a *lot* of influence on these decisions. First, how important would it be to you to have influence in (ITEM)?" (very important, somewhat important, not too important, not important at all).

41 percent said it was very important to have influence in deciding general pay raises; this gives a range in the desire for influence of 35 percentage points. Relatively many workers also said that it was very important to have influence in deciding the training workers get and the kind of benefits the firm offers them. Averaging the responses across areas, 55 percent of employees report that it was *very important* to have a lot of influence on these decisions.

Column 2 records the proportion of workers who said they actually had "a lot" of influence in an area. The proportion of workers reporting that they have a lot of influence in an area also varies across items. Just 6 percent of workers said they have a lot of influence setting pay or benefits at their workplace, as compared with 57 percent who said they have a lot of influence deciding how to do their particular job. This gives a 51-percentage-point range across areas, which is larger than the range in the desire for say. The implication is that people are more alike in what they want than are workplaces alike in providing them what they want. Finally, averaging the responses in Column 3 across areas, we see that 27 percent of employees reported that they had a lot of influence on these decisions. That twice as many workers consider it "very important" to have influence in workplace decisions than who say that they have "a lot" of influence in workplace decisions supports the notion that firms are not giving workers their desired say at the workplace.

Column 3 measures the gap between wanting say and having say as the difference between the percentages for whom having influence is very important and the percentages who have a lot of influence. Averaged across items, this influence gap is our bottom-line indicator of how the U.S. job market is falling short of meeting employee desires for say at their workplace. The average gap is a valuable summary statistic, but it is also an imperfect one — imperfect because it collapses four responses to each question (and thus sixteen possible combinations of answers) into a single number based on whether the respondents answered "very" to both items. This lumps together people who, for instance, said influence is "somewhat important" to them with those who said it was "not at all important."[10] The summary statistic is also imperfect because workers who have less influence than they want on items are grouped with workers who have more influence than they want on items.[11] Both of these imperfections imply that the summary gap understates the degree to which workers want more say on the job than they have.

To resolve this problem, we calculate in Column 4 the proportion of workers who want more influence in an area than they report having. Because many workers say it is somewhat important to have an influence on workplace decisions (and thus do not fit into the group in Column 1) but do not have much influence on decisions, this measure shows much greater representation/participation gaps than Column 3 does. Averaging across items, 53 percent of workers have less involvement in a workplace decision than they want — almost twice the difference in the average gap in Column 3.[12]

So, in which specific areas do workers want more say at their workplace? The biggest individual gaps involve deciding on benefits and pay raises for their group. These are issues regarding the division of the pie in the firm, where more influence for workers might benefit them at the expense of management or shareholders. The next largest gap is for something quite different: deciding on the training needed for workers, as the right training can improve productivity, profits, and wages. The gap is large here not because workers have exceptionally little influence on outcomes, as in determining benefits and pay, but because they have an exceptional desire for influencing this outcome. The representation/participation gap is smallest in the area of deciding how to do one's job and in setting work schedules, although for different reasons. Many workers have a great deal of direct influence in deciding how to do their job and organize their work, while relatively few workers regard setting schedules as being very important to them.

Differences in the Influence Gap
Does the gap between wanting and having an influence on workplace decisions vary among workers with different demographic or economic characteristics?

To answer this question, we formed a *summated rating* of the amount of influence each worker wanted and the amount that he or she had across all of the items discussed. A summated rating[13] is a simple scale that scores answers on each item and then sums the scores across items. Because the WRPS used a four-point scale, we accorded a 4 to a respondent's highest influence category and a 1 to his or her lowest influence category. The split design of the WRPS meant that each worker was asked about four items, so the scale takes a value from 4 (when the worker either had or wanted the least influence) to 16 (when the worker either had or wanted the most influence).

Exhibit 3.6 contrasts the value of our summated rating for workers of different types. Column 1 gives our measure of the influence workers want to

EXHIBIT 3.6. Summated rating measures of how much influence workers want and have on workplace decisions (by groups of workers).

	Measure of influence they want	Measure of influence they have	Influence gap
	On a scale from 4 to 16		
Sex			
Men	13.6	10.3	3.2
Women	13.6	9.7	3.9
Race			
White	13.5	10.0	3.5
Black	14.2	9.8	4.4
Education			
College graduate	13.5	10.5	3.0
High school graduate	13.7	9.9	3.8
Occupation			
Professional	13.6	10.8	2.8
Laborer	13.7	9.6	4.1
Union status			
Nonunion	13.6	10.0	3.6
Union	13.6	9.6	4.0
Employee involvement (EI)			
EI participant	13.8	11.2	2.6
Nonparticipant	13.5	9.4	4.1
Weekly earnings			
Upper quartile	13.6	10.8	2.8
Lower quartile	13.5	9.3	4.2

Note: The summated rating scale is based on a coding that gives the highest category a 4, the next highest a 3, the next highest a 2, and the lowest a 1. It simply sums these values for the four items about which we asked each worker. Thus it has a maximum value of 16 and a minimum value of 4. The higher the score in the text, the more a worker said that he or she wanted or had influence in decisions in the areas covered. *Source:* Tabulated from WRPS questions listed in Exhibit 3.5.

have. It shows that diverse groups have similar desires for influence on decisions. Men and women, union and nonunion workers, professionals and laborers all get the same score in terms of the amount of influence they want. Where differences occur, they are relatively modest: high school graduates want a bit more influence than college graduates; blacks want more than whites; participants on EI committees want more than nonparticipants. The overriding impression, however, is that, regardless of how we divide the workforce, employees want comparable amounts of influence on workplace decisions. Column 2 measures the influence that workers say they actually have. Here we find considerable variation. Workers in weaker positions in terms of their education or occupation, earnings, or sex or race have less influence on decisions than workers in stronger positions. Union workers report somewhat less influence than nonunion workers, while participants on EI committees report considerably more influence than do nonparticipants. (We examine these two groups in detail in Chapters 4 and 5.)

Similarity in the amount of influence people want and differences in the amount of influence they have necessarily translates in Column 3 into differences in the magnitude of the influence gap among workers. Most striking here is that influence gaps are large for all groups. To appreciate the magnitude of the summated scale, note that a four-point gap implies that, on average, a worker's influence on the job falls short of that worker's desire for influence by one category — that is, the worker wants a lot of influence and has only some influence, or wants some and has only a little, or wants a little and has none.

However we measure the difference between the say workers want in workplace decisions and the influence they actually have, the gap turns out to be large.

Collective or Individual Voice?

Workers can have a say on workplace decisions as individuals or as part of a group. Individually, employees can exert influence at their workplace by speaking directly with a supervisor. In companies with open-door policies, they can take a problem to higher management. In companies with internal grievance mechanisms, they can use a formal complaint procedure when they have a problem. In many large firms, workers can also voice their concerns through the opinion surveys of workers that these firms regularly conduct. They can also send e-mail or use suggestion boxes.

Collectively, employees can affect decisions by meeting as a group with management or by electing representatives to meet with management. In some companies, management gathers all workers together in "town meetings" to discuss common workplace problems. In other companies, management might set up committees of employees to deal with problems. Independently of management, workers might form unions to represent their collective interests. In most European countries, national law establishes works councils in which all workers — white collar as well as blue collar, nonunion as well as union — elect representatives to meet regularly with management.

When U.S. workers express a desire for more say about their jobs, do they want greater say only as individuals, or as part of a group?

This is a critical question in American labor relations because most employers prefer that employees speak out as individuals and are uneasy dealing with workers as a group. Groups invariably have greater power than the individuals who constitute them, and the strongest worker group in capitalism, the trade union, forces management to negotiate decisions rather than to decide as management feels best.

The WRPS examined the preferences of workers for these forms of exerting influence on workplace decisions in various ways. In one part of the survey, we asked half of the respondents, "Do you agree or disagree with the following statement: 'I'd feel more comfortable raising workplace problems through an employee association, rather than singly.'" We asked the other half: "How would you prefer to solve a workplace problem of your own? Would you feel more comfortable dealing directly with management yourself, or would you feel more comfortable having a group of your coworkers help you deal with management?" We asked the question in two ways to eliminate possible biases owing to differences in wording, context, or sequencing. The first question put the group process first and refers to workplace problems in general. The second question put individual action first and refers to a problem faced by the individual worker.

As Exhibit 3.7 indicates, the sequencing, context, or precise wording of the questions affected the responses. When the first response in the question was *through an employee association*, 56 percent of employees said they preferred to deal with a workplace problem through an association. When the first response was *by self*, 55 percent said they preferred dealing with their problem directly with management, with 43 percent preferring the group approach. The safest conclusion is that workers are evenly divided in their preferences between individual and group ways of dealing with problems.

The preference for a group or an individual solution to problems depends on the particular problem workers face. Most elected to deal with instances of sexual harassment, unfair treatment, and insufficient job training directly with management, whereas for issues involving workplace heath and safety and benefits, they wanted the help of other employees. Many who favored collective voice in general still preferred to deal with harassment/unfair treatment issues individually, while many who said they

EXHIBIT 3.7. Some employees prefer individual voice; others prefer group voice.

Percentage who feel more comfortable raising workplace problems . . .

Through an employee association	56
As an individual	38
Don't know	5

Percentage who prefer to solve a workplace problem of their own . . .

With the help of fellow employees	43
By self	55
Don't know	2

		Depending on the problem		
	Benefits	Health/ safety	Training at job	Unfair treatment	Sexual harrassment
---	---	---	---	---	---
Percentage who prefer to solve workplace problems					
With the help of fellow employees	66	53	44	39	34
By self	33	36	54	59	65
Don't know	1	1	2	3	1

Source: Based on these WRPS questions: (W1.34a) "Do you agree or disagree with the following statement: 'I'd feel more comfortable raising workplace problems through an employee association, rather than as an individual'?"; (W1.34b) "How would *you* prefer to solve a workplace problem of your own? Would you feel more comfortable dealing directly with management *yourself*, or would you feel more comfortable having a *group* of your fellow employees *help* you deal with management?"; (W2.36a–e) "How do you prefer to deal with any complaints you might have about something at work? For each of the following problems, please tell me whether you would prefer to deal directly with management *yourself* or prefer to have a *group* of your fellow employees help you deal with management."

favored individual voice in general preferred to deal with health and safety/benefits collectively.[14]

How much meaning should we attach to workers saying that they want collective input in workplace decisions? After all, it's one thing to say, "Yes, I want to participate in decisions that affect the overall workplace"; it's another matter entirely to put time and effort into such an activity. We asked workers if they would be willing to volunteer two to three hours per month to participate in an employee organization that met with management. One-third of employees said they would definitely be willing to do so; 44 percent said they would probably be willing to meet with management. Because you don't need many folks to represent employees in discussion with management, even if workers vastly exaggerated their willingness to give time to such an activity, there would seem to be an ample supply of employees to serve in any workplace organization.

In sum, employees want greater say at the workplace not simply as individuals but as a group as well. They differentiate between those areas in which they prefer to deal with problems by themselves and those in which the collective or public-goods nature of the decision — health and safety, benefits, a system for resolving problems — would seem to require a group input to be effective.

Cooperation and Independence

In the focus groups, the survey, and the follow-up probes, employees consistently said they wanted a cooperative relationship with management, and that they preferred workplace arrangements that produced such cooperation. The first indication of how sensitive workers were to management's attitude toward an employee organization came in response to a question toward the end of the survey: "Thinking now about any kind of employee organization, not just unions, how would *you* like it to work? If it was your decision alone to make, and everybody went along with it, would you prefer . . . ?" On governance, we offered two choices: one run jointly by employees and management or one run by employees alone. We imagined that most workers would choose "by employees alone," but an overwhelming majority of nonmanagerial employees chose an organization "run jointly" by employees and management (85 percent) to one run "by employees alone" (10 percent). Even union members supported the jointly run organization (82 percent favored this, as compared with 14 percent who favored the employee-run organization). This floored us.

Recognizing that there are two potential determinants to workers' having an influence on workplace decisions — the strength of any employee organization and the attitude of management toward that organization — we asked employees to choose between two hypothetical organizations, "one that management cooperated with in discussing issues, but had no power to make decisions," and "one that had more power, but management opposed." Exhibit 3.8 shows that 63 percent of nonmanagerial employees favored management cooperation and no power, as compared with 22 percent who wanted more power even if management opposed it. Unionized employees, whom we expected to be less concerned about managerial attitudes, gave almost identical responses, preferring the weak organization with cooperation to the stronger organization.

EXHIBIT 3.8. Management cooperation perceived as essential.

Percentage of workers who think that an employee organization cannot be effective without cooperation

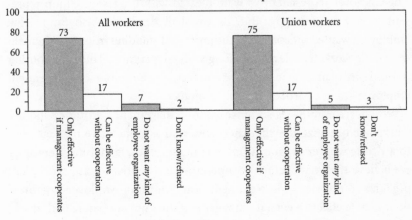

Percentage of workers who prefer management cooperation to a powerful employee organization

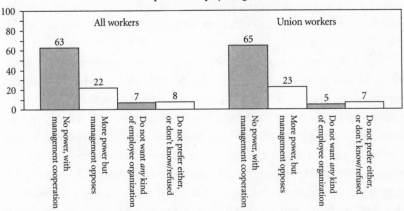

Source: Based on these WRPS questions: (W1.49b) "Do you think employee organizations can be effective *even if* management does not cooperate with them, or do you think they can *only* be effective if management cooperates?"; (W1.49c) (TO NONMANAGERS) "Which *one* of these employee organizations would you prefer (ROTATE ORDER): one that management cooperated with in discussing issues, but had no power to make decisions, or one that had more power, but management opposed?"

Finding that workers prefer a cooperative management to a powerful workplace organization by such an overwhelming number stunned us, as it did the business and labor groups to whom we presented this discovery. The employer representatives were pleased with the result. Union representatives were unhappy. But, as we shall detail, we also found that employees wanted independent authority and standing from management in making workplace decisions along with cooperation. This runs counter to the desire of most management to prevent the formation of independent employee groups, particularly trade unions.

Why were employees so sensitive to management's attitudes about a workplace organization that they preferred a cooperative management to a strong worker organization? The main reason is that most employees believe that management cooperation is essential for any workplace organization to succeed. We asked, "Do you think employee organizations can be effective even if management does not cooperate with them, or do you think they can only be effective if management cooperates?" Three-fourths declared employee organizations could "only be effective with management cooperation" — four times the percentage who thought management cooperation was not required. And once again, union members responded similarly to nonunion members (see Exhibit 3.8).

But what do employees mean by "cooperative management"? A management that smiles and says nice words while it does what it wants? A management that lets workers do what they want? Had the WRPS been a one-shot poll we would have been left wondering or speculating. But we were able to question workers about how they interpreted cooperation on our Wave 2 follow-up. We asked, "what do you think employees get when management is cooperative?" Thirty-one percent said some power to influence company decisions; 66 percent thought employees got a chance to give their opinions and ideas. This pattern of response suggests that most employees expect a cooperative management simply to hear employee views. But we asked further, "If a company always listens to what employees have to say but doesn't follow their advice, is management being cooperative or uncooperative?" Seventy-one percent declared such a management to be uncooperative. Even those who said that the most that employees get from a cooperative management is the chance to give their opinions and ideas thought that a management that listened but never followed employee advice was uncooperative.

We conclude from these responses that employees choose a cooperative management over a strong workplace organization and want workplace organizations to be jointly run by labor and management, because they believe that this gives them a genuine influence on decisions, either through group decision-making or by management's listening to what they have to say and following their advice at least some of the time. Most workers believe that management must be on board for any workplace representation or participation system to work effectively. Management cooperation implies real employee influence.

At the same time, preference for influence through a cooperative management rather than through a strong worker organization does not mean that workers reject an independent organization. In fact, most workers wanted an organization with some independent authority. This opinion came out strongly when we asked employees to specify the characteristics of any workplace organization that dealt with management (see Chapter 7). The majority of workers said that they wanted an organization in which

- either management or employees can raise problems for discussion as opposed to one in which management alone decides the problems that should be discussed.
- employees and management have to agree on decisions as opposed to one in which management makes the final decision about issues.
- conflicts are resolved by an outside arbitrator rather than by management.
- employee representatives are elected or volunteer themselves rather than being chosen by management.

A similar pattern of preferences emerges when we ask employees their views of different existing organizations at the workplace, including unions. Current union members, for example, overwhelmingly prefer a cooperative management to a powerful workplace organization, but they want to keep the organization they have: 90 percent of them would vote to keep their union if a new election were held today. A cooperative management and a union would presumably be their ideal world.

Thirty-two percent of nonunion/nonmanagerial employees would vote for a union "if an election were held today to decide whether employees like [them] should be represented by a union." For these workers, the ideal would also presumably be a union and cooperative management.

Finally, as Chapter 7 shows, many nonunion workers favor a worker organization that is independent of management rather than one that is more compliant to management, while relatively few favor an organization that is management-dominated.

Perhaps we should not have been so surprised at worker sensitivity to management attitudes at the workplace. A workplace has many of the features of a marriage. Cooperation is as essential for a pleasant working environment and high productivity at a workplace as it is for a successful marriage. In most work settings, management has most of the power to effect changes. If you are in a room with a 900-pound gorilla, better that it be good-natured and friendly than hungry and angry. And, to return to the question whose answer first stunned us, workers did not choose an organization run by employees; they chose an organization run *jointly* by management and labor.

One Important Bottleneck: Management Resistance

So why don't workers have the workplace influence they want? We asked employees, "Given the way things are set up now in your company, how likely is it that you could get the influence you want, if you tried to get more influence?" Fifty-six percent of those who wanted more say in workplace decisions indicated that it was "not too likely" or "not likely at all" that they could get the influence they wanted, "even if [they] tried." Only 10 percent thought it "very likely."

Most workers believe that the bottleneck is management. Most believe that management will not voluntarily give them more voice and representation than they currently have. Most believe that management will actively resist employee attempts to establish the one form of independent workplace organization nominally encouraged by U.S. labor law — unions. As with virtually all of the findings in this chapter, this conclusion is based on responses to several questions rather than to a single one.

Consider first how workers grade management's willingness to share power and authority. We asked workers to give a report card to their management in various areas using a five-grade school scale (A, B, C, D, and F). We have all been graded in this manner long enough to have a similar notion of the difference between an A and an F. As Exhibit 3.9 shows, employees gave management high grades in their understanding and knowledge of the business, and reasonably high grades on overall company leadership. If your kids came back with mostly A's and B's, you'd be pleased.

EXHIBIT 3.9. Report card for managers.

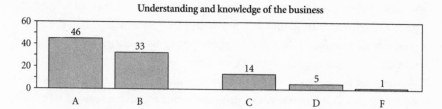

Understanding and knowledge of the business

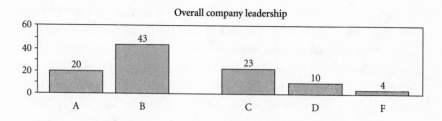

Overall company leadership

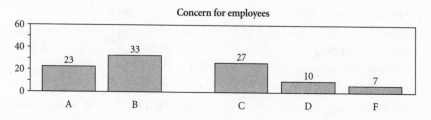

Concern for employees

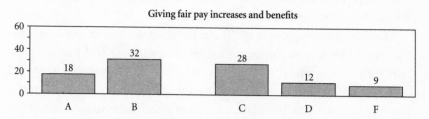

Giving fair pay increases and benefits

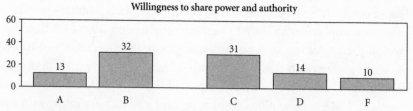

Willingness to share power and authority

Note: Numbers represent percentage of workers who assigned each grade.
Source: Based on this WRPS question: (W2.16aa–ae) "If you were to rate the performance of management on a scale similar to school grades — A for excellent, B for
good, C for fair, D for poor, and F for failure — what grades would you give management in the following areas?" (overall company leadership; concern for employees; giving fair pay increases and benefits; understanding and knowledge of the business; willingness to share power and authority).

But the grades drop precipitously when it comes to issues about how management treats workers. Forty-four percent of workers gave a C grade or lower for management's concern for employees. Forty-nine percent gave a C or worse in giving fair pay increases and benefits. But the worst grade of all was for willingness to share power or authority: 55 percent of workers awarded management a C or lower in this area. Workers see management as hogging power in their organization. If your kids came back with mostly C's or lower, you'd probably want to have a serious talk with them about their future.

This is not, moreover, an aberrant finding: It comes up repeatedly throughout the survey. In the part of the WRPS focused on employee involvement, we asked those workers who believed that greater employee participation would be good for their company's performance[15] why they didn't have this participation. Fifty-five percent cited the reason as management's unwillingness to relinquish power. In the part of the WRPS focused on unionization, we asked respondents who had worked at a company or organization at a time when employees were trying to form a union[16] how management had responded. Two-thirds said that management had opposed the organizing campaign in ways that ranged from information campaigns to threats against or harassment of union supporters.[17] Nonunion employees, most of whom had not experienced a union campaign, also expected significant management opposition to any union drive: 55 percent who said they wanted a union gave management opposition as the central reason for not having one.

Managers tell a similar story. The majority in nonunion firms said that they would oppose any unionization effort; one-third said that it would hurt their advancement in the company if the employees they managed formed a union; and most of them said that it would hurt their career a great deal. Under U.S. labor law, a manager who refuses to oppose a union can be summarily dismissed. Three-fourths of managers said that they felt more comfortable dealing with workers on workplace problems individually, as compared with only 14 percent of managers who said that they would prefer dealing with workers in a group. By contrast, about half of workers preferred to deal with management as a group rather than on a one-to-one basis. Most managers reported that they were willing to meet with employee organizations,[18] but 55 percent said that in dealing with any employee group, they wanted to maintain final decision-making powers in cases of dispute. Twenty percent wanted to pick employee representatives for any joint employee/management committee, as compared with 12 percent of employees who wanted management to pick representatives. In fact, in nonunion companies with employee committees, management picks committee members in 27 percent of the cases, fills the committee with volunteers in 43 percent of the cases, and allows employees to elect them in 17 percent of the cases.

In short, the chief reason that workers have less influence at their workplaces than they want is that management is unwilling to cede power or authority to them. Because management has effective hegemony over workplaces, it is easy to understand why workers so highly emphasize managerial cooperation as the key to any successful employee organizational activity.[19]

Conclusion: Employee Voice in a Competitive Market

This chapter shows that workers want more influence or say in workplace decisions than they have, and that this unsatisfied desire for influence pervades U.S. labor-management relations. It also shows that workers want to express this influence through a more cooperative relationship with management, as well as a more equal one. That workers in the most flexible labor market in the advanced world want greater say in workplace decisions will surprise competitive market theorists who believe that market forces solve all problems. That workers in the labor market with the most unequal income distribution in the advanced world want to work cooperatively with their management will distress those who still believe in zero-sum class struggle.

But this chapter's findings fit well with a view of the labor market in which management and employees are intrinsically linked in a relationship that is both cooperative and conflictual — cooperative because both sides are needed to produce output, and conflictual because people invariably disagree about the best way to execute different activities and about the division of the output from those activities.

Considering workplace disagreements, the economists' favorite solution is to increase the possibilities of *exit* — the ability of dissatisfied workers to quit a firm ("take this job and shove it") or of dissatisfied bosses to fire them ("you're toast, buddy"). But exit is an incomplete solution to workplace problems, and it's one that most workers and management reject in favor of some form of dialogue. Exit creates search costs, as workers look for a new job and management looks for new workers; it obviates the firm-specific skills that workers acquire through experience; and it is a poor way to communicate the precise nature of problems, and thus to learn how to correct them. This is as true for disagreements between managers and employees as it is for disagreements between spouses, or children and parents.

As discussed in Chapter 1, the alternative to exit is *voice* — talking about a problem and seeking to resolve it through discussion, argument, and bargaining. Political scientists, sociologists, psychologists — perhaps everyone but economists — like voice.[20] While voice has its own costs (Another committee meeting? Help!), in many circumstances its benefits outweigh its costs. Voice is far more informative than exit, because it permits the exploration of problems. And the process of exploration itself often helps induce the mutual trust needed to act together on new information. Voice is also more democratic, because it requires the cooperation of both sides: It takes one to exit but two to voice. Both sides need to talk, and both sides need to listen.

That most American workers want more individual and collective voice at the workplace, and believe they cannot get it, tells us that most workers feel they do not have enough of that conversation. At least in the view of workers, the current U.S. labor-relations system is generally failing to support this productive way of dealing with workplace problems.

CHAPTER 4

How Workers Judge Unions

Three different institutions govern American workplaces and the relations between labor and management: collective bargaining between unions and management, management-initiated personnel policies, and state and federal government laws and administrative regulations. We asked what workers thought about these different governing institutions, and this and the next two chapters report what workers told us.

Because we found that most workers want more say at their workplaces, and that many are dissatisfied with existing labor-management relations, one critical thing to learn in these chapters is *why these institutions have not met worker desires for greater say.* It could be that existing institutions are inadequate or defective in some way — that unions, firms, and governments are not competent enough to deliver what workers want. It could be that these institutions are simply inadequately supplied — that more unions, more management-led human-resource programs, more laws and government regulators would solve the problem. Or it could be that the mix of these institutions is off-kilter — that strengthening or weakening one might induce the others to provide what workers want.

Another focus of these chapters is how worker attitudes toward these institutions depend on the worker's personal attributes — for instance, age, sex, ethnicity, or income — and on the work conditions he or she experiences. Perhaps different kinds of people want different kinds of voice, for systematically different reasons. Maybe professionals desiring a greater voice want more private dealings with management, whereas office workers seeking greater voice want more regulations and shop-floor workers want unions. Perhaps if you are employed by a good firm that is open to worker input, a consultative committee can give you your desired voice. If your employer is a mean SOB, however, you might want a full-fledged union. What, in short, explains the variation among workers in their attitudes toward current institutions? Is it you or your workplace that makes you favor or oppose unions, employee involvement (EI) committees, or greater governmental regulation of labor market outcomes?

This chapter examines attitudes toward unions and collective bargaining; Chapter 5 turns to attitudes toward management-led policies; Chapter 6 treats attitudes toward legal regulations.

Unionization and Collective Bargaining: Headed for Oblivion?

Remember "big labor" — George Meany with his cigar, Walter Reuther bargaining against General Motors, Jimmy Hoffa with his National Master Freight Agreement? In the 1950s and 1960s, and in some industries through the 1970s, private-sector unions were powerful actors in the U.S. economy. American labor law, grounded in the National Labor Relations Act (NLRA) of 1935, formally encourages collective bargaining as the preferred mode for determining the rules of work and governing labor-management relations. In the aftermath of World War II, collective bargaining arguably influenced the wages job rules for most workers. Some 40 percent of private-sector workers were organized into unions. Nonunion firms widely copied union workplace conditions such as grievance procedures, seniority rules on job bidding, competitive wages and benefits — if only to keep their own workplaces "union free." Although pay and benefits differed markedly between highly organized sectors such as manufacturing and construction and largely nonunion sectors such as services and the retail trade, many experts believed that the broad direction of American labor outcomes was set in those primary sectors in which unions were key actors. If the United Automobile Workers (UAW) set a contract with General Motors, many other unions and firms would follow the UAW-GM pattern, at least in part, and GM would give its nonunion employees wage and benefit increases matching the collective-bargaining agreement. If GM didn't give all workers the union-won increases, the nonunion workers might want to unionize, or they might suffer from morale problems. In Canada, where collective bargaining is more prevalent than in the United States, union wage settlements still greatly affect nonunion wages. In 1997 workers in the only unionized Canadian Starbucks store gained a $0.75 wage increase (roughly 10 percent); Starbucks extended the increase to the chain's 95 nonunion stores, presumably to reduce the incentive for those workers to organize.

But as the United States enters the twenty-first century, collective bargaining outside the public sector is no longer a major force in the economy. Unions represent less than 10 percent of the private-sector workforce and are concentrated in declining industries such as manufacturing and in older firms and plants within those industries. With union density so low, collective bargaining no longer takes wages and benefits out of competition among firms. The greater number of nonunion competitors reduces the spillover of union gains to nonunion workers by increasing nonunion managerial resistance to matching union wages and benefits. If most of your competitors are low-paid nonunion firms, you face market problems if you follow union contracts and pay higher wages and give better benefits. For the same reason, the decline in unionism reduces the ability of unions to win wage and benefit gains for their members. How can you ask for a large wage gain if it is going to put union firms at risk of going out of business or losing market share? And the diminished threat of unionization reduces the pressure on nonunion firms to match union wages or benefits so as to convince workers that they do not need a union to represent their interests.

Despite the great decline in unionism in the private sector, however, the status of unions still lies at the heart of disputes over national labor policy. From one perspective, this is understandable. Unions are the *only* major workplace institution that workers control. To the extent that national labor policy is about guaranteeing workers the right to associate inside the firm (which is the expressed intent of the NLRA), the ability of workers to form and defend unions is the best test of that guarantee. But the current marginality of unions also makes the discussion a little odd. De facto, it excludes labor policy toward 90 percent of private-sector workers even as it does nothing to relieve the intensity of the union-management argument in Washington.

What reconciles these observations is that the diminished position of unions is exactly what makes that discussion so heated. Most firms welcome the steady decline of private-sector unions and oppose any reform that might reverse the decline, however justifiable the reform. Once only Neanderthal ideologues dreamed of a "union-free" economy; now, however, as that reality approaches, many businesses support this goal and are prepared to expend substantial resources to achieve it — lobbying to prevent union-friendly changes in existing law and resisting attempts at new organizing. For unions, reciprocally, the stakes could not be higher. They are in the fight of their lives, and they're losing. They blame current law and policy for providing them little protection against management attack, and they blame management attack for their problem in organizing workers.

This is not an atmosphere conducive to rational debate about what might best serve American workers. It's more a war zone than a policy discussion. Nor does it help that in that zone, the voices of organized interests (labor or management) fully dominate. The views of average American workers are not heard, or are ignored, even though in principle they should be the governing force in national policy.

So how do American workers view unions? What do members like and dislike about them? Given a choice between working union and working nonunion, how many unorganized workers would want unions to represent them? And why don't those workers, however many or few they are, have the union representation they want?

To Know Unions Is . . . to Love Them?

Our entry into the war zone is a simple question that we asked nonunion and union workers alike: Would they vote for or against a union in an National Labor Relations Board (NLRB) election at their workplaces? The question has two virtues. It requires respondents to give a bottom-line assessment. You can recognize the benefits of unions and still decide to vote no, or you can recognize the flaws of unions and still decide to vote yes. And, while it is hypothetical, the question relates to a choice that people have or might readily make at some point in their working lives. The precise question we asked nonmanagerial/nonunion employees was, "If an election were held today to decide whether employees like you should be represented by a union, would you vote for the union or against the union?"

Exhibit 4.1 shows that nearly one-third of respondents said they would vote for the union. Finding that one-third or so of nonunion workers say they want unions in response to questions of this sort is nothing new. Similar figures are reported in many other studies, including those conducted by management groups.[1] We added a twist to the standard question, however, by also asking nonunion workers how they thought their colleagues would vote in such an election. We asked this because if the one-third of the workforce that wanted a union was evenly distributed among workplaces, unions would lose all NLRB elections by a two-to-one majority, whereas if those workers were in workplaces where most workers wanted unions, unions could win elections at those sites. The results show that 82

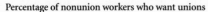

EXHIBIT 4.1. Who wants unions? One-third of nonunion workers and almost all union members.

Percentage of nonunion workers who want unions

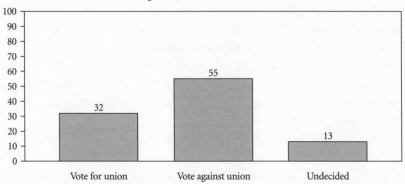

Percentage of union members who want unions

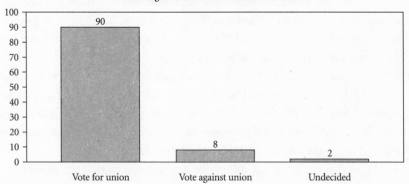

Source: Based on these WRPS questions: (W1.41a) (TO CURRENT UNION MEMBERS) "If a new election were held *today* to decide whether to keep the union at your (company/organiza-tion), would you vote to keep the union or get rid of it?"; (W1.41b) (TO NONMANAGERS WHO ARE NOT CURRENT UNION MEMBERS) "If an election were held *today* to decide whether employees like you should be represented by a union, would you vote for the union or against the union?"

percent of pro-union unorganized workers thought a majority of their col-leagues shared their views, while 10 percent of unorganized workers who opposed unions thought themselves in the minority in their workplace in that view. Putting these numbers together, one-third of disorganized workers believe that were an election held tomorrow, workers at their firm would support a union. This is roughly identical to the share of workers who would themselves vote union.

We also asked union members a nearly identical question about their attitude toward their union: "If a new election were held today to decide whether to keep the union at your company, would you vote to keep the union or to get rid of it?" Few surveys ask union members whether they would vote to keep their union or to disestablish it.[2] The reason is that analysts and practitioners generally believe that most members support their union. After all, votes to disestablish unions are rare; workers queue up for union jobs, and those who do not like a union setting can readily move to a nonunion job, as most jobs are nonunion. The figures in Exhibit 4.1 show that this assumption is true: The vast majority of union members support their union.

The surprise in the exhibit is not that union workers support their union but that they support it so much more than nonunion workers. Nearly 90 percent of current union members said they would vote for the union if an election were held tomorrow. Just 8 percent said they would vote against the union. Underlying these voting intentions are the personal experiences of workers with the union at their firm. More than 70 percent of union members described those experiences as positive, 26 percent described them as very good, and 45 percent described them as good. By contrast, just 5 percent of union members described their experiences as bad, and 2 percent described them as very bad. The remaining 22 percent reported mixed ("neither good nor bad") experiences, but a majority also said they would vote to keep the union were a new election held, indicating that the good outweighed the bad in their bottom line.[3]

The 58-percentage-point difference between the 90 percent support for unions from current union members and the 32 percent support from nonmembers contrasts sharply with the broadly similar attitudes of union and nonunion workers on many other Worker Representation and Participation Survey (WRPS) questions. Recall that we found that union members were just as likely to prefer a cooperative management over a powerful employee organization as were nonunion members, and that union members were nearly as likely as nonunion members to want any workplace organization to be jointly run by management and workers rather than to be run solely by workers. The only issue on which union and nonunion workers' views differ by anything approaching 58 percent is in worker desire for a union. What gives? If we are to understand how American workers view unions, it is essential to explain why union workers are so much more supportive of unions at their workplace than are nonunion workers.

The first explanation that comes to the mind of a social scientist is that

EXHIBIT 4.2. Percentage of workers who want unions (by characteristics of workers).

Sex		
	Men	27
	Women	35
Age		
	18–24	44
	25–34	32
	35–44	26
	45–54	32
	55 +	24
Race		
	Nonblack	28
	Black	59
Education		
	Less than high school	44
	High school graduates	34
	Some college	32
	College graduates	21
Occupation		
	Professional	25
	Laborer	42
Weekly earnings		
	Upper quartile	22
	Lower quartile	45

Source: Tabulated from WRPS for all nonunion/nonmanagerial workers (W1.41b).

union members and nonmembers are different types of people working in different types of jobs. In the private sector, union members substantially differ from nonmembers in several demographic and economic characteristics.[4] They are, for instance, more likely than nonunion workers to be blue-collar and less educated and male. Could it be that workers with these or related characteristics favor unions more than others?

Exhibit 4.2 shows that nonunion member support for unions varies by occupation, education, income, age, and race. The highest level of demand for unionization is by black workers, the majority of whom would vote union today in an NLRB election. Disproportionately large numbers of lower-wage workers, blue-collar workers, and younger workers also support a union. These data indicate that, in general, employees in weak labor market positions tend to favor collective representation. But demographic factors do not explain the huge difference in the desire for unionism between organized and unorganized workers. The reason is simple. Because union members almost unanimously would vote union, there is almost no variation among members for demographic factors to explain.

To document statistically the (in)ability of demographic factors to explain the union/nonunion difference in the desire for a union, we used a linear probability model to relate workers' intention to vote union (1 = vote for the union; 0 = vote against the union) to measures of the individual's demographic characteristics and whether the person was a union member. As Exhibit 4.3 shows, this regression does not reduce the difference between member and nonmember pro-union response at all: The difference actually rises to 60 percentage points.

A second possibility is that an "innate" desire for collective action to obtain a say at their workplace is greater among union members than nonunion workers. Union members might want workplace influence to a greater extent than do observationally equivalent nonunion workers. Or, wanting the same say, union members might prefer solving problems through groups of workers than individually. Perhaps persons with a bent for dealing with problems through collective action are more likely to seek union jobs than are persons who prefer to deal with problems individually. These are variants of the "different types of people" explanation, although in this case the difference between union and nonunion workers is in terms of preferences rather than demographic and economic characteristics.

We examined the extent to which differences in the desire for collective action might explain why union workers are so much more favorable to unions than are nonunion workers by comparing the likelihood that union and nonunion employees would vote for a union contingent on their desire for say and on their preference for group solutions to workplace problems. The results summarized in Exhibit 4.3 fail to explain why union members and nonunion workers view unions so differently. After we take into account the attitudes toward collective action and say, we have a difference between union and nonunion worker opinions that is just 1 percentage point less than it was in the raw data.[5]

A third possible explanation is that workers who are unhappy with unions leave them, so that members consist only of workers who approve of unions. Because about 85 percent of all U.S. jobs are nonunion, workers who don't like unions have a lot of jobs to choose from and can easily vote with their feet. This is a selectivity or sorting argument: People who like unions end up in unions, whereas those who don't like unions work nonunion. But differences in the typical wages and benefits associated with

EXHIBIT 4.3. No simple explanation for why union members are more likely to vote union.

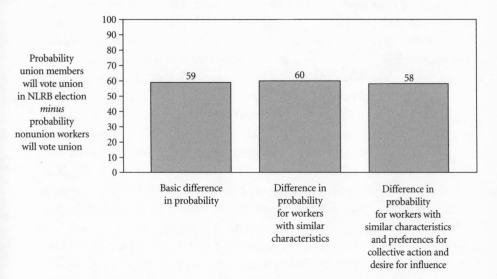

(NLRB = National Labor Relations Board.)

Source: Based on linear probability regression. The "basic difference" is from the regression of the 0/1 dichotomous variable voting for a union on union membership. The "difference in probability for workers with similar characteristics" adds a set of dummy variables for five age groups (18–24, 25–34, 35–44, and 45–54), for two race groups (black and nonblack), for sex, and for five education groups (less than 12 years, high school graduate, technical school post-high school/some college, college graduate, and postcollege graduate). Workplace characteristics were a set of three dummy variables for whether workers were very, somewhat, or not satisfied with their influence on workplace decisions (W1.14_1,2,3,4); two dummy variables for whether they participated in an employee-involvement program (W1.24) or were in a company with a program (W1.23); three dummy variables for the quartile of their weekly earnings in the earnings distribution; one dummy variable for those who did not report earnings; and one dummy variable for worker preferences for preferring to deal with workplace problems with a group of employees rather than as an individual. The latter variable is based on persons who answered that they preferred the help of fellow employees to the WRPS question (W1.34b), "How would *you* prefer to solve a workplace problem of your own? Would you feel more comfortable dealing directly with management *yourself,* or would you feel more comfortable having a *group* of fellow employees *help* you deal with management" (ASKED OF HALF THE SAMPLE), or to the WRPS question (W1.34a), "Do you agree or disagree with the following statement: 'I'd feel more comfortable raising workplace problems through an employee association, rather than as an individual'?" (ASKED OF THE OTHER HALF).

union and nonunion jobs could push the selectivity in the reverse direction. A worker unhappy with a union might stay in that job anyway, as it will generally offer better pay and benefits than a nonunion job would. By contrast, a nonunion worker unhappy with her job might more readily switch employers. The net effect would be more disgruntled workers in the union setting. The democratic nature of unions also argues against explaining the difference in views in terms of sorting. After all, if you don't like how your union works, you can campaign against the leadership and vote for new policies.

One way to assess the selectivity effect is to examine the views of workers who had previously been in a union but were now working nonunion. If people who leave unions do so because they don't like unions, they would be exceptionally likely to vote against a union at their new workplace. Because union density has been falling, there are many more former union members than union members in the WRPS. But former members do not appear to have voted with their feet in leaving unionized settings. Asked how they would vote in an NLRB election, former union members said they would support a union at a moderately *higher* rate than would nonunion workers with no experience of unions: 35 percent of former members said they would vote union, as compared with 30 percent of workers who had never been in a union. Even when we compare workers with the same economic demographic characteristics, we find that former members are slightly more favorably inclined to unions than are persons with no experience with them.[6]

Still, former union members are much closer to other nonunion workers in their intention to vote union than they are to union workers. A 5-percentage-point differences is not a 50-percentage-point one. Why?

One reason is that former members report their union experience less favorably than current members. A smaller share describe their experiences as "very good" (14 percent versus 26 percent) or "good" (24 percent versus 45 percent), and a larger percent describe it as "bad" (13 percent versus 5 percent) or "very bad" (12 percent versus 2 percent). Exhibit 4.4 shows that both current members and former members who say they had good experiences with a union are more likely to vote union than those who say they had a bad experience. These differences in experiences help to explain some of the lower support for unions among ex-members than current members. But ex-union members and current members who had the same experiences with their union differ greatly in their attitudes toward the union. Among workers who report their union experience as "very good," *all* union members would support the union, compared with 74 percent of former members. Among workers who report "bad" or "very bad" union experiences, 44–47 percent of union members would still vote union compared with very small proportions of ex-members.

So the puzzle deepens. Two workers with comparable experiences with

EXHIBIT 4.4. Union members are more likely to vote union than are former members with similar union experiences.

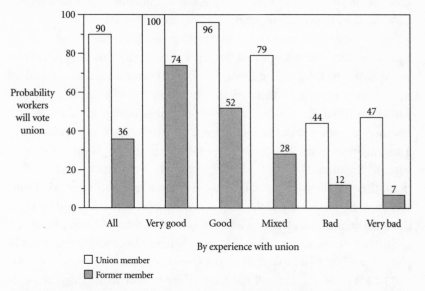

By experience with union

□ Union member
■ Former member

Source: Based on these WRPS questions: (W1.39b) (TO NONMANAGERS) "Have you *ever* been a member of a union?" or (W1.39c) "Before you said there is no union at your (company/organization). Have you *ever* been a member of a union?"; (W1.40a) (TO CURRENT UNION MEMBERS) "How would you describe your personal experience with the union at your (company/organization)?"; (W1.41a) (TO CURRENT UNION MEMBERS) "If a new election were held *today* to decide whether to keep the union at your (company/organization), would you vote to keep the union or get rid of it?"

unions report different intentions to vote depending on their current union status. What is going on?

We think the best explanation for the huge difference in support for unions between members and nonmembers is the "to know them is to love them" hypothesis. This hypothesis is grounded in a well-established psychological phenomenon called the *endowment effect.*[7] Psychologists have found that, in general, people are conservative in their preferences, in the sense that they value what they have more highly than something else of identical value that they don't possess, *simply because they have the former.* Say you are indifferent between two *What Workers Want* coffee mugs: a blue mug and a green mug. You are indifferent between blue and green (it's the gross pink mugs you can't tolerate). You'd just as soon take a blue mug as a green mug. We give you the blue mug, and you use it for a week. We come back and offer to trade you a green mug for your blue one. If you are like most people, you decline the trade. Simply possessing the blue mug raises its value to you. In experiment after experiment, people show that they become attached to what they have or are initially endowed with.

What does the endowment effect imply for our problem?

Assume that workers with neutral feelings about unions are placed into a union setting, and assume that the union is doing a reasonable job at that workplace. Then, by the endowment effect, these workers would end up more favorably inclined to the union than they would otherwise be. They would find that the union does some valuable things for them — for instance, ensuring that the employer treats them fairly in various ways. They might wonder, "How can I be sure the employer will treat me fairly without my union?" In fact, in workplaces where unions win NLRB elections, they usually win by a small majority, but after a short period of time they gain the confidence of the bulk of the workers, with the result that neither management nor workers who opposed the union will seek an election to disestablish the union. This has certainly been the experience at a workplace one of us knows well, Harvard University, where after many years and NLRB votes, clerical and technical workers chose to organize by a slim majority, but where today most workers strongly support the union.

But the same endowment effect should operate on nonunion workers as well. If we put workers with neutral feelings about unions into a nonunion setting, and if the nonunion workplace operates essentially as well as the union workplace, these workers would end up more favorably inclined to the nonunion workplace. They would find that the employer's labor policies did valuable things for them, such as ensuring that supervisors treated them fairly and giving them direct access to management. They might wonder, "How can I be sure things will work well if there is a union intervening between me and the employer?" Maybe the workplace will be rife with conflict.

Assuming that both settings produced the same well-being for workers, and that the endowment effect was working, we would expect that the proportion of workers in the union setting who would vote to keep the workplace union and the proportion of workers in the nonunion setting who would vote to keep the workplace nonunion would be roughly the same. In each case, workers would prefer the mug that they had. It held their coffee without leaking. Who knows if the other mug would do the same?

But the statistics do not show that equal proportions of workers favor the status quo at their workplace. Using the argument that the endowment effect predicts a positive response to the current workplace, we treat workers who are uncertain about how they vote as opposing their current status. Some 55 percent of nonunion workers said they would vote to remain nonunion, as compared with 90 percent of union workers who would vote to remain union. This contrast gives a smaller (35-percentage-point) gap than that in Exhibit 4.1, but it is still huge.

That proportionately more union than nonunion workers want to maintain their current workplace institution suggests that the endowment effect must be working on different outcomes. On average, union workplaces must be fulfilling the desires of their workers better than nonunion workplaces are fulfilling the desires of theirs. Because, contrary to the "let's stay put" endowment effect, 32 percent of nonunion workers want to change the status quo at their workplace as compared with just 8 percent of union workers, unions must be doing something right. That in nonunion settings former union members are more desirous of unions than workers with no experience with unions is consistent with this explanation.

. . . But Not Blindly

When we first conceived the WRPS, we did not intend to ask union members to judge their union. We believed that we had enough on our plate trying to figure out what workers wanted from their workplace than to also try to figure out what they wanted from their union. Our sample of organized workers would necessarily be relatively small — 250 or so union members — which is not enough to permit the type of detailed cross-tabulations and comparisons that we would ideally want to make. And individual unions survey their own members regularly and thus can probe in greater depth the various issues faced by workers in their jurisdiction.

But both the business and labor representatives advising us thought that failing to ask union members about attitudes toward say in their union would be a serious omission. The business representatives said, "It won't look right to the business community if you find that workers are dissatisfied with their say in companies, and you never ask the same things about unions. You're giving workers a chance to gripe about us but not about them." The union representatives said, "It won't look right to unions if you ask union workers a lot of questions about their dealings with management and not about their union. We're part of the workplace, too."

So we asked union members how satisfied they were with the influence they and their union coworkers had in union decisions in several areas. We worded this question similarly to the questions we had asked about worker satisfaction with influence on workplace decisions. This gave us a natural

EXHIBIT 4.5. Percentage of union members satisfied with their union.

	Very satisfied	Somewhat satisfied	Not too/ not satisfied	Don't know
Satisfied with say in local issues				
Choosing local leaders	35	44	17	4
Bargaining about wages and benefits	31	41	25	3
Less satisfied with national leaders				
Choosing national leaders in your union	20	49	35	6
Least satisfied with say in union political process				
Union positions on national political issues	15	53	25	7
Endorsements of candidates in political campaigns	13	50	29	8

Source: Based on this WRPS question: (W1.43a–e) (TO CURRENT UNION MEMBERS; N = 282) "How satisfied are you with the influence you and fellow union members have in union decisions about (VARIOUS ITEMS; ROTATE)?" (very satisfied, somewhat satisfied, not too satisfied, not satisfied at all).

measuring rod for comparing employee attitudes toward their say in union decisions and in their say in workplace decisions. The results, reported in Exhibit 4.5, show that union members are relatively satisfied with their influence on local leadership and on wage and benefit negotiations. Because unions are democratic organizations that elect local leaders, whose performance and their performance on wage and benefit negotiations is the key to their staying in office, union members can rightfully feel they have considerable influence in these areas. By contrast, union members are not particularly satisfied with their influence on national union operations, and are least satisfied with union endorsement of political candidates and the union position on national issues. One reason is that there is more division within the ranks of labor on political issues than is reflected in national union behavior. Whereas national union leadership almost invariably supports Democrats, only one-third of union members on the WRPS consider themselves Democrats. In the national election that immediately preceded the WRPS, 33 percent of union members in the survey reported having voted for Bill Clinton, as compared with 14 percent who voted for George Bush and 16 percent for Ross Perot. What happened to the rest? Like many other groups, a large number of union members simply did not vote.

That union members are happier with their influence on local leadership than national leadership is not a new finding. The result showed up in the 1973 Quality of Work Survey, which was one of the first national surveys to ask union members about their satisfaction with their union.[8] It also shows up in surveys that individual unions take of their members.[9] And it is consistent with American attitudes toward local versus national leadership in other areas. Voters usually express greater support for their House representative or local government than for the Congress or other Washington-based government bodies, and they like their local school more than the quality of education in America.

The different evaluation by union members of local and national unions might also suggest another factor behind the difference in the attitudes toward unions by union members and nonmembers. When union members are asked whether they would vote to maintain the union at their workplace, they probably think about the local union. When nonunion workers are asked about whether they want a union, they might think more about the national union, about whom even members express less satisfaction. We did not ask the questions that would test this story. We did, however, ask workers to tell us what they thought unions do for members. Exhibit 4.6 shows that while many workers cite the bread-and-butter issues of better pay/working conditions as the first thing, many also cite the voice issues of respect/fair treatment on the job and some cite giving workers a greater say in workplace decisions. Around 1 in 11 nonunion workers and 1 in 16 union members don't believe that unions offer anything for their members. The biggest difference in the opinions between union members

EXHIBIT 4.6. What do unions do for members?

	Union members	Nonunion employees
Better pay/working conditions	48	39
More say in workplace issues	11	14
More respect/fair treatment on job	31	22
Unions don't do anything	6	9
Don't know	3	13

Source: Based on this WRPS question: (W2.37) "What is the *most* important thing a union does for its members?"

EXHIBIT 4.7. Percentage of union members satisfied with influence on local union and on workplace decisions.

Degree of satisfaction with influence in choosing local union leadership		
Very	35%	Of these workers 27% were very satisfied with their influence on workplace decisions 25% were not satisfied with their influence on workplace decisions
Not	17%	Of these workers 7% were very satisfied with their influence on workplace decisions 44% were not satisfied with their influence on workplace decisions
Degree of satisfaction with influence on workplace decisions		
Very	20%	Of these workers 47% were very satisfied with their influence on workplace decisions 6% were not satisfied with their influence on workplace decisions
Not	29%	Of these workers 29% were very satisfied with their influence on workplace decisions 26% were not satisfied with their influence on workplace decisions

Source: Satisfaction with influence on union is based on this WRPS question: (W1.43a) "How satisfied are you with the influence you and fellow union members have in union decisions about choosing local leaders?" Satisfaction with influence on workplace is based on this WRPS question: (W1.14_1,2,3,4) "Overall, how satisfied are you with the influence you have in company decisions that affect your job or work life?"

and nonmembers is that nonmembers were more likely to say they didn't know what unions did.

How do employees' satisfaction with their say at their workplace stack up against their satisfaction with their influence on their local union?

Exhibit 4.7 shows that union members are more satisfied with their influence on their local union than they are with their influence on company decisions affecting their job. But this does not mean that satisfaction with the union competes with satisfaction with the firm in employee feelings. To the contrary, the exhibit shows a positive relationship between satisfaction with the union and satisfaction with say at the firm. Twenty-seven percent of union members who are satisfied with their influence on the union report that they are satisfied with their influence at the workplace. By contrast, just 7 percent of members who are dissatisfied with their say at the union are satisfied with their say at the workplace. Our data cannot determine whether satisfaction with say at the firm or say at the local union comes first, or whether (as we suspect) a positive labor-management relationship requires openness from both the firm and the union. But the correlation is consistent with the notion that good labor relations produce workers satisfied with both the firm and the union. In any case, at the local level, unions seem to be doing all right, and when they do all right, so does the firm in giving workers influence at the workplace.

The One-Third Who Want Union Representation

Thus far, we have focused on the 14 percent of the WRPS who are union members. But more than twice as many workers are nonunion members who say they want union representation. Who are these workers? What explains their desire for unionization? Why are workers who want to be unionized not represented by unions?

Two factors should determine worker desire for unions: the personal characteristics of workers and the way management treats workers at their workplace. Exhibit 4.2 showed that the personal characteristics of people affect their desire for unions, but not overwhelmingly so (except for race). In Exhibit 4.8 we look at the other part of the workplace equation: how management treats workers. This exhibit shows that employee desires for a union do in fact depend greatly on how management treats workers. Workers who report poor labor-management relations at their firm or who give management low grades in concern for workers and willingness to share power or who find management not trustworthy or who report that they do not look forward to work (presumably because their workplace is an unpleasant environment) are all especially likely to say that they would vote for a union.

To see whether the characteristics of workplaces or the characteristics of workers most affect the desire of nonunion workers to vote union, we estimated how well we would predict the votes of workers who differed in these two dimensions separately and together. Again, we used a linear

EXHIBIT 4.8. Percentage of nonunion employees who want unions.

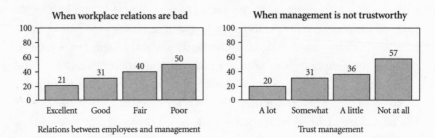

When workplace relations are bad

Excellent	21
Good	31
Fair	40
Poor	50

Relations between employees and management

When management is not trustworthy

A lot	20
Somewhat	31
A little	36
Not at all	57

Trust management

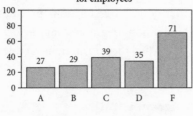

When management shows little concern for employees

A	27
B	29
C	39
D	35
F	71

Grade management on concern

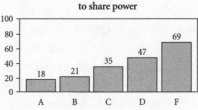

When workers dislike jobs

Look forward	27
Don't care	24
Wish didn't have to go	43

Feeling about going to work

When workers are dissatisfied with influence

Very	23
Somewhat	28
Not too	44
Not at all	54

Satisfaction with influence at workplace

When management is unwilling to share power

A	18
B	21
C	35
D	47
F	69

Grade management on sharing power

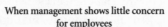

Source: Based on the following WRPS questions: (W1.10b) "Overall, how would you rate relations between employees and management at your (company/organization)?"; (W1.10a) "In general, how much do you trust your (company/organization) to keep its promises to you and other employees?"; (W2.16ab) "If you were to rate the performance of management in your company on a scale similar to school grades — A for excellent, B for good, C for fair, D for poor, and F for failure — what grade would you give *management* in its concern for employees?"; (W1.8) "On an average day, what best describes your feeling about going to work?" (W1.14_1,2,3,4) "Overall, how satisfied are you with the influence you have in company decisions that affect your job and work life?"; (W2.16ae) "If you were to rate the performance of management in your company on a scale similar to school grades — A for excellent, B for good, C for fair, D for poor, and F for failure — what grade would you give *management* in its willingness to share power and authority?"

probability model to predict how workers would vote. We classify workers with the highest estimated probabilities as "vote union" and those with the lowest estimated probabilities as "vote nonunion" (here "highest" and "lowest" are defined so that the model accurately predicts the proportion who actually voted union). If the model perfectly accounted for worker votes, it would assign a higher probability for voting union to all those workers who in fact said they would vote union than to workers who said they would vote against the union. If, by contrast, we randomly assigned workers to a "vote union" group in proportion to the actual proportion who voted union, we would correctly classify around one-third.[10] So the success of our model can be judged by the extent to which it exceeds the 0.31 percent correct classification from the random model and the closer it is to giving a 100 percent correct classification.

The results, summarized in Exhibit 4.9, show that personal factors (age, education, race, and gender) and the nature of the workplace (employees influence on workplace decisions, their pay, and whether their firm has EI committees) determine the probability of voting union roughly equally. By themselves, measures of personal characteristics correctly classify 67 percent of the sample, while measures of workplace characteristics by themselves correctly classify 68 percent of the sample.

The most powerful personal characteristic[11] that affects the vote for union is race. Conditional on other factors, nonunion black workers are 27 percent more likely to favor a union than are white nonunion workers. This is nearly the same as the unconditional black/white difference shown in Exhibit 4.2. That blacks favor unions more than whites with the same characteristics and workplace experiences might reflect the exceptional vulnerability of blacks in the job market, their need for protection against discrimination, or their historical reliance on collective action, such as through the civil rights movement, to improve their situation.

On the workplace side, employees dissatisfied with their influence are more likely to support unions than other workers. By contrast, workers in firms with EI committees are less likely to support a union.[12]

Taken together, the two factors correctly classify 69 percent of the sample. In the analysis with both sets of variables, the measures of workplace characteristics are more statistically important, save for the huge effect of race on the desire to vote union.

There is yet another way in which the WRPS allows us to examine the preferences of nonunion workers toward unions. We can compare the characteristics of a workplace organization that nonunion workers want with the charac-

EXHIBIT 4.9. Predicting which nonunion employees would vote union.

Model used for prediction	Percent of workers whose vote was correctly predicted
Random model	31
Personal characteristics of workers	67
Workplace characteristics	68
Both personal and workplace characteristics	70
Perfect model	100

Source: Based on linear probability models, with 1 for employees who said that they would vote union and 0 for employees who said they would vote against the union or didn't know/refused on the WRPS question (W1.41b), "If an election were held today to decide whether employees like you should be represented by a union, would you vote for the union or against the union?"

The sample size for the regression was 1,666. Personal characteristics were a set of dummy variables for five age groups (18–24, 25–34, 35–44, and 45–54), for two race groups (black and nonblack), for sex, and for five education groups (less than 11 years, high school graduate, technical school post-high school/some college, college graduate, and postcollege graduate). Workplace characteristics were a set of three dummy variables for whether workers were very, somewhat, or not satisfied with their influence on workplace decisions; two dummy variables for whether they participated in an employee-involvement program or were in a company with a program; three dummy variables for the quartile of their weekly earnings; and one dummy variable for those who did not report earnings. To estimate the proportion of workers whose vote was correctly predicted, we ranked workers by the estimated probability they would vote union and determined a cut-off point that divided the sample, so that the number of workers with a probability greater than or equal to the cutoff was equal to the number who said they would vote union. We then gave all workers a predicted 0/1 for voting union, depending on how their predicted probability compared with the cutoff. The percent of workers whose support is correctly predicted is the sum of those for whom the model correctly predicted a 1 or 0 relative to the entire sample.

teristics that union workers want. If nonunion workers who would vote union are being deprived of the representation they want, they should have similar preferences for an organization as union members. By contrast, nonunion workers opposed to unionization should want workplace organizations that operate much as management wants. Exhibit 4.10 provides such a comparison.

In sum, there is thus nothing odd about the one-third of the nonunion workforce who say they want unions. They cannot readily rely on the job market outside their firm to give them bargaining power, and the management at their workplaces seems to show little respect for them. Their preferences for an independent organization are similar to those of workers who are represented by a union.

EXHIBIT 4.10. Percentage of workers who want a strongly independent workplace organization (electing representatives and using arbitration to settle issues).

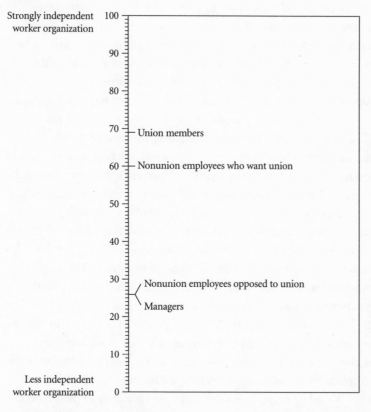

Source: Calculated from this WRPS question: (W1.48) "Thinking now about any kind of employee organization, not just unions, how would you like it to work? If it was your decision alone to make, and everybody went along with it, would you prefer (W1.48a) an organization that can use an *outside* referee or arbitrator to settle issues, or one in which management makes the final decisions about issues? (W1.48c) An organization in which the key participants are *volunteers*, are *elected*, or are *appointed* by management?" We have omitted workers who said they don't know/refused or did not want any kind of organization. Strongly independent organization is defined as one wanting to elect representatives and to use arbitration to settle issues.

What about the majority of workers who do not want union representation or who reported that most workers at their workplace would vote against a union? Because unions raise wages and benefits, are they being irrational? What reasons do these workers give for opposing union representation?

Management often argues that the reason unions are declining is that unions are not providing adequate services to members. Enlightened firms, governmental protections, and a flexible labor market provide the services that workers once needed unions to give them. Unions blame much of their decline on management resistance to workers' efforts to unionize. They stress that anti-union managements bring in high-powered consultants, run expensive campaigns that impugn union supporters, and create a literal war at the workplace when workers try to organize.

The responses to the WRPS suggest that both claims have some validity. Many workers who said most employees at their workplace did not want a union said that collective representation was inferior to taking care of workplace problems on their own (27 percent); that having a union would create too much tension in the company (25 percent); that they didn't like the way unions operate (22 percent); and that unions were too weak to help workers (10 percent). The 27 percent who favored dealing with workplace problems on their own and 22 percent who said they didn't like how unions operate would seem to fit management's view. The 25 percent who cited tension with management fit the view of unionists. The 10 percent who considered unions too weak could be cited by other side: With less management resistance, unions would be stronger and thus might win the support of these workers, but perhaps the perceived weakness of unions relates more to their organizational deficiencies than to management.

What about the workers who reported that a majority of employees at their workplace would vote union? Why are they not organized when they want to be? We asked employees who said that a majority of their coworkers favored a union why their workplace was not organized. The biggest single explanation was management resistance to unions (55 percent), as opposed to unions not being interested in organizing employees like them (22 percent) or unidentified other reasons.

How much weight should we attach to this answer? Voting in NLRB elections about unionization is done through secret ballot administered by the government. We Americans like to think of ourselves as tough independent folk, pioneers of sorts, not easily cowed in our decisions. Can management resistance really be that important? While most analysts, including us, attribute a significant role to management opposition in the decline in unionization, there are skeptics.[13] For instance, in its analysis of the reasons for union decline, the management-oriented Employment Policy Foundation estimated that managerial opposition had very little effect on the trend in union density.[14] In fact, it is not easy to take limited quantitative data and parse the precise decomposition of the factors that underlie the decline in union density, any more than it is easy to determine the reasons for slowdowns or accelerations in productivity, the increase in U.S. income inequality, the low level of inflation despite surging employment and tight labor markets, or rises or falls in the stock market.

How, then, might we better resolve this argument? One approach is to call on commonsense economic theory, which provides an unequivocal answer. As one of our conservative colleagues said, "Of course, management resistance is important. If it didn't matter, why does management put so much of its resources into fighting unions? And why is management so opposed to any labor-law reform that might restrict its ability to run anti-union campaigns? Shareholders don't pay managers millions to blow money on something that doesn't matter."

But our approach is not to rely on theory but on empirical evidence. We asked workers on the WRPS if their vote on unionizing their workplace would change if management signaled a different attitude on unionization. Although we initially doubted that very many workers would admit that their vote would depend on management, even if that was the case, a sufficiently large proportion said, "Yes, I would switch, depending on management's views" to swing many NLRB elections. Some 12 percent of workers who said that they would vote anti-union told us that they would vote pro-union if management was not hostile to the union; some 8 percent of pro-union voters said that they would change their vote and oppose the union if management was opposed to the union. Because NLRB representation elections are often won or lost by swings of 5–10 percent of the vote, these numbers are enough to change the outcomes of many such NLRB elections. The fact, noted earlier, that workers value management cooperation so highly in assessing the form of labor organization they would want at their workplace strengthens this conclusion.

How Management Sees Unions

Given that worker attitudes toward unions are influenced by management's position, it is important to find out how management views unions. In U.S. labor law, workers are supposed to decide by themselves without management interference whether they want to be unionized. But while management doesn't vote in the election, it tries to influence results, and in the view of workers, competitive theorists, and most empirical analysts, it does in fact do so. Management can influence whether workers want a union and how they vote in an NLRB election by treating workers well or poorly. And management can influence results by using its free-speech rights to try to convince workers to vote one way or the other. In fact, in the vast majority of NLRB representation elections, management not only gives its opinion that unionization is not in the workers' interest but also conducts an aggressive expensive campaign to convince workers that they should vote against the union. In many cases, management pays lawyers and consultants who specialize in union prevention to run their anti-union campaigns and convince workers that a union is not in their interest. Nor is illegal "campaigning" — for example, firing workers for supporting the union — uncommon.

We asked the managers on the WRPS their views about unionization at their workplace: "Mr. or Ms. Nonunion Manager, how would you and your firm respond to worker efforts to unionize?" Fifty-three percent of the managers in nonunion firms said they would oppose any effort by their employees to form a union; 27 percent said they wouldn't care; and 15 percent said that they would welcome the effort. When we presented these results to AFL-CIO leaders, they salivated to know the names of the 15 percent of managers who were pro-union, "so we can send out some organizers today." When we presented the results to business leaders, they were equally interested in the 15 percent of managers who were pro-union, "so we can get them fired immediately." In fact, nearly one-third (32 percent) of nonunion managers thought it would hurt their career if the employees they managed succeeded in forming a union, with more than half of those thinking it would hurt their career a great deal.[15]

Are most managers in union firms also opposed to unions? Mr. or Ms. Union Manager, are unions good or bad for workers at your firm? Are they good or bad for the firm itself?

Some 64 percent of managers in firms with unions thought unions made the lives of workers in their firm better.[16] Twice as many managers in unionized companies also reported that in recent years unions were more cooperative rather than more confrontational with the firm.[17] The vast majority of managers in union firms reported that top management in their firm accepted the union as a partner in workplace decisions. But nearly one-quarter said that management wanted to get rid of the union. Most managers in union companies said that the union did not affect their day-to-day work, but of those who said that the union did affect them, more reported that the union made their job harder than reported that the union made their job easier.[18] Eight percent of managers in union firms thought the union hurt the performance of the firm "a lot"; 25 percent thought the union hurt the firm "a little." On the other side of the spectrum, 19 percent of managers in union firms thought the union helped the firm "a lot"; 8 percent thought it helped "a little." The remaining managers thought the union had no effect on firm performance.

So what's the one-paragraph sound-bite that summarizes how workers judge American unions? Taking union and nonunion workers together, the bottom line for this chapter is that *looking upon unionization as a good produced by the market, the United States is producing too little.* Despite the widely publicized flaws of unions and the unease that many members feel about the role of unions on the national scene, 44 percent of private-sector American workers would like to be represented by a union, more than three times the 14 percent share of our sample who reported union membership. The workers who want a union but do not have one receive lower wages, are disproportionately black, report particularly poor labor-management relations at their workplace, and have similar attitudes toward the independence of any workplace organization as union members. In short, they seem to be just the sort of folks who could truly benefit from union representation. As far as our evidence goes, the main reason these workers are not unionized is that the managements of their firms does not want them to be represented by a union.

CHAPTER 5

How Workers Judge Management

With the decline in collective bargaining as a means of governing workplaces and a forum for discussion between labor and management, management-led human-resource policies have become the chief determinant of how most employees fare at their workplace and how much say they have about their job. Virtually all large firms have sizable and sophisticated human-resource or personnel departments. Many have introduced innovative labor practices — employee involvement (EI) committees and worker teams — to harness employee skills and effort to improve firm performance.

The business press offers much advice about how to manage employees. Some consultants advise management to operate "lean and mean"; to run things like Attila the Hun or to follow the strategic precepts of Musashi, the famous Samurai swordsman; or to master Sun Tze's *Art of War*.[1] Others tell management to listen more closely to what employees say and to involve workers in the firm's decision making;[2] to support EI programs of different kinds; and to let workers have real responsibility in self-managed work teams. Some argue for gain-sharing or other profit-sharing schemes, while others advocate stock-ownership plans to align the interests of employees with those of the firm. The goal is to give workers control over the decisions about which they have the most information and to develop incentive systems so that the workers make decisions that produce the most value for the firm. At the end of this rainbow of competitive democratization is the high-performance workplace — a near mythical organization in which workers make continuous improvements in product quality or productivity for the mutual advantage of themselves and the firm, without much supervision.

How Common Are Advanced Human-Resource Systems?

The question of how many advanced human-resource practices exist in the job market occupied the initial deliberations of the Commission on the Future of Worker-Management Relations. The chair of the commission, former labor secretary and Harvard Professor Emeritus John Dunlop thought the high-performance stuff was vastly exaggerated. He recalled wave upon wave of revolutionary "new" ways of managing — from the workplace cooperation movement of the 1920s through the quality circles of the 1970s and 1980s. Taking a long-term perspective, he was less impressed with the new kid on the block than were others. CEOs might tell his commission or Congress that their firm had the latest employee-empowerment programs, but that didn't mean middle management had implemented the program on the shop floor, much less that any worker saw the firm as operating differently.

Still, the business people who testified before the commission swore that their companies could not compete in global markets without employee involvement, teamwork, total quality management, decentralized decision-making, the whole shebang. And they said everybody was doing it.

There are three ways to discover what firms are doing in human-resource management: ask knowledgeable managers at particular sites about practices at that workplace, visit workplaces and observe how they operate, or ask employees themselves — the human resources that management is managing — what is going on at their workplace. We, of course, did the third.

Exhibit 5.1 shows that a large proportion of American workers report that their firm has a given advanced human-resource practice or policy. More than two-thirds report that their firm has a personnel/human-resource department. Nearly as many say the firm holds town meetings in which management discusses issues with the whole workforce.

Most workers report that their firm has an open-door policy for individual employees to talk directly to top management, and nearly half say that their firm has an open-door policy for groups of employees who want to do the same. One-third report that their management meets with committees of employees to discuss problems. One-third have a grievance system to resolve individual problems that involve an outside referee. Most important to us, 56 percent of respondents reported that their firm has some form of EI system, and nearly one-third reported that they themselves participated in it.

On the pay front, U.S. firms reward workers in ways that go far beyond traditional hourly or monthly wage and salary checks. Many employees report that they receive bonuses based on profit sharing or based on meeting workplace goals. Some 22 percent of nonmanagerial employees report

EXHIBIT 5.1. Modern human-resource policies are widespread.

Personnel practices	Percentage of employees with given practice
Personnel or human-resource department	68
Open door to management	
For individual problems	85
For group problems	63
Regular "town" meetings	47
Committee of employees that discusses problems with management on a regular basis	37
Employee-involvement program at firm	52
Participated in program	31
Grievance system with outside arbitrator	32
Modes of pay/share participation	
Bonuses through profit sharing	30
Bonuses based on workplace goals	27
Participates in employee stock-ownership plan	23
Employee-owned	11

Source: Tabulated from background questions and from these WRPS questions: (W1.36) "Which of the following, if any, does your (company/organization) have to deal with issues that affect employees as a group? (W1.36a) Regular 'town' meetings with employees, called by management, (W1.36b) An open-door policy for groups of employees to raise issues about policies with upper management, (W1.36c) A committee of employees that discusses problems with management on a regular basis, (W1.36d) A union that negotiates with management on a regular basis."; (W1.29) "Which of the following, if any, does your (company/organization) have? (W1.29a) A *personnel* or human resource department, (W1.29b) *An open-door policy* so employees can tell upper management about problems with their immediate supervisors, (W1.29c) A *grievance* procedure that uses an outside referee or arbitrator to settle disputes between an employee and management."; (W1.d16) On your (main) job, do you (W1.d16a) Receive any bonuses based on profit sharing? (W1.d16b) Receive any bonuses based on meeting workplace goals? (W1.d16c) Participate in an employee stock-ownership plan? (W1.d16d) Work in an employee-owned (company/organization)? "The percentages are for the entire sample, including that small percentage who responded "don't know" or refused to answer.

that they participate in some form of employee stock-ownership plan, and 12 percent describe their firm as employee-owned.[3]

Advanced human-resource practices are found to some degree throughout the U.S. labor market.[4] As Dunlop suspected, these programs are more prevalent in large firms and in manufacturing, but they are not limited to those high-profile enterprises.[5]

Do Human-Resource Programs Work?

The programs work tolerably well, although not perfectly, according to employees. Some 28 percent of our respondents said that their firm's policies toward the problems faced by *individuals* at the workplace were "very effective"; 49 percent rated the policies as "somewhat effective"; 21 percent rated them as "not too effective" or "not effective at all."

Asked separately about each policy that deals with problems that face workers as a *group*, most employees gave a comparable assessment. Thirty-three percent judged open-door policies as "very effective" in dealing with group problems, as compared with 17 percent who saw their firm's open-door policies as "not too effective" or "not effective." Twenty-nine percent judged employee committees as "very effective," as compared with 10 percent who saw them as "not too effective" or "not effective." Twenty-four percent judged town meetings as "very effective," as compared with 17 percent who judged them as "not too effective" or "not effective."

To get some perspective on these numbers, compare them to workers' assessment of unionization as a means of dealing with workplace problems. Some 30 percent of unionized employees report that their union is "very effective" in resolving group problems, as compared with 15 percent who report it as ineffective. This puts the most highly rated firm-based policy — the open-door policy — in the same range of effectiveness as unions. Nonunion workers in unionized firms, however, rate the effectiveness of the union less favorably than do union members: 18 percent judge the union as effective, and 20 percent judge the union as ineffective. But union members judge firm-based policies as less effective than do nonunion members, so that on average union members view the union as the most effective way of resolving group problems. We see the endowment effect at work once again.

High-Performance Workplaces?

There is no single definition of a high-performance work organization. Business analysts often identify these organizations as those that apply many advanced human-resource practices to a large portion of their workforce. The argument is that no single practice does much for productivity or worker well-being, much less transforms a workplace into the high-performance mode. It is the combination of practices as complementary synergistic parts of a new work system that produces high performance. In this view, the high-performance workplace is a bit of an all-or-nothing proposition — qualitatively different from other workplaces.

The idea that these workplaces are something special is intuitively appealing. It tracks what workers told us in the focus groups. Recall that in most groups, only one or two workers reported that their firm involved employees in decisions, and that the other workers looked enviously on them as inhabiting a different universe than themselves.

If high-performance workplaces differ qualitatively from others, how might this show up in our data? By the existence of a distinct cluster of firms having many effective advanced practices; this should separate them from the pack. High-performance firms should have many effective practices, whereas other firms should have very few, with few organizations in between. To examine this issue, we needed to form some sort of scale from the various human-resource practices about which workers reported. But how should we group the practices, and how should we treat worker reports on their effectiveness?

Our first thought was to use the Guttman scaling technique developed in the 1940s. A Guttman scale assumes that responses to yes/no questions have a cumulative property that allows the analyst to rank them on a scale from highest to lowest, and that people answer these questions so that they themselves can be similarly ordered. Think of 20 questions on a test, ranked from easiest to hardest. If the ranking is valid and you answer 10 questions correctly, you should answer Questions 1 through 10 correctly, not the harder ones that follow or some mixture of hard and easy questions. If you can correctly answer Question 20, which is the hardest, you should answer all the questions correctly. Knowing how many questions you answered thus tells us exactly where you fit on a scale of 1 to 20.[6] But the system does this only if the responses fit the model perfectly, which is rare in practice. Maybe you answered the hardest question because you got lucky. Maybe you missed some easy ones because your mind wandered. Maybe the single scale does not truly capture the variation of difficulty among questions.

For questions with multiple responses — say, 1 is the lowest answer and 4 the highest — there is natural analogue to the Guttman scale. This is the same summated rating technique that we used in Chapter 3, which is simply the sum of the answers to the relevant questions, all ordered in the same direction. Say we ask you to assess fairness at your workplace with four related questions. Each question has three possible answers, with 1 being the least fair and 3 the most fair. If you answer 1, 3, 1, 2, the summated rating for your workplace would be 7. If you answer 3, 2, 3, 2, the summated rating for your workplace would be 10 — higher in the fairness scale. Summated rating works perfectly when variables are measured in common units, so that each item contributes equally to overall fairness and when the differences among responses (for instance, between "not important," "somewhat important," and very important") across items have the same meaning. Neither of these is likely in questions that ask people for subjective judgments. The answer "somewhat important" might be closer to "very important" on one question but closer to "not at all important" on another question.

As psychologists at a seminar pointed out to us, however, educational psychologists had developed measures that allowed for responses to diverge from the rigid Guttman or summated rating pattern. The key was to assume that an individual has a probability of answering questions in a particular way depending on his or her characteristics and the item. They told us that the Rasch scale (invented by a Danish researcher of that name) was the appropriate measurement tool for what we wanted. This procedure effectively orders responses from high to low, adds them up, and then rescales the sum of responses depending on where the score fits in the distribution of outcomes. Instead of giving you a 7 when you answer 3, 1, 1, 2 on four questions, the Rasch scale gives you a score that depends on how many people scored higher or lower than you.[7]

The Rasch procedure treats the least frequent practices as the most advanced (that is, as the hardest questions on the exam). If a firm has the most advanced practice, it should have all the less advanced practices, and thus have more practices than a less-advanced firm. If the firm has few practices, these should be the most common and thus the least advanced practices. And as with practices, so, too, with effectiveness. Given two firms with the same practice, the scaling places the one in which the practice is judged most effective as more advanced. We proceeded to develop a Rasch scale for human-resource practices reported on the WRPS. The data supported this formulation, indicating that this scaling captures the major interrelations among the practices.

As noted earlier, if "high-performance" firms are truly separate from other firms, we would anticipate finding a sharp divergence in the position of firms on the scale of advanced practices: the high-performance firms at one end and the rest at the other. But when we made a histogram of practices and their effectiveness, we obtained the results in Exhibit 5.2.

The distribution does not fit the expected pattern. It resembles more the bell-shaped normal curve, with a central tendency around which firms cluster. There are firms having more practices and more effective practices at the upper tail and firms with fewer and less effective practices at the lower tail. But there are many firms in the middle.

EXHIBIT 5.2. Distribution of advanced human-resource practices.

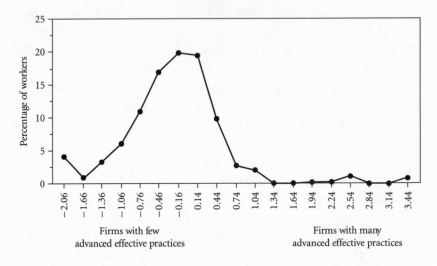

Firms with few
advanced effective practices

Firms with many
advanced effective practices

Source: Calculated by forming a latent variable for advanced human-resource practices from ten WRPS questions regarding the presence and effectiveness of practices.

Six of the questions related to how firms deal with problems that affect workers as a group: (W1.36) "Which of the following, if any, does your company/organization have to deal with issues that affect employees as a group? (W1.36a) Regular 'town' meetings with employees, called by management, (W1.36b) An open-door policy for *groups* of employees to raise issues about policy with upper management, (W1.36c) A committee of employees that discusses problems with management on a regular basis."; (W1.37) "How effective were (THE PRECEDING ITEMS a, b, AND c) in resolving group problems or concerns?" (very effective, somewhat effective, not too effective, not effective at all).

Four of the questions related to how firms deal with problems faced by individuals: (W1.29) "Which of the following, if any, does your company/organization have? (W1.29a) A personnel or human resources department, (W1.29b) An open-door policy so employees can tell management about problems with their immediate supervisor, (W1.29c) A grievance procedure that uses an outside referee or arbitrator to settle disputes between employees and management."; (W1.32) "Overall, how effective is your company's/organization's system for resolving the problems *individual* employees have at work?"

Two of the questions related to employee-involvement programs: (W1.23) "Some companies are organizing workplace decision-making in new ways to get employees more involved — using things like self-directed work teams, total quality management, quality circles, or other employee-involvement programs. Is anything like this now being done in your company/organization?"; (W1.27) "How effective would you say these programs have been in improving productivity or quality?"

The latent variable was formed in two steps. First, we gave a value of 0 to 4 to each of the seven practices based on its existence and effectiveness: A 0 meant the firm did not have the practice; a 1 meant it had the practice and that the practice was not effective at all; a 2 meant that the practice was not too effective; a 3 meant that it was somewhat effective; and a 4 meant that it was very effective. We summed these variables to get a single number and then transformed that number into a Rasch score, as discussed in the text.

Are high-performance workplaces not magically transformed firms but the upper tail of a continuous population of all firms? This interpretation is enough at odds with popular business discussion that we decided to examine the distribution of human-resource practices in two other data sets and found that the distribution of firms by number of advanced practices looks more like a normal distribution than a discontinuous one in those data sets also.[8] To say that the distribution of effective practices resembles a normal distribution does not mean that it is randomly generated, natural, or fixed in shape. Some kinds of workers and some kinds of firms have more human-resource management practices than others. The mean practice in a normal distribution of practices can change, and firms can be clustered closer to or farther from the average. What is important is that firms do not appear to cluster neatly into "high-performance firms" and "all others" in the way that the popular understanding suggests.

Who Has Advanced Practices?

Exhibit 5.3 shows the proportion of workers with differing characteristics who are in firms with many effective advanced human-resource practices (those in the upper decile of our measure) and those in firms with few effective advanced human-resource practices (those in the lowest decile).

Worker characteristics have only a modest effect on the prevalence of advanced human-resource management. There are no race or sex differences to speak of, relatively modest variation by education, and, save for the youngest workers, who are less likely than others to be in a firm with advanced practices, relatively little variation by age. What matters significantly are (1) the worker's position in the earnings distribution, with higher-paid workers more likely to be in firms with advanced human-resource management; (2) union status, with unionized firms having more advanced practices;[9] and (3) size of firm or workplace, with more advanced practices in larger firms and workplaces.[10]

Do Advanced Human-Resource Practices Improve Worker Well-Being?

One way to judge the effectiveness of advanced human-resource policies is to compare how workers in firms with differing practices rate labor-management relations at their company and their own job satisfaction. If the policies are effective, employees should be happier at their

EXHIBIT 5.3. Percentage of workers in the upper decile of firms with advanced human-resource practices.

Sex		
	Male	10
	Female	10
Age		
	24 or Less	5
	25–34	9
	35–44	10
	45–54	14
	55–64	12
Race		
	Black	9
	Nonblack	10
Education		
	College graduates	10
	Some college	12
	High school	9
	Less than high school	8
Earnings		
	Upper quartile	13
	Second quartile	9
	Third quartile	9
	Bottom quartile	6
Union status		
	Member	17
	Nonunion employee	9
Number of employees in firm		
	Less than or equal to 99	3
	100–499	10
	500–999	9
	1,000 or more	14
Number of employees in workplace		
	Less than 25	7
	25–29	7
	100–499	11
	500–999	13
	1,000 or more	20

Source: Calculated using the human resource practices measure described in Exhibit 5.2 and in the text. This measure takes seven human resource practices and workers' assessment of their effectiveness to form a single "latent variable." The top decile consists of workers in firms that score in the upper 10 percent. Workers in groups that score below 10 percent are thus underrepresented in firms with advanced human resource practices. Workers in groups that score above 10 percent are disproportionately in firms with advanced practices.

EXHIBIT 5.4. Effective advanced human-resource practices and worker satisfaction go together.

	Position of firms in distribution of advanced practices	
	Upper decile	Lower decile
Attitude toward work		
Look forward	78	44
Wish didn't have to go	15	46
Labor-management relations		
Excellent	21	5
Good	62	30
Fair	15	33
Poor	2	32
Labor-management relations compared with average		
Better	59	12
Average	40	50
Worse	1	37

Source: Calculated using the human resource practices measure described in Exhibit 5.2 and in the text. This measure takes seven human resource practices and workers' assessment of their effectiveness to form a single "latent variable." The top decile consists of workers in firms that score in the upper 10 percent; the bottom decile consists of workers in firms that score in the lowest 10 percent.

job and report more pleasant labor-management relations at firms with those policies than at firms lacking those policies. Exhibit 5.4 shows that, in fact, workers in firms with more advanced and effective human-resource practices are more likely than workers at less-advanced firms to say they look forward to going to work, to report that labor-management relations are excellent, and to believe that management shows concern for workers.

This association of employee satisfaction with advanced human-resource practices does not prove that the practices themselves create better workplace relations, or even better worker perceptions thereof. Good firms with relatively worker-friendly cultures might treat workers well even in the absence of such practices, with the practices simply being the least-costly or the au courant way of doing the right thing. Correlation does not mean causality. Still, even if the link between advanced human-resource practices and worker satisfaction simply means that advanced practices are a good indicator of a more worker-friendly culture, we will have identified a measurable indicator of the often fuzzy notion of corporate culture.

The Open-Door Policy

You think your firm is doing something wrong. It does not respond properly to customer complaints; it fails to take advantage of a new technology or market opportunity; it fails to deal with an employee whose coughing might make the entire workforce sick. Or perhaps the firm is not paying you the salary you deserve, or your supervisor is picking on you or sexually harassing you.

A direct way to deal with these or any other problem is to march into top management's office, explain the problem, and ask management to rectify it. Firms with open-door policies encourage such individual expression of voice. Initially we viewed open doors skeptically. We thought that few workers or groups of workers would bring serious problems to higher-ups for fear of antagonizing their immediate superior or being labeled a malcontent. In the focus groups, workers did not volunteer "open door" as a policy that meant all that much to them.

But so many workers on the WRPS reported that their firm had an open-door policy and said that this policy was effective that we thought we ought to find out something more about it. In our follow-up survey we asked employees how much they used the open-door policy and what issues they brought to the open-door manager.

About one-fifth of employees said they went to high-level management with problems three or more times in the previous twelve months.[11] About one-fourth reported using the policy once or twice a year. The majority reported that they had not used it at all in the past year. Workers with individual market power are more likely to use an open-door policy than are workers in a weaker position in the job market. A large number of managers and college-educated workers used the policy during the year.[12] The workers *least* likely to walk through the open door are those with the least market power: younger workers (ages 18 to 24), those 55 and older, and those who are semi-skilled or manual laborers.[13] Just 40 percent of black workers reported that they had used the open door.

In addition, the workers who described their firm's open-door system as relatively effective used it more frequently.[14] For instance, 42 percent of workers who said that their system was very effective used it three or more times in the past year, and just 9 percent said that they had not used it in the last year. By contrast, of the workers who judged the open door as ineffective, 17 percent did not use it at all, while 33 percent used it three or more times over the year. The implication is that when the policy is real, it creates a steady flow of complainants to management.

We asked workers to tell us about the problem they raised *the last time* they used the open door. The majority of problems were in the areas of production/procedures/operations and general working conditions.[15] Very few workers used the open door to discuss problems with their immediate supervisors or wages or benefits. Managers and union members are most likely to bring up money problems.[16] Workers who used the open door for problems with operations or general working conditions reported most favorably on its effectiveness.[17]

Open doors increase communication between workers and higher management in regard to day-to-day production problems or working conditions. They are not widely used, however, to deal with issues that have more potential to cause conflict — for instance, employee-supervisor difficulties and wages and benefits — or for larger questions regarding company governance or policy.

Employee Involvement

The firm-based policies or programs of greatest interest to us are EI programs, as such programs are specifically designed to increase worker influence on workplace decisions. EI programs come in various flavors: quality circles and discussion groups, total quality management, self-directed work teams, safety committees, production committees, Christmas party committees, and diverse small groups that work on sundry other issues. What places these disparate programs under a single rubric is their goal of giving workers more say in decision making. Consider them the firm's response to the representation/participation gap.

More Is Better

The extent to which EI resolves the representation/participation gap depends on the types of committees management sets up and on how these committees function. Despite occasional business claims that committees are primarily short-term groups that deal exclusively with specific problems, many EI participants report that their firm's program includes long-term committees that deal with different problems. Sixty percent of workers said that their firm had both long-term and short-term EI committees, and of those workers who said that their firm had only one type of committee, nearly the same proportion reported it as being long term (18 percent) as those who reported it as being short term (19 percent). Adding the 60 percent of workers who said their firm had long-term and short-term EI committees and the 18 percent who said their firm had only long-term committees, we see that 78 percent of firms with EI have committees that discuss different problems over a long period of time. Even when management limits EI to short-term committees, moreover, the range of issues covered by all of the short-term committees taken together might be quite wide.

Most EI committees of whatever duration focus on issues relating to production. Approximately half of workers participating in long-term committees and half of those on short-term committees reported discussion of quality assurance, safety, and technology/new products. By contrast, only 14 percent of workers on long-term committees and only 8 percent on short-term ones reported discussing issues relating to job advancement/performance.

This does not mean, however, that there is no substantive distinction between EI committees that are short term and those that are long term. Twenty-four percent of workers on the long-term committees said that the committee discussed *issues of corporate direction*, as compared with 8 percent of workers on short-term committees. Firms with the longer-term EI committees seem to give workers greater say in the broader operation of the firm, and thus to come closer to the ideal high-performance workplace than those firms whose committees are short term.

U.S. labor law limits, in theory, what an employer-controlled EI committee can do. Under Section 8(a)(2) of the NLRA, firms cannot set up groups of workers to help set policy on issues such as wages, benefits, and working conditions covered by collective bargaining. The intent of this section was to outlaw company unions of the type that firms established in the 1930s and 1940s to subvert workers who wanted to form independent unions. Paradoxically, perhaps, this effort to protect workers allows EI committees to discuss productivity and other matters that might benefit the firm, but does not allow them legally to do much that might benefit workers.[18]

The extent to which EI committees step over the legal line and operate as illegal company unions is an area of contention between management and labor. Management's belief that the law is too restrictive has motivated the various teamwork bills that Congress has considered but has not enacted into law. To get some notion of how much illegal discussion goes on, we asked workers who participated on an EI committee whether the committee discussed wages and benefits. Twenty-eight percent of the participants reported discussing wage and benefit issues. We then asked those who discussed these issues if continuing such discussion was very important to the success of the program: 72 percent said it was. Initially, we also intended to ask workers whether they discussed working conditions in their EI committees, but our management and union advisors convinced us that this would be redundant. In reality, it is nearly impossible to talk about productivity without discussing working conditions.

Productivity Effects and Voice

Employee involvement supposedly raises productivity by encouraging workers to make more suggestions about how to improve their job environment and committing management to take those suggestions seriously and act on them. If EI works this way, EI participants should report that they make more suggestions and that management acts on them more frequently than do other employees.

Exhibit 5.5 shows that they do. Measured in percentages, nearly twice as many EI participants as nonparticipants say that they make suggestions often, and nearly twice as many EI participants as nonparticipants report that management takes the suggestions seriously. Managers tell the same story. One-third of managers involved in an EI program said that they almost always find worker suggestions useful, as compared with one-fourth of managers not involved in an EI program.

As a crude indicator of the greater flow of useful suggestions from EI participants than from other employees, we multiply the proportion of workers who say they make suggestions "often" by the proportion who say that management "almost always" takes their suggestion. This gives us a measure of the likelihood that employees regularly make suggestions that in fact improve their workplace. By this measure, EI participants are *three times* more likely to report being in this position than are nonparticipants.[19] Our data cannot determine, however, whether this in turn means that firms with EI programs are more likely to make continuous quality improvements than other firms, justifying the expense of an EI program. It is possible that managers in non-EI firms discover comparable improvements in their firms as workers do in EI firms, or that the value to the firm of employee suggestions generated by an EI program does not meet the

EXHIBIT 5.5. The value of employee involvement (EI) to the firm.

EI participants make more suggestions that management take seriously

	Percentage of workers who make suggestions		Percentage of managers who find suggestions useful		Chance that employees make potentially valuable suggestions (%)
	Often	Hardly ever/never	Almost always	Hardly ever/never	
EI participant	57	6	45	9	26
Nonparticipant in EI firm	30	22	27	19	9
No EI at firm	33	21	23	31	8

EI participants are more involved in the firm's success

	Percentage of workers who rate employees				Percentage of workers who say EI raises productivity/product quality	
	Willingness to work hard		Care about success of firm		Very effective	Not too effective
	A	D/F	A	D/F		
EI participant	38	2	30	3	32	11
Nonparticipant in EI firm	35	3	28	6	14	21
No EI at firm	33	5	20	12	—	—

Source: Based on these WRPS questions: (W1.17) (TO NONMANAGERS) "How often, if ever, *do you* make suggestions to your supervisor or to management about how to improve quality or productivity?"; (W1.17a) (TO MANAGERS) "How often, if ever, *do you get* suggestions from the people you manage about how to improve quality or productivity?"; (W1.22a) "Imagine that *more* decisions about production and operations were made by employees, instead of by managers. How do you think this would affect your (company/organization) in the following areas?"; (W1.22b) (BASED ON FORM B) "Would the *quality* of the (company's/organization's) products or services get *better or worse?*"; (W2.16b) "If you were to rate the performance of employees in your company on a scale similar to school grades — A for excellent, B for good, C for fair, D for poor, and F for failure — what grade would you give *employees* in their

program's costs. This is possible but unlikely — at least in our view and in that of management at companies with EI.

Employee involvement might also improve a firm's performance by inducing greater effort. If you are involved in making a decision, you might try harder to carry it out. We asked employees to grade the willingness of their coworkers to work hard, using the easily recognizable school grade scale. The lower panel of Exhibit 5.5 shows that proportionately more participants in EI programs than other workers gave high grades to the work effort of their coworkers and believe that their coworkers were concerned about the success of the company, although the differences are not large. As nearly half of EI participants report that they supervise other employees or tell others what to do (as compared with many fewer of nonparticipants in firms with EI and employees in other firms), these grades are presumably based on direct knowledge, not hearsay.[20]

Most employees who participate in EI programs believe that EI raises productivity, although with varying degrees of effectiveness. Nearly one-third of nonmanagerial EI participants rated the programs as very effective in improving productivity or quality; a majority viewed them as somewhat effective, while just one in nine people found them ineffective.[21] And although we did not ask about EI's direct effect on company success, a larger proportion of EI participants described their company as successful (79 percent) than did nonparticipants (65 percent).[22]

Several studies have compared productivity between firms or establishments with and without various forms of EI, ranging from formal programs to employee-ownership programs. Some researchers have examined the same firm before and after introduction of programs designed to increase worker participation in decision-making. As a broad summary, employee participation raises productivity modestly — say, by 2 percent to 5 percent. Studies based on small numbers of firms or observations sometimes find that these effects are not "statistically significant,"[23] but this appears to be more a problem of sample size than lack of an effect. Several small samples that give weak results in the same direction can cumulate into statistically significant results when considered as a whole.[24] Thus it appears that the moderately positive views that workers express on this issue are consistent with what economists and business experts find in their studies.

Why Doesn't Every Firm Do It?

Productivity increases of 2 percent to 5 percent may seem modest to some readers, but in fact they are not. Productivity growth of the United

States has been on the order of 1.5 percent per year, so that 2 percent to 5 percent translates into 1 to 3 years of growth. Productivity improvements of 2 percent to 5 percent can greatly increase the value of profits to the firm and its shareholders. In the U.S. economy as a whole, capital's share of output (value added) is around 25 percent. An increase in productivity that raises output by, say, 3 percent, *all* of which went into capital in the form of profits, would raise profits by 12 percent.[25] Multiply this by typical price-earnings ratios, and the value of shares could more than double.

If EI is generally found to raise productivity, why doesn't every firm do it? One explanation is a "market knows best" theory. Managers know what they are doing. EI works for some firms, and managers in those firms adopt it. In other firms, EI would not work, and managers there reject it. Different strokes for different folks. There must be some truth to this explanation. Even if management isn't all that bright, surely it is more likely to introduce EI where it works than where it doesn't. If this explanation is right, firms for whom EI pays off more ought to make greater use of EI than firms for whom EI pays off less.

Going beyond argumentation, there is some evidence for this. EI appears to be more effective in union settings than in nonunion settings,[26] and unionized firms are more likely to have an EI program than nonunion firms. But this explanation also has a Dr. Pangloss flavor. It suggests that everything management does is the best in this best of all possible worlds. Every firm knows what it should do, and it goes about doing it. This may fit an Economics 101 blackboard model of the economy, but not the dynamic world of modern capitalism.

Another explanation is that EI programs might give a firm a competitive edge when few firms institute them but lose their advantageous effects as more and more firms adopt them. If, say, 30 of 100 firms implement a successful EI program that gets them to the high-performance ideal, they might benefit; to the thirty-first firm, however, the rewards from adopting the strategy might be negligible. There are too many good employers in the market, and the thirty-first firm may find it wiser to go lean and mean. In a well-functioning market, the returns to different human-resource strategies ought to be the same for the firm on the margin between the alternatives, and possibly to all firms as well.

There is probably some truth to this explanation. Innovators in EI might garner most of the gains — for instance, by attracting the best workers or those most likely to be more productive when they participate in decisions. Imitators might find imitating an EI strategy to be less profitable for them. We know of no evidence for this sort of explanation, however.

The most important reason that EI is not universal is that it is not easy to implement. Management can't simply prance into the office or shop floor and announce, "Workers, we want you to be involved and participate in decisions," and expect results. EI succeeds by getting workers to look at their jobs differently, by getting managers to look at workers differently, and by getting managers and workers to interact differently. In many firms this requires change in corporate culture. If the company cannot transform the way people see themselves and behave in workplaces, then EI can fail.

Indeed, while the business press publicizes EI successes, there are also EI failures. We know one major firm that introduced EI and found that workers simply took advantage of less supervision to slack off. It had to kill the program to get back on track. In the mid-1990s, Levi Strauss introduced a teamwork system in its apparel plants, which seems to have created as many or more problems than success for the firm and its workers.[27] It can also take a long time to find the right EI program for a given firm at any given time. What works for Motorola or Xerox (two firms with highly publicized EI programs) in 1990 might not work at XYZ production or even at Motorola or Xerox in 2000. We visited one establishment in which a manager favored EI for moral reasons. For years he tried different types of involvement programs, but nothing worked until, finally, he found a way that struck a chord with workers and succeeded in getting them involved.

Do Employees Want It?

To determine worker attitudes toward EI, we first asked if workers personally benefited from involvement in their firm' EI program. If they benefited, they presumably would favor continuing the program. The vast majority of nonunion/nonmanagerial participants in EI programs reported that they had personally benefited from their involvement in the program by getting more influence about how they did their job.[28] Thirty-six percent said they benefited from an increase in pay (although EI committees are not supposed to discuss issues of pay).

Second, we asked EI participants how they would feel if the company dismantled the program. Although most EI participants told us that they thought that their management was committed to the firm's EI program,[29] there is always the risk that the firm might decide that some other way of managing is more profitable. Perhaps the CEO will read the new business best-seller *Managing the Queen Ant Way* and decide that success requires turning workers into drones rather than empowered EI participants.

We posed the issue to workers in terms of a takeover: "Imagine your company was taken over tomorrow by new managers who did not want to continue the employee involvement program. If your company got rid of these teams or committees, how would it affect you personally?" The vast majority of EI participants said that eliminating the EI program would make their work lives worse. Twenty-three percent said that closing the program would be very bad for them, and 48 percent said it would be bad, as compared with 22 percent who said it wouldn't affect them one way or the other. Just 5 percent thought this would be good for them.

If we assume that workers who say that eliminating EI is bad for them would vote for continuing their firm's EI program if the firm polled them on the decision, the level of support among EI participants for EI approaches the level of support among union workers for their union. Because voting on EI is not an option, in hindsight we should also have asked the workers who said the elimination of their firm's EI program would be bad or very bad for them what, if anything, they might try to do to save the program. But we didn't think that far ahead.

One other way of assessing employee attitudes toward EI is to compare overall attitudes toward workplaces between workers in EI programs with workers in firms without such programs or nonparticipating workers in firms with EI programs. If employees value EI as much as they claim, participants in EI programs should have more positive attitudes toward their firm, its management, and its labor relations policies than nonparticipants.

Exhibit 5.6 shows that this is the case. Compared to nonparticipants, workers in EI programs express more loyalty and trust toward the firm, rate employee management relations better, are more likely to think their firm has better than average labor relations, are more likely to look forward to going to work, and give their employer higher grades in concern for employees and giving fair pay increases/benefits.

Note, moreover, that the difference in attitudes is nearly as substantial between participants and nonparticipants in firms with EI programs as between participants and nonparticipants in firms without EI programs. This implies that the EI effect is not simply a difference between workers in firms with good labor practices and workers in firms with bad labor practices. Rather, it is an effect within firms associated specifically with EI.

Sixty-four percent of workers without an EI program said they wished that their firm had one. These workers have a mixed set of characteristics.

EXHIBIT 5.6. Employee-involvement (EI) participants have more positive attitudes toward their work and management.

	Percentage of workers loyal to firm		Percentage of workers who trust firm		Percentage of workers who report labor-management relations			
	A lot	Only a little/none	A lot	Only a little/none	Excellent	Fair/poor	Better than average	Worse than average
EI participant	63	8	49	12	21	25	50	5
Nonparticipant in EI firm	52	15	36	18	14	36	35	8
Firm has no EI program	49	17	30	28	17	36	31	13

	Percentage of workers who grade management on				Percentage of workers with attitude toward work	
	Concern for workers		Giving fair pay increase			
	A	D/F	A	D/F	Look forward to work	Wish didn't have to go
EI participant	26	9	23	12	74	19
Nonparticipant in EI firm	19	15	23	18	63	25
Firm has no EI program	22	25	12	29	61	30

Source: Based on these WRPS questions: (W1.9c) "How much loyalty would you say you feel toward your (company/organization) as a whole?" (a lot, some, only a little, no loyalty at all); (W1.10a) (BASED ON FORM A) "In general, how much do you trust your (company/organization) to keep its promises to you and other employees?"; (W1.10b) (BASED ON FORM B) "Overall, how would you rate relations between employees and management at your (company/organization)?"; (W1.8) "On an average day, what best describes your feeling about going to work?"; (W2.16A) "If you were to rate the performance of management in your company on a scale similar to school grades — A for excellent, B for good, C for fair, D for poor, and F for failure — what grade would you give *management* in (W2.16aa) Overall company leadership? (W2.16ab) Concern for employees? (W2.16ac) Giving fair pay increases and benefits? (W2.16ad) Understanding and knowledge of the business? (W2.16ae) Willingness to share power and authority?"

They are higher paid than the workers in non-EI firms who told us that they did not want a program at their firm. The workers who wanted an EI program are more likely to be hourly paid than salaried. They are disproportionately black and especially likely to be employed in manufacturing and in large firms and at large work sites.

What seems to unify this disparate group is their desire for more say at their job. The representation/participation gap for these workers is larger than it is for workers who said they did not want their firm to introduce an EI program. Similarly, 81 percent of workers without an EI program who were very dissatisfied with their influence on decisions at their workplace said they wanted an EI program, whereas just 50 percent of workers who were satisfied with their influence on workplace decisions said that they wanted an EI program. So among those most desirous of more say, EI is seen as part of the solution.

It Reduces But Doesn't Close the Representation/Participation Gap

As the major employer-initiated effort to give workers more say on the job, EI should increase worker participation in all sorts of decisions relating to their job. While we do not have a before-and-after research design to test this, we can compare EI participants with nonparticipants. Exhibit 5.7 shows that proportionately more EI participants say they have a lot of direct influence on a workplace decision than do nonparticipants in firms with EI and workers in firms without an EI program. More than one-third of EI participants report that they are "very satisfied" with the influence they have in company decisions that affect their job or work life, as compared with 12 percent who are "not too satisfied" or "not at all satisfied." By contrast, nonparticipants are more likely to report that they are "not too satisfied" or "not at all satisfied" with their influence than those who say they are "very satisfied." Because nonparticipants in firms with EI programs report similar say on the job and satisfaction with their influence on decisions as workers in firms with no EI program, we interpret these results as reflecting the impact of EI rather than of being employed in a good firm.

But EI does not eliminate the representation/participation gap. Exhibit 5.8 contrasts the representation/participation gap between workers with and without EI.[30] Item by item, EI participants have smaller gaps than nonparticipants in firms with EI programs and nonparticipants in firms without programs. But even among EI participants, a sizable representation/participation gap remains.

EXHIBIT 5.7. Employee-involvement (EI) participation gives workers more influence on the job.

| | EI participants have more influence on the job | |
	Lots of influence	Only a little/none
EI participant	46	24
Nonparticipant in EI firm	32	36
Firm has no EI program	29	38

| | Are more satisfied with their influence on decisions that affect their work life | |
	Very satisfied	Not too satisfied/ not at all satisfied
EI participant	34	12
Nonparticipant in EI firm	19	24
Firm has no EI program	19	29

| | Think that speaking up against company policy would help/hurt their career | |
	Help	Hurt
EI participant	39	23
Nonparticipant in EI firm	25	39
Firm has no EI program	27	47

Source: Respondents' involvement with decisions is based on WRPS question W1.12aa–ah, as described in Exhibit 3.5. We exclude responses on deciding on raises in pay or on kinds of benefits in this question, as these are legally proscribed issues for employee-involvement committees.

The satisfied-with-influence panel is from this WRPS question: (W1.14_1,2,3,4) "Overall, how satisfied are you with the influence you have in company decisions that affect your job and work life?" (very satisfied, somewhat satisfied, not too satisfied, not satisfied at all).

The speaking-up-against-company-policy panel is from this WRPS question: (W2.17) "If there was some company policy that you *spoke up against* in your company/organization, how would that affect your chances for advancement in the company/organization? Would it *help* you or *hurt* you in getting ahead?"

One possible reason that EI falls short of closing the gap is that having a say in decisions increases the desire for say. Workers who participate in EI programs are more likely to report that it is very important to have an influence on workplace decisions than are persons who do not participate in EI. This is most striking with respect to deciding how to do one's job: 86 percent of EI participants say that this is very important to them, as compared with just 70 percent of workers in non-EI firms and 73 percent of

EXHIBIT 5.8. Representation/participation gap (by employee-involvement [EI] status).

	Difference between percentage who say it is very important to have influence and percentage who have a lot of direct involvement on workplace decisions		
Workplace decision	EI participant	Nonparticipant in EI firm	Non-EI firm
Setting work *schedules*, including breaks, overtime, and time off	1	15	18
Setting safety standards	9	20	28
Deciding what *training* is needed for people in the work group	26	30	37
Deciding what kinds of *benefits* employees get	47	53	59
Deciding how to work with new *equipment* or *software*	19	21	28
Deciding how much of a *raise* in pay people in the work group get	32	29	39
Setting *goals* for group or department	17	22	23
Deciding *how* to do your job and organize the work	18	21	20
Average of all items	21	26	32

Source: Based on these WRPS questions: (W1.12a) "How much direct involvement and influence do *you* have in (ITEM)?" (a lot, some, only a little, no direct involvement at all); (W1.13a) "Suppose you *could* have a lot of influence in these areas at work, regardless of whether you do now or not. How important would it be for you to have *a lot* of influence on these decisions? First, how important would it be to you to have influence on (ITEM)?" (very important, somewhat important, not too important, not important at all).

nonparticipants in EI firms. EI raises the proportion of workers who have a lot of influence on deciding how to do their job, but it also raises the proportion of those to whom this is important, producing only a modest difference in the gap.

Another reason that EI leaves a sizable representation/participation gap might be that EI programs simply do not go far enough in empowering workers. Eighty-two percent of EI participants believe that giving employees a greater say would make their firm's EI program work better, and many EI managers tell much the same story: that their programs are not as advanced as they could be, or that they're not as advanced as top management would like.

It Reduces Worker Desire for Unionization

Many union activists are uneasy about EI programs because they believe that nonunion firms introduce them in part to reduce worker interest in unions and that unionized firms introduce them to undermine the union role in decision-making. Even if firms are less Machiavellian in introducing EI programs than the activists think (nonunion firms have more direct ways to keep a workplace nonunion if they so desire, and most union firms seek cooperative relations with their union), EI may still reduce interest in unions by giving workers more say at the workplace outside the union venue.

Exhibit 5.9 shows that union activists' concern about the effect of EI on nonunion workers' desire for unionization is well-placed. EI participants are much less likely to say that they would vote for a union in an NLRB election than are nonparticipants. But even nonparticipants in a company with an EI program are less likely to say that they would vote union than workers in companies without programs, perhaps because of the other good labor-relations practices in EI firms. And EI participants are less likely to think that the majority of workers at their workplace would vote union than are nonparticipants.

Consistent with these results, EI participants also show less desire for group decision-making than do nonparticipants. On our split questions that probed attitudes toward group or individual voice, EI participants did not want to deal with management through a group or employee association as much as nonparticipants did. And EI participants are more favorably inclined than nonparticipants to employee organizations that are management-dominated. For example, while a majority of EI participants prefer that disagreements between management and workers be settled by an arbitrator rather than by management, that majority is much less

EXHIBIT 5.9. Employee Involvement (EI) reduces workers' desire for an independent organization.

	Support for union in NLRB election	
	For union	Against union
EI participant	23	66
Nonparticipant in EI firm	27	61
Firm has no EI program	39	47

	Belief that employee representatives would improve firms' system for solving employee problems	
	More effective	Less effective
EI participant	65	31
Nonparticipant in EI firm	75	19
Firm has no EI program	71	22

	Desire for arbitrator to reach final decision when committee of workers and management disagree on workplace issue	
	Arbitrator decides	Management decides
EI participant	49	43
Nonparticipant in EI firm	58	33
Firm has no EI program	61	33

(NLRB=National Labor Relations Board.)
Source: Based on these WRPS questions: (W1.41b) "If an election was held *today* to decide whether employees like you should be represented by a union, would you vote for or against a union?"; (W1.38c) "Imagine employees chose their own representatives to meet with management and discuss the problems employees have as a group. Do you think this would be *more* effective or *less* effective (as compared with your current system) to resolve employees' concerns?"; (W1.48a) "If it was *your* decision alone to make, and everybody went along with it, would you prefer an organization that can use an outside referee or arbitrator to settle issues or one in which management makes the final decisions about issues?"

among EI participants than among nonparticipants. Indicative of the more positive attitude that workers in EI firms have toward their management than workers in non-EI settings, just 11 percent of workers in firms with EI believed their management would break the law to bar the union, as compared with 21 percent of workers in non-EI firms.[31]

It Is More Likely with Unions, and Member Satisfaction Rises

While EI programs reduce the desire of nonunion workers for unions, they are found more frequently at union workplaces than at nonunion

EXHIBIT 5.10. Unionized workers with employee involvement (EI) are more satisfied with their union.

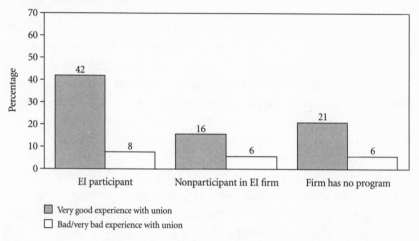

Source: Based on WRPS question (asked to union members only:) W1.40b "How would you describe your personal experience with the union at your company?"

workplaces. On our survey, 55 percent of unionized workers had an EI program at their workplace, and 33 percent participated in it, as compared with 49 percent of nonunion workers with an EI program and 28 percent participating in the program. Perhaps because unions give workers an independent source of authority or strength to deal with management, or perhaps because EI makes it easier for management to deal cooperatively with union workers, EI complements unionism.

Consistent with this, there is general agreement among managers that EI programs work well in unionized settings. Whereas managements from nonunion companies usually claim that they can run their business better without a union, when it comes to EI committees, nonunion managers who testified before the Commission on the Future of Worker-Management Relations claimed only that they could run an EI program as well as unionized managements, implicitly recognizing that unionized firms set the standard.[32] Econometric evidence[33] goes even further, suggesting that in fact EI produces greater gains in union settings.

Finally, contrary to the fears of some union activists, EI does not undermine worker support for unions at union workplaces. In fact, it has the opposite effect. As Exhibit 5.10 shows, workers in unionized workplaces who participate in EI programs describe their experiences with their union as markedly better than unionized workers who are not EI participants. A unionized workplace with EI makes workers more satisfied with both the union and management.

Employee-involvement programs make workers' lives better. Workers believe that EI improves company performance as well, and studies of worker participation in company decision-making suggest that, at a minimum, such programs do not harm productivity on average and, more likely than not, raise it. Most workers want these programs and want them to become more extensive, giving workers greater say. While workers in EI programs are less likely to want unions, EI is more prevalent under unionism, and unionized workers are happier with their union in EI settings. EI represents a road toward a new mode of labor-management relations that most workers want, but given competing managerial paradigms and fads, it is doubtful that management alone can travel far enough down that road to give workers what they want.

CHAPTER 6

How Workers Judge Government Regulations

Faster than a speeding bullet. Stronger than the strongest steel. Able to leap into your workplace to rescue you from an unfair supervisor, sexual harassment, discrimination, dangerous work conditions. Willing to battle million-dollar corporate lawyers to guarantee your employment rights in court. Is it a bird? Is it a plane? Is it Superman? Spiderman? The Incredible Hulk? The U.S. cavalry? No, it's your federal government regulator!

You haven't seen the advertisement? You wouldn't believe it if you did? It sends shivers up your spine?

At one time the United States had a largely unregulated labor market. American unions opposed laws that would protect workers on the notion that the government should not substitute for unions. American management opposed regulations requiring businesses to treat workers decently on the notion that the government should not substitute for voluntary business activities.

But this is no longer the case. The Great Depression and New Deal introduced labor legislation covering unionization, minimum wages, and hours worked, among other things. The civil rights revolution created a new corpus of individual rights at workplaces. Problems with pension funds, health and safety on the job, and other workplace-related issues ranging from family and medical leave to employer use of lie-detector tests generated additional labor-market regulations.[1] From the 1960s through the 1990s, under Republican as well as Democratic administrations, legislation governing the workplace has grown. Decisions and problems once dealt with at the workplace now often wind up before regulatory agencies or in court.

If regulatory agencies or courts remedied problems quickly and restored good working relations between employees and firms at low cost, legal regulation would be a fine way to treat workplace problems. But if regulatory agencies take years to reach decisions, if court suits are so expensive that only the well-heeled and their lawyers or the lucky few gain from them, and if regulations extract a huge cost on business, legal regulation is a poor way to govern workplace relations. Assuming, that is, that some alternative exists.

On this issue, as on most other aspects of labor regulations, business and labor are at odds about which of the "ifs" are valid. Business complains about a litigation explosion that is invading their bottom line and sapping American productivity. Unions and consumer groups point to areas in which workers need greater regulatory protection and complain that much critical workplace regulation is poorly enforced.

How do workers see growing legal protections at the workplace? How many regard regulatory agencies and the courts as their ultimate protector at the workplace? Do employees want more or less legal protection? What is their response to possible reforms in the system of legal protection?

Do Workers Know What Protections They Have?

Is it legal or illegal for your employer to

- Fire you for no reason?
- Move you to a lower-paying job because you wanted to form a union?
- Refuse to let you take time off from work to take care of your sick baby?
- Fire you for refusing to do hazardous work?
- Permanently replace you if you went on strike?
- Avoid hiring minorities for "good business reasons"?

Exhibit 6.1 summarizes the responses on the WRPS to these questions. It shows that employees vastly exaggerate their workplace rights. For instance, most workers believe that it is illegal for a manager to discharge an employee at will or for refusing to do hazardous work. But both forms of discharge are perfectly legal under U.S. labor law. More than half of employees believe that a firm cannot legally replace permanently striking workers. This, despite the fact that shortly before the survey Congress had rejected a bill that would have outlawed permanent replacement of strikers.

On the other hand, most employees correctly recognize that firms cannot legally discriminate against someone for trying to form a union, that "good business reasons" do not excuse racial discrimination in hiring, and that an employer cannot legally refuse unpaid family leave to an employee to care for a sick child (although workers might not have known that an

EXHIBIT 6.1. Employees believe the law protects them when it doesn't.

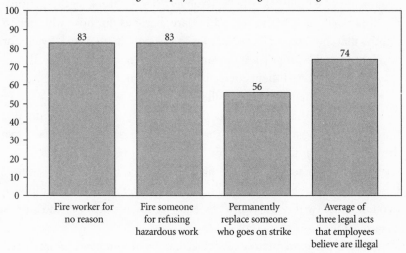

Percentage of employees who believe legal acts are illegal

- Fire worker for no reason: 83
- Fire someone for refusing hazardous work: 83
- Permanently replace someone who goes on strike: 56
- Average of three legal acts that employees believe are illegal: 74

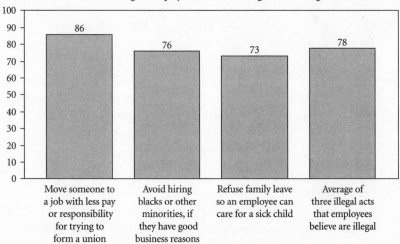

Percentage of employees who believe illegal acts are illegal

- Move someone to a job with less pay or responsibility for trying to form a union: 86
- Avoid hiring blacks or other minorities, if they have good business reasons: 76
- Refuse family leave so an employee can care for a sick child: 73
- Average of three illegal acts that employees believe are illegal: 78

Source: Based on this WRPS question: (W1.50) "Federal law guarantees employees certain protections in the workplace. To the best of your knowledge, please tell me if you think it is now legal or not legal for employees to do each of the following: (W1.50a) Fire an employee for no reason; (W1.50b) Move someone to a job with less pay or responsibility for trying to form a union; (W1.50c) Refuse family leave so an employee can care for a sick child; (W1.50d) Fire someone for refusing to do hazardous work; (W1.50e) Permanently replace someone who goes on strike; (W1.50f) Avoid hiring blacks or other minorities, if they have good business reasons for doing so."

employer could refuse unpaid family leave to a worker until August 1993, when the Family Leave Act took effect).

Indicative of employee misperception of labor law, a nearly identical proportion of employees believe, wrongly, that the three legally permissible unfair actions listed in the exhibit are illegal as do those who believe, rightly, that the three unlawful actions in the exhibit are illegal. Even more striking, a smaller proportion of workers answered the items correctly than would have answered them correctly had they simply guessed.[2]

Worse than chance in getting all items correct? What gives?

What gives is that people think that anything that is blatantly unfair at the workplace must be illegal — a kind of "there's got to be a law" syndrome. Surely it must be illegal for an employer to order a worker to stick his head in a furnace and then to fire the worker if he or she refuses to do this. Surely it must be illegal to walk into the worker's office and simply say, "You're gone," without giving a reason, with no due process, and with no chance for the worker to appeal.

In fact, the employment-at-will doctrine that dominates U.S. labor relations allows the employer to say "fired" without giving any reason.[3] Seventy-eight percent of the errors in the "quiz" were errors in which workers thought they were legally protected from ill treatment when in fact the law was silent on the issue.

Do more highly educated workers have better knowledge of the labor laws than other workers? Not much actually. Most college graduates think that all unfair acts are illegal, just as do most other workers, although college graduates do a bit better than nongraduates on the quiz.

Do union members have better knowledge of their rights as members of a union than other workers? No. The majority of union members think it is illegal to hire permanent replacements in a strike, just as do the majority of nonmembers.

Do managers have better knowledge of the laws that might restrict their power at workplaces than nonmanagers? Not much. Seventy-six percent of managers thought that firing someone for no cause was illegal, as compared with 88 percent of nonmanagers. Averaging across laws, 68 percent of managers believe erroneously that the legal "unfair" actions in Exhibit 6.1 are illegal, whereas 80 percent of managers believe correctly that the illegal actions in the exhibit are illegal. No bonus or bananas here.

There is nothing odd about our results, however. Researchers on law and society have long pointed out that people are generally ignorant of their rights and of the system that protects them. Ask citizens about the terms of U.S. senators or the difference between various types of courts or the division of the federal budget among various uses, and they will show similar lack of knowledge. Perhaps you would expect managers to know better, but your average manager is not a human-resource or personnel expert, much less a labor law expert. If you would never dream of firing someone for no reason, it's easy to think that such an act is unfair. If you discuss workplace problems with committees of your workers, it's hard to imagine that using those committees to help set policy about wages and benefits is illegal, at least until someone charges you with violating Section 8(a)(2) of the National Labor Relations Act.

That workers have incorrect perceptions of labor regulations and law creates a problem for this chapter. If workers don't know what they have in the form of legal protections, why should you, or we, take seriously their views about legal regulation? What value is there in finding out what workers think about "Washington" issues as opposed to the individual workplaces on which the rest of the book focuses? Maybe this is a situation in which it is better to leave things to the experts.

Our defense for asking workers their views of legal protections and possible reforms in the way the regulatory system works is threefold.

First, that workers overstate legal protections at the workplace can be viewed as a "blessing in disguise," if — as turns out to be the case — we find that workers say they want more regulatory protection than they currently have. Because workers think that they have greater legal protections than they have, we can be pretty sure that their desire for more regulations would be greater than they report to us if they were informed about the true state of the law. In social science, a bias that works against a result is much better than one that works for it.

Second, in this chapter as elsewhere in the book, we direct several questions only to workers who have in fact experienced the situation under examination — in this case, going to court or an agency to seek legal remedies for workplace problems. Workers' assessment of these personal experiences should be as valid as their assessment of how their workplace functions, even though the workers do not know the ins and outs of the law.

Third, when it comes to assessing *reforms* in labor regulations, we sought to reduce the lack of knowledge of workers by sending them written materials describing those reforms in some detail. Hence, in those parts of the chapter we report the views of relatively informed respondents, some of whom told us that they had discussed the issues with friends or relatives. To be sure, the material we gave to workers did not go into legal fine points or lay out the full spectrum of thought on the various reforms. It did, however, give them the basic facts from which they could form judgments.

In any case, here is what we found about how workers assess legal regulations.

See You in Court, Boss

Have you or anyone you know personally ever gone to court or to a government agency because of a possible violation of workplace rights? Six percent of Worker Representation and Participation Survey (WRPS) respondents answered "Yes" when asked whether they had gone to court or to an agency at least once in their lives because of a possible violation of workplace rights. An additional 17 percent said someone they knew had done so.

Because people have many acquaintances, and like to talk about their workplace and legal problems, the 17 percent figure did not surprise us. The 6 percent did. With a private-sector workforce of some 100 million people, this implies that around 6 million workers at one point in their lives felt sufficiently aggrieved about a workplace problem to go to an agency or court. That's an awful lot of people seeking legal redress for workplace problems. Given that the average worker has been employed for about 15 years, the 6 million court or agency "visits" implies roughly that workers make 400,000 *complaints* or so per year.[4] But because the number of complainants has risen over time with the increased regulation of the labor market, the number of complainants in the mid-1990s should exceed the 15-year average, whereas the number in earlier years should be smaller. Roughly, we estimate that the respondent reports of "ever" going to court or an agency are consistent with workers making around 600,000 *complaints* annually in the 1990s.[5]

Is 600,000 complaints to courts/agencies a plausible number? Given the many agencies and court jurisdictions involved in labor disputes, and the multiple administrative complaints or judicial actions arising from the same underlying dispute, it is not easy to find an answer. To see whether the WRPS respondents have the right "order of magnitude" answer, we had to piece together statistics from federal and state agencies, using Wisconsin for our state data.

Start at the top of the court and agency system. In 1995, some 290,000 complaints were made to federal agencies charged with workplace regulations, and some 20,000 federal district court filings were issued on labor-related matters. Because states are responsible for unemployment and worker-compensation claims, and most have state-specific antidiscrimination, occupational health and safety, or other labor regulations, they deal with many employment-related complaints from workers as well. Extrapolating from the 5,000 or so labor disputes that come to Wisconsin, we estimate that states deal with around 200,000 cases a year.[6] Two hundred thousand federal agency complaints, plus 20,000 court filings, plus 200,000 complaints to states brings us to 420,000 complaints — a *large number, although short of our estimated 600,000.*

But not all the complaints reported by workers on the WRPS will be counted in the official data. Workers might bring problems to agencies that the agency does not pursue because of lack of evidence, staffing, or legal basis, and thus does not list in its reports. The most popular complaint brought to field offices of the National Labor Relations Board (NLRB), for instance, is about being discharged for no particular reason (as we just saw, most workers believe this to be illegal). Such a complaint will not show up on the NLRB records as a formal complaint, as it is in fact invalid, but it might show up in a worker's mind as bringing a complaint to a government agency.

Again looking at Wisconsin, the state department of labor reports that its Milwaukee and Madison field offices alone receive some 90,000 inquiries annually. Extrapolated to other states, this turns into about 2.25 million inquiries per year. Field offices of the NLRB estimate comparable numbers of inquiries. Extrapolating to the entire nation and other agencies, government regulatory agencies receive on the order of 4 million to 5 million law-related inquiries a year about workplace problems. If only 10 percent to 15 percent of these are genuine attempts to take an issue to an agency, we are again in the ballpark of the 600,000 or so complaints per year that would validate what workers said on the WRPS.

Another way to judge whether our respondents overstate their reliance on courts and agencies to protect them at workplaces is to consider the situation from the employers side. According to the U.S. Society of Human Resource Management, a majority of firms have been sued by employees, and one-fourth of managers have been individually named in a lawsuit, largely in cases of alleged discrimination.[7] Every firm deals regularly with complaints about the myriad of government health and safety, pension and welfare benefits, and wage and hour regulations.

In short, the WRPS estimate that 6 percent of workers have tried to sue their firm in court or have brought the firm before a government agency for alleged violations in legal rights at the workplace is not excessive. See you in court, Mr. or Ms. Boss.

And Then What Happens?

Are workers satisfied with the outcomes of the legal process for dealing with alleged violations of workplace rights?

Exhibit 6.2 shows that a high proportion of employees who went to court or to a regulatory agency were dissatisfied with the outcome. One-third of workers said that they were very satisfied with these government processes. This figure is in the same range as the proportion of workers who find unions or employer modes of dealing with workplace problems "very effective." Relatively fewer workers, however, said that they were "somewhat satisfied" with their trip to court or a regulatory agency than said that union or firm-based systems of resolving problems were "somewhat effective."

Most striking, one-third of workers who went to courts/agencies reported that they were not satisfied with the outcome of their complaint. Contrast this to the 6 percent of workers who viewed their firm's system for dealing with the problems workers have as "not at all effective" or the 4 percent who viewed their union as "not at all effective" in dealing with problems.

Why are so many workers who take job-related problems to agencies or courts so dissatisfied with the outcomes?

One reason might be that many of these workers are disgruntled people in general — the kind who find all systems of dealing with workplace problems ineffective. In fact, 10 percent of workers who went to courts/agencies reported their firm's policies for resolving individual problems as being "not at all effective," and 10 percent reported their union as being "not at all effective." These proportions exceed those reported by other workers, but they do not approach the 23 percent who reported themselves "not at all satisfied" with courts/agencies. Workers who take problems to courts/agencies are more dissatisfied with that method than with other modes of resolving problems.

A second reason that so many workers are unhappy with the way courts or agencies resolve workplace problems might relate to the nature of administrative or judicial proceedings. Legal processes are often zero-sum games, with distinct winners and losers. Go to court and win, and you are very satisfied with the outcome; go to court and lose, and you are very dissatisfied. Equally important, taking your employer to court or an agency

EXHIBIT 6.2. Legal system produces many unsatisfied complainants compared with union and employer systems for solving problems.

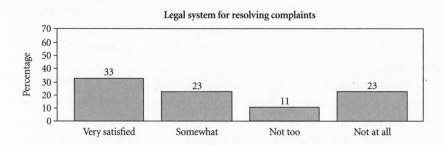

Legal system for resolving complaints

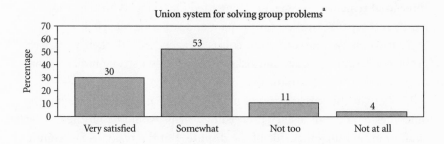

Union system for solving group problems[a]

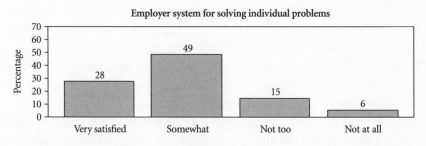

Employer system for solving individual problems

Source: Tabulated from these WRPS questions: (W1.53) (TO THOSE WITH WHO WENT TO COURT OVER WORKPLACE RIGHTS) "How satisfied were you with the outcome of your complaint?"; (W1.37d) (TO ALL WHOSE COMPANY HAS UNION) "How effective has union been in resolving group problems or concerns?" (very effective, somewhat effective, not too effective, not effective at all); (W1.32) "*Overall,* how effective is your (company's/organization's) system for resolving the problems *individual* employees have at work?"
[a] These percentages are based only on union workers.

usually involves a decisive break. Win or lose, your firm is going to hold it against you for having sued it in court or complaining about its practices to a government agency. The winner-take-all nature of court/agency proceedings explains why a relatively large number of workers report themselves as "not at all satisfied," and a relatively large number also report that they are "very satisfied" with outcomes, with few workers in between.

Finally, another reason for worker unhappiness with resolving disputes through courts or agencies is that the legal system can take a long time to reach a final resolution and might not recompense the worker for the time and pain of going through the legal process even if he or she wins. Huge backloads exist in many agencies. Court dockets are filled to capacity. And some legal remedies — say, for being fired for trying to form a union — hardly recompense workers for the pain and suffering incurred.[8]

That so many American go to courts or agencies with their workplace problems despite the costs and risks of doing so is a strong indicator that they have nowhere else to turn.

You might think that because many workers are dissatisfied with the outcomes of court or agency proceedings, firms would be satisfied. After all, they are on the other side of the dispute. But the reality is far from it. Firms regularly complain about the expense of regulations and are eager for new ways to adjudicate problems with workers. Many argue that the threat of lawsuits hampers the way they manage employees who are slacking off or whose competence has deteriorated. Everyone at the workplace might know that Q does nothing useful, but if Q fits into a protected group by reason of age, race, gender, or the like, Q can threaten an expensive lawsuit if the firm demotes or fires him or her on the grounds of discrimination. Wishing to avoid a court battle, the firm may decide that there is nothing to do about Q or might "bribe" Q to leave with some early-retirement bonus.[9] Other firms say that they have settled cases out of court even when they believe they were completely in the right because the cost of defending themselves in court is so high.

Thinking about It

Have you or anyone you know ever *thought about* going to court or to a government agency because of a possible violation of workplace rights but then decided *not* to go? Nine percent of workers on the WRPS told us that they had thought about going to court or to a government agency but decided not to; 19 percent said that someone they knew had considered complaining to a court or agency about their workplace rights. Adding the number of employees who have gone to the government and the number who have thought about going but didn't (adjusted for the overlap in responses), 14 percent of American workers have used or considered using legal remedies for workplace problems. Adding the number of employees who know people who have gone to the government and the number who know people who have thought about going but didn't go (adjusted for the overlap in responses), some 30 percent of American workers know others who have gone to or considered seeking legal remedies. Consequently, many workers in the putatively deregulated U.S. job market have lawsuits or regulatory appeals on their mind.

Why do some workers choose to go to court or to an agency while others do not?

One reason workers go is because they have a serious problem at their workplace. Exhibit 6.3 shows that the probability of taking a problem to court/an agency is higher for workers who report that employee-management relations at their workplace are poor or who do not trust their management — which suggests that they have a serious problem at work.[10] But having a problem is not by itself enough to bring a case to an agency or court. Unionized workers and high wage workers are more likely to go to an agency or court than are other workers, presumably because they have greater access to the resources needed to bring a case forward or protect them during the process.[11] Consistent with this interpretation, roughly 40 percent of workers said that they did not bring forth a complaint because the regulatory/court system was too expensive in various ways. One in ten could not find or afford a lawyer. Nearly one in five was frightened by what their employer would do in reprisal. One in eight was intimidated by the process of making a complaint.[12]

On the other side, workers in firms with effective systems for resolving individual problems are less likely to bring a workplace problem to court or a government agency. These are "good" firms that generate few serious labor problems and in which aggrieved workers can get a fair resolution of their problem at their workplace.

Employees Want More Legal Protection

Before we undertook our survey, the Employment Policy Foundation (EPF), a business-supported group in Washington, D.C., sponsored an opinion survey designed in part to determine if workers wanted more or less protective legislation. This survey asked a question of the form "Gov-

EXHIBIT 6.3. Percentage of employees who go to the courts/agencies.

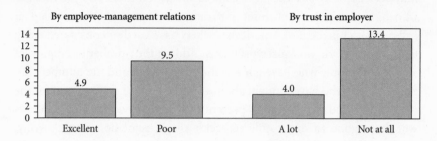

By employee-management relations / By trust in employer

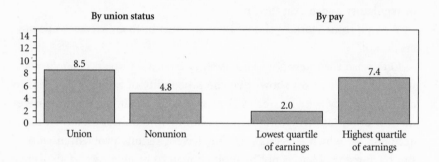

By union status / By pay

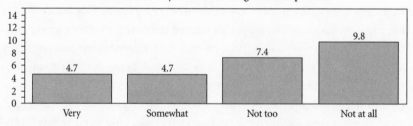

Effectiveness of systems for resolving individual problems

Source: Tabulated from this WRPS question: (W1.52) "Have you or anyone you know personally ever gone to court or to a government agency because of a possible violation of workplace rights?"

ernment regulation imposes severe costs on business. Do you think that there should be more government regulation of the workplace?"

You probably can guess how most people answered this question: "No more regulations!" When we saw these results, we thought we could increase the credibility of our study by asking the EPF question, followed by a more even-handed question. But Princeton Research Associates refused to ask the leading question. To do this went against their professional integrity and might lead some respondents to wonder whether our survey was the academic research instrument we told them it was. So we decided to ask a single "correct" question that recognized that regulations protect people at the workplace as well as restrict business in ways that could be costly.

This, we learned, is easier said than done on a telephone interview. If you phrase the question so that the costs of regulations are foremost in respondents' minds, they are likely to oppose regulations. If you phrase the question so that the protections are foremost in their minds, they are likely to favor protections. If you fill in all the "on the one hands" and "on the other hands," you have lost the respondent. Maybe you can come up with a short question that does the trick, but we could not.

To the rescue came the split-question design. We asked half of the sample, "Do you think current laws give employees too little legal protection or more protection than is necessary?" This wording stressed the protection given workers by the laws. We asked the other half, "Do you think current laws put too few legal restrictions on management or more restrictions than are necessary?" This wording stressed the restriction on business under the laws. We expected that the differing stress on protection or restrictions in the two questions would tilt answers in different directions.[13]

Exhibit 6.4 shows that posing the issue in these ways did indeed produce differences in the proportions wanting more or less legal protection in six different areas. Use the word "protections" and many people want more; use the word "restrictions" and fewer people want more. On average, 59 percent of workers believe that current laws provide too little protection, as compared with 45 percent who believe that current laws put too few restrictions on management — a difference of 14 percentage points.

On both designs more employees said that there is too little labor regulations than too much or about the right amount in all areas but one. The exception is employment discrimination. Phrased in terms of protecting workers, the majority see protections as too little; phrased in terms of restricting management, the majority sees too much restriction.

In three of the areas covered in Exhibit 6.4, there is in fact little or no protection: "firing without cause," "layoffs and plant closings," and the "use of temporary or part-time employees to replace full-time employees." In three areas, there is some legal protection: "conflicts between work responsibilities and family responsibilities," "rights to form unions and employee associations," and "job discrimination based on race, sex, or age." If workers' views have some basis in reality, we would expect more to

EXHIBIT 6.4. Workers want more legal protection.

	Percentage of workers who believe protection in area is			Percentage of workers who believe restrictions on managers are		
	Too little	About right	Excessive	Too few	About right	Excessive
Average of all areas	59	11	19	45	8	35
Without legal protection						
Being fired without cause	67	9	16	55	7	31
Use of temporary or part-time employees to replace full-time employees	64	8	18	46	5	36
Layoffs and plant closings	63	7	17	50	8	29
With legal protection						
Conflicts between work responsibilities and family responsibilities	60	13	18	41	8	40
Rights to form unions and employee associations	53	11	24	39	7	37
Job discrimination based on race, sex, or age	45	16	33	41	15	38

Source: Based on these WRPS questions: (W1.51a) "In the following areas, do you think current laws give employees *too little* legal protection or *more protection than is necessary?*"; (W1.51b) "In the following areas, do you think that current laws put *too few legal restrictions* on management or *more restrictions than are necessary?*"

Exhibit 6.5. Percentage of workers who say laws give too little protection to employees or put too few restrictions on management (by worker characteristics and workplace characteristics).

Worker Characteristics	
Female	30
Male	26
Black	43
Nonblack	26
Less than high school education	35
College graduates	21

Workplace characteristics	
Satisfaction with influence on job	
Not at all satisfied	43
Very satisfied	19
Feelings toward job	
Wish you didn't have to go	37
Look forward to it	25
No EI at firm	34
Nonparticipant at EI firm	25
EI participant	23
Union member	33
Nonunion employee	28

Workers who've brought complaints to court/agency want more laws	
Went to court/agency	38
Know someone who went to court/agency	30
Never went to court/agency	27

(EI = employee involvement.)
Source: Based on the following WRPS questions: (W1.51a) "In the following areas, do you think current laws give employees *too little* legal protection or *more protection than is necessary?*"; (W1.51b) "In the following areas, do you think current laws put *too few* legal restrictions on management or *more restrictions than are necessary?*" These questions were cross-tabulated with other relevant questions.

---

say protection/restrictions are too little/few when laws are nonexistent than when they are. This is in fact the case. Workers overstate the extent to which the law protects them, but they want more laws in precisely the areas where legal protection is lacking.

What kinds of workers want more legal protection?

Exhibit 6.5 shows that workers who have troubles at their workplace and who have little influence are more likely to want more laws than other workers while, by contrast, workers in firms with EI see less need for additional protections. Workers in relatively weak positions in the job market — blacks, women, and the less educated — also want more laws. More surprising, union workers, who have independent protection at the workplace, also want more legal protections than other workers. We interpret this as reflecting the fact that the union gives workers greater ability to make use of legal protections than other workers.

Finally, despite the fact that many workers who went to court/an agency were not happy with the outcomes from the legal or regulatory system, these workers want more legal protections than those who never went. If you felt sufficiently mistreated at work to bring a complaint to court or an agency, you feel a need for greater state protection, even though the system of enforcement might not have served you well.

All told, the desire of workers for more protection at the workplace fits a sensible pattern.

But Not If There Is Something Else

When you have a problem at your workplace, would you prefer to go to court or an administrative agency or to resolve the dispute through an alternative dispute-resolution system based at your workplace?

What, you ask, is "an alternative dispute-resolution system"? It is a system in which a third party — a neutral arbitrator — has the final word in determining the outcome. Many firms use arbitration to resolve arguments about interpretation of commercial contracts. Almost all collective-bargaining contracts use arbitration to resolve disputes about the application of the contract. Professional sports use arbitrators to deal with the complaints of athletes that they have been mistreated by leagues. Alternative dispute-resolution systems of various forms are a growing mode of resolving problems outside the judicial system.

In Wave 1 of the WRPS, we asked employees their views of arbitration at their workplace: "Going to court or to a government agency can be expensive and time-consuming. Here is an alternative system . . ."; then we gave a one-sentence description of arbitration. Most respondents said they thought arbitration could effectively resolve disputes between workers and management. About one-fourth thought arbitration would be "very effective" in resolving disputes over legal rights, a bit more than half thought it would be "somewhat effective," and about 20 percent thought it would be "not too effective" or "not effective at all."[14] Asked to choose between this sort of a system and courts or agencies, more than half of the workforce preferred going to an arbitrator. Workers who had in fact been to court or to an agency favored arbitration as well, but they differed in their views from other workers in one important way. Many of them told us that arbitration would be "very effective" *if an elected committee of workers was involved in selecting the arbitrator*; they said they would choose this option if this were the case more so than if management selected the arbitrator. Other workers did not make such a distinction.[15]

But how much credence, you ask, should we give to these responses? We did not describe how the alternative system would work in any detail. We did not ask workers what type of problem they would bring to the system or the type of arbitration system they would prefer. We introduced arbitration in a leading way, reminding workers that going to courts or agencies could be expensive or time-consuming. Arguably, we had done here what we had tried so hard to avoid throughout the WRPS — posing an issue in a leading manner. Perhaps if workers heard arguments for and against arbitration, they might find the arguments against more compelling.

Concerned about these problems, we mailed a six-page description of an arbitration system (see Appendix D) to half of the population in our follow-up survey. We detailed the problems the system would cover, gave arguments for and against the system, and asked workers to think about how effective such a system would be at their workplace. Several days later we called and asked workers if they had read the material, if they understood how arbitration worked, and finally what they thought about arbitration of disputes over workplace rights.

The majority reported that they had taken the material seriously: 57 percent said they had read *all* of the material; 24 percent said they had read *most* of it. More than one-fifth said they had an excellent understanding of the arbitration system, and most said they had a good understanding.[16] One-third said they had discussed the system with someone else. Although workers might have exaggerated the attention they paid to our material, they surely were more informed than otherwise. And, most important, they were sufficiently interested in the issue to bear with another telephone interview.

As in the main survey, the majority of workers reacted favorably to the idea of arbitrating disputes at their workplace (see Exhibit 6.6). Most viewed arbitration to be a "very good idea" or a "good idea," as compared with just 8 percent who viewed it as a "bad idea" or a "very bad idea." Most thought arbitration would work well at their firm, although the percentage who said it would work well fell short of the percentage who said it was a

EXHIBIT 6.6. Workers' views on using arbitration to settle legal disputes.

	Percentage of workers who think committees would
Overall use of arbitration	
Very good idea	17
Good idea	66
Bad/very bad idea	8
Mixed feeling/don't know	9
Would work at their company	
Well	62
Not well	27
Depends/don't know	11
Complaints against employer	
More	59
Fewer	17
Stay the same	19
Fairness in dispute settlement	
More fairly	62
Less fairly	13
Stay the same	17
Ease of workers getting fair hearing	
Easier	71
Harder	15
Stay the same	11
Effect on workers	
Better off	73
Worse off	13
Stay the same	10
Effect on management	
Better off	71
Worse off	15
Stay the same	10

Note: Numbers do not add to 100 percent for items 3–7 because some respondents answered "Don't know" or refused to answer.
Source: Based on these WRPS questions: (W2.5) "Overall, what do you think about using arbitration to settle legal disputes? Do you think it is a very good idea, a good idea, a bad idea, or a very bad idea?"; (W2.6a) "Suppose [*an arbitration*] system was set up in your (company/organization). That is, employees who felt their *legal* rights had been violated would take the case to a neutral arbitrator to be decided, rather than to court. Do you think this system would work well, or not well, at your (company/organization)?"; (W2.7A) "If arbitrators replaced the courts in solving most employee disputes about legal rights, (W2.7aa) Would *more* employees or *fewer* employees bring complaints against their employers? (W2.7ab) Would disputes be settle *more* fairly or *less* fairly? (W2.7ac) Would it be *easier* or *harder* for ordinary workers to get a fair hearing of their complaints? (W2.7ad) Would *workers* overall be *better off* or *worse off* with this kind of system? (W2.7ae) Would *management* overall be *better off* or *worse off* with this kind of system?"

very good or good idea in general. Most thought that more employees would bring complaints to an arbitrator than to court, that disputes would be settled more fairly, and that arbitration would make both management and workers better off and save them money.

Comparing the arguments for and against arbitration, the majority of workers found arguments for arbitration more convincing than those who did so for arguments against arbitration. We do not think that this reflects any tilt in the pro and con arguments that we offered, but you can judge that for yourself by looking at Appendix D.

Employees do not favor arbitration blindly, however. Workers rejected the practice of some firms that insist on employees relinquishing their right to go to court and agreeing to use a management-appointed arbitrator for disputes over legal rights as a precondition for getting a job. Three-fourths said that such a practice should be illegal.

Finally, we asked workers to choose the features of an arbitration system themselves: "Suppose Congress passed a law that encouraged companies to use arbitration to settle employment disputes about legal rights. If it were your decision to make, and everyone went along with it, what type of system would you like Congress to encourage?" Exhibit 6.7 shows that the majority of workers favor an arbitration system in which

- the procedures for using it are set up by management and employees together;
- expenses are paid by management and employees or by them with a government contribution;
- workers receive expert advice and assistance preparing their case; and
- arbitrators' decisions are not subject to government review.

What surprised us is that workers want to contribute to the costs of an arbitration system. Where is the economists' "free rider" principle of letting the other guy pay the costs of a public good? Why didn't workers simply say, "Let the firm pay from the savings it will get from avoiding expensive lawsuits?" The most likely reason is that workers recognize that if the firm pays arbitrators' fees, even the most fair-minded arbitrator will probably tilt decisions toward the firm.

Does an alternative dispute-resolution system based on what workers want constitute a feasible way to deal with disputes over workplace rights? Absolutely. Is this the type of system firms are introducing at workplaces? Not entirely. Most firms do not involve workers in the design and administration of their dispute-resolution system. And some firms hire em-

EXHIBIT 6.7. The "ideal" arbitration system to settle employee disputes about legal rights.

Percentage of workers selecting systems with given characteristics

Set up jointly by employees and management	95
Set up by employees or management alone	5
Allows employees to use arbitration or court	78
Must use arbitration alone	18
Provides expert advice/assistance to employees	82
Makes employees responsible for own case	17
Expenses paid by management and employees	43
Expenses paid by management, employees, and government	39
Expenses paid by management alone	15
Operates without government review	56
Decisions reviewed by government	42

Source: Based on this WRPS question: (W2.10A) "Suppose Congress passed a law that encouraged companies to use arbitration to settle employment disputes about legal rights. If it was your decision to make and everyone went along with it, what type of system would you like Congress to encourage?"

ployees only if they sign away their right to go to court for violations of labor laws.

Workplace Committees to Monitor Labor Regulations?

We asked workers about one other explicit workplace reform: the use of workplace committees of employees and managers to enforce compliance with legal workplace standards, such as occupational health and safety regulations, antidiscrimination laws, and the like. While the idea of devolving regulatory authority to workplace committees was not on the national policy agenda, it is not a far-out idea.[17] In the area of occupational health and safety, ten states mandates joint committees as of 1994;[18] Canada mandates such health and safety committees nationwide; and most European Union countries have similar workplace-based committees in health and safety and other areas.

We mailed a four-page description of how workplace committees might function to the one-half of the follow-up survey who had not received our arbitration module. We gave arguments for and against the system; we asked workers to think about whether a workplace-committee system would be better or worse than the current system of enforcing legal stan-

EXHIBIT 6.8. Employees' views of workplace committees for workplace standards.

	Percentage of employees who think workplace committees would
Overall view of committees	
Very good idea	21
Good idea	64
Bad/very bad idea	7
Mixed feelings/don't know	8
Would work at their company	
Well	64
Not well	29
Depends/don't know	7
Standards enforced compared to government regulators	
More often	64
Less often	12
Stay the same	19
Ease for companies to meet standards	
Easier	58
Harder	23
Stay the same	14
Standards of enforcement	
Stricter	57
Weaker	19
Stay the same	16
Effect on workers	
Better off	80
Worse off	7
Stay the same	9
Effect on management	
Better off	73
Worse off	15
Stay the same	8

Note: Numbers do not add to 100 percent because some answered "don't know" or refused to answer.

Source: Based on these WRPS questions: (W2.7B) "What do you think would happen if workplace committees were given some responsibility for enforcing workplace standards? (W2.7ba) Would standards be enforced *more often* or *less often* than they are now? (W2.7bb) Would it be *easier* or *harder* for companies to meet standards in a way that fits well with how they operate? (W2.7bc) Would enforcement be *more strict* or *less strict?* (W2.7bd) Overall, would *workers* be *better off* or *worse off* with this kind of system? (W2.7be) Overall, would *management* be *better off* or *worse off* with this kind of system?"

dards; and, finally, we asked how workers would like such a committee to operate. Several days later we called the workers. As with the workers who received the arbitration module, most said they had read the material and had a good to excellent understanding of how committees for workplace standards would function.

Overall, employees were favorably inclined toward workplace committees to enforce labor standards (see Exhibit 6.8). As a general policy matter, 85 percent of workers thought workplace committees were a "very good idea" or a "good idea." When it came to their own workplace, however, the percentage favoring committees fell to 64 percent, as a significant minority of 29 percent thought standards committees would not work well. That more workers viewed the committees unfavorably at their workplace than in the abstract suggests that we made the right choice in directing most WRPS questions at employees' views of their workplace rather than of the American labor scene in general. People might favor something in the abstract that they reject as unworkable in their particular situation.

Exhibit 6.8 also shows that the majority of workers thought committees would enforce standards more often and more strictly than regulators, would make it easier for companies to meet standards, and would make both workers and management better off. The pro-committee argument that resonated most with workers was that committees would give workers more say in workplace decisions, followed by the argument that committees would give companies more choices about how to meet standards. Most workers found less convincing the arguments against committees for workplace standards. The anti-committee argument that carried the most weight was the cost of training committee members and giving them time off to attend meetings. The idea that committee members would be less knowledgeable than government inspectors or that committee members might not enforce standards as strictly as government inspectors carried less weight.

Finally, we asked workers their ideal design for a system of workplace committees: "Suppose Congress passed a law encouraging companies to set up workplace standards committees. If it were your decision to make and everyone went along with it, what type of committee would you like Congress to encourage?" The responses, given in Exhibit 6.9, show that workers want to resolve workplace problems cooperatively with management but that they want some independent standing as they do so. The majority favor committees in which (1) employee members are elected by employees, (2) outside experts give advice and help to the committee, and (3) the committee is responsible for all types of workplace standards.

EXHIBIT 6.9. The "ideal" workplace committee system to enforce workplace standards.

	Percentage of workers selecting committee with given characteristics
Commitees with elected employee members	85
Commitees with members chosen by management	11
Committees responsible for all workplace standards	63
Committees cover only a few standards	35
Committees get advice/help from outside experts	83
Committees operate on their own	14
Committees that have power to enforce regulations	49
Committees that only give advice to management	47

Source: Based on this WRPS question: (W2.10B) "Suppose Congress passed a law encouraging companies to set up workplace standards committees. If it was your decision to make and everyone went along with it, what type of committee would you like Congress to encourage?"

By contrast, workers are roughly evenly divided between committees that have the power to enforce regulations and committees that only advise management.[19] Determining the powers that a standards committee should have is critical to any reform, so more needs to be explored here. Still, there is no gainsaying that workers prefer a more decentralized mode of regulating workplaces than the United States currently has — conditional on their having a significant input into the process.

The bottom line is that these responses show that, given a bit of information, workers can assess possible new workplace institutions and design what seems to be a reasonable supplement to government regulators enforcing standards.

CHAPTER 7

If Workers Could Choose

If, more generally, workers were free to choose the institutions that would give them their desired representation and say in workplace decisions, as well as settle disputes about legal rights and to enforce workplace standards, what kind of institutions would they pick? What sort of labor-relations system would they like to see in the United States?

This chapter moves from reporting how workers view existing workplace institutions to examining what they want in the form of new or expanded institutions of representation and participation. It gives what are arguably the most conjectural but important results in *What Workers Want*. Conjectural, because determining preferences for institutions or policies that workers have not experienced pushes survey methodology to its limits. Important, because we cannot imagine how private or public policy-makers could improve the U.S. labor system without taking account of the design features that workers want.

To discover the institutions that workers believe would best increase their workplace representation and participation, we used two different types of questions. First, as we did in the questions about arbitration systems and workplace committees in Chapter 6, we asked about the attributes or characteristics that workers would like to see in a workplace organization. Here, however, rather than specifying the particular institutions among which workers could choose, we gave them a checklist and simply asked if they preferred an organization with attribute X or Y. Second, we presented them with three alternative institutions: increased legal protection, unions or a workplace organization that negotiated with management, and a potentially new institution — an employee-management committee that discussed workplace problems but did not collectively bargain. We asked workers to select one of the three institutions, even though it might not be their ideal.

Both approaches have strengths and weaknesses. The first approach identifies the functions and attributes that workers want in a workplace organization without reference to any particular existing institutions. Ideally, it captures their preferences without any distortions that might come from their associating particular attributes with existing institutions. The downside of this is that it doesn't tell us how workers would react to a choice between different institutions with different clusters of attributes. Preferences on individual items might not add up to a valid composite organization. You like pepper and you like ice cream, but you probably don't like pepper on your ice cream.

The second approach forces respondents to look at a workplace institution in its entirety and to make something that approaches a real choice between potentially imperfect institutions. The disadvantage of this approach is that different workers might have different ideas of how the three institutions we gave them would actually function. This is particularly the case for the option of a joint workplace committee, which some employees may see as a near-union in which they have considerable independence from management, whereas other employees might see it as a more management-run operation.

By asking both sorts of questions, and working back and forth between their responses, we are able to fill in some of the gaps in each. The result is a coherent picture of the new or expanded workplace institutions that different groups of workers want.

Desired Organizational Attributes

To determine the attributes of an ideal workplace organization we asked employees, "Thinking now about any kind of employee organization, not just unions, how would *you* like it to work? If it was your decision alone to make, and everybody went along with it, would you prefer . . . ?" We listed six items[1] and asked workers if they thought employees who participated in an organization with the attributes they chose would need legal protection from discrimination or harassment, and whether they would volunteer time to the organization. Column 1 of Exhibit 7.1 gives the average response for all nonmanagerial employees to the six items. Column 2 shows how union workers answered the question. Column 3 shows how managers answered the question. Ignore Column 3 for the moment and focus on the preferences of workers in Columns 1 and 2.

The most striking fact in the exhibit — sufficiently striking that we raised it in Chapter 3 — is that the vast majority of workers want an organization run jointly by employees and management. This overwhelming preference reflects employees' desire for cooperative labor relations with

EXHIBIT 7.1. Percentage of employees choosing attributes of an ideal organization.

The "ideal" employee organization should . . .	Nonmanagerial employees	Union members	Managers
Be run jointly by employees and management	85	83	90
Be run by employees alone	10	14	3
Have elected employee representatives	59	76	47
Have volunteer representatives	25	16	25
Have management select representatives	10	6	20
Include similarly situated workers	55	57	48
Include everyone but top management	31	30	32
Have arbitrator make final decisions in cases of conflict	59	86	37
Have management make final decisions in cases of conflict	34	10	55
Have access to confidential company information	47	50	38
Rely on public records	39	38	48
Draw on company budget and staff	52	37	57
Rely on own budget and staff	34	48	31

Source: Tabulated from these WRPS questions: (W1.48a–f) "Thinking now about any kind of employee organization, not just unions, how would *you* like it to work? If it was your decision alone to make, and everybody went along with it, would you prefer (ITEMS)?"

their firm and their recognition that management must be deeply involved in any workplace institution if workers' say is to affect decisions. That most union members — whom, as we have seen, would vote overwhelmingly to maintain their union — support such joint governance tells us that workers' preference for a jointly run organization does not imply that they favor a management-dominated organization. The key phrase is *jointly run*.

The responses to the other items makes this point clearly. They show that the majority of workers favor an organization with more independent rather than less independent authority. The majority want to elect employee representatives to the group and to use outside arbitrators to make final decisions when management and workers disagree. In addition, they want the organization to have access to confidential company information, to be limited to employees doing the same kind of work, and to receive company budget and staff for the organization. They are almost exactly evenly split on whether workers involved in the organization would need legal protection.

On all these questions, union members favor an organization that is more independent of management in greater numbers than do nonunion workers. More than three-fourths of union members want to elect employee representatives, and 86 percent want an arbitrator to make final decisions when management and labor disagree. The majority of union members who responded to the question want the organization to rely on its own budget and staff (as unions do), rather than to draw on company resources.

The "Just Say No" Respondents

When we asked workers the attributes of their preferred organization, we did not offer them the option of saying they wanted no organization of any kind. In fact, a number of respondents volunteered that they were opposed to any workplace organization, and we recorded their answer as a kind of write-in response. Depending on the attribute, as many as 7 percent volunteered that they did not want any organization. In addition, up to 9 percent of workers either "didn't know" what they wanted or refused to answer various questions. If, to be conservative, we assume that those who "didn't know" or refused to answer actually oppose any workplace institution, we would conclude that about 16 percent of American workers reject any workplace organization.

But even these figures might understate the proportion of workers who want no workplace organization. Some respondents opposed to any organization might have answered the attributes question out of politeness to the interviewer. We can get a fix on that number by looking at responses to a succeeding question: "How willing would *you* be to volunteer two or three hours a month to participate in an employee organization to discuss workplace issues with your management?" Seventy-seven percent said they would "definitely" or "probably" be willing to do so; 10 percent said they were "probably not willing," 5 percent said that they would "definitely not participate," and 7 percent said that they did not want any kind of employee organization. If, again to be conservative, we assume that anyone who was not "definitely" or "probably" willing to volunteer two or three hours a month to participate in an employee organization was truly against it, we get an upper bound of 23 percent on the "just say no" proportion of the workforce. Put positively, American workers want some sort of organization to represent them at their workplace by a better than three-to-one ratio.[2]

Management Preferences

Imagine that workers came to management asking for an organization with the characteristics of the composite given in Exhibit 7.1 How might management respond? Does management have a similar or dissimilar notion of the ideal workplace organization as do workers? The right-hand column records the type of employee organization managers prefer to deal with, given that the workplace has some organization. Managers favor an organization that differs in some critical respects from that chosen by workers. The majority of managers want to make a final decision when employees and management disagree, and they do not want an organization to have access to confidential company information. These are bottom-line issues of who has power and authority at workplaces. Because management has power, and people do not relinquish power readily, we do not find this pattern of preferences surprising.

What is perhaps surprising, though, is that nearly half of managers report that they would prefer to deal with elected employees if their firm had an employee organization, and 37 percent say they would prefer an outside arbitrator to resolve disagreements with employees in such an organization. One reason these managers favored electing workers to committees is that they think it would increase the effectiveness of labor relations. Sixty-nine percent of the managers who favored employees electing representatives thought that their firms' method for resolving workplace problems would be more effective if employees chose their own representatives to meet with management, as compared with 21 percent of managers whose ideal workplace organization depended on management selecting workers or on volunteers. Managers from union firms, which regularly negotiate with elected representatives of workers, were moderately more favorable to electing employee representatives than managers from nonunion firms.[3]

The managers who wanted employees to elect representatives to joint workplace committees also seem to be reacting to the way their firm manages employees. They expressed less satisfaction with their influence on workplace decisions than did those managers who opposed the election of worker representatives; they trusted their firm less than others to carry out its promises to workers;[4] and they were more likely to rate labor-management relations at their firm as fair or poor or as below average than were other managers.[5] The message from these managers seems to be that their firm (and maybe they themselves) needed an independent workplace organization to improve working conditions and give workers a say in decisions.

Variation in Preferences

The composite workplace organization in Exhibit 7.1 is based on average responses, item by item. But averages can be misleading. That a majority of workers say that they want to elect workers to an organization on one item and that a majority say that they want the company to fund the organization on a second item does *not* imply that a majority favors the two attributes together. Perhaps the two majorities barely overlap, so that only a minority favor the composite.[6] In fact, workers who desire elected representatives are less likely to want the company to fund a workplace organization than other workers. By contrast those who favor company funding are less favorable to electing representatives than are other employees.[7] What is true for two attributes holds even more so for a composite of six attributes.

To determine the actual configuration of workplace features that individual workers want, we tabulated the distribution of worker preferences for combinations of workplace characteristics. Because each respondent has selected one of two choices for five features and one of three for one feature, ninety-six outcome configurations are possible.[8] With this large number of possibilities, it would be remarkable indeed if the majority selected the composite. In fact, only 8 percent of workers selected the majority items on the composite, but many chose something close to the composite: 23 percent chose an ideal institution that differs in just one feature from the composite, and 38 percent chose an institution that differs in two features, so that 61 percent of workers selected an institution in the neighborhood of the composite. By contrast, less than 4 percent had an ideal organization that had only one feature in common with the composite, and 13 percent had an ideal organization that had only two features in common with composite.[9]

The six attributes listed in the exhibit are not, however, equally important in determining the character of a workplace organization. The independence and relative power of workers and management depends fundamentally on two attributes of an organization: the mechanism for selecting worker representatives and the way the organization resolves disputes between management and labor. Whether all employees below top management or only similarly situated employees are members of the group, access to confidential company documents, and even the mechanism for funding the organization, are less central to guaranteeing workers an independent say in decisions. If workers have a coherent view of the authority a workplace organization ought to have, we would expect their opinions on selection of representatives and resolving disputes to overlap. Indeed, 71 percent of workers who want to elect employee representatives also want an arbitrator to decide disputes, whereas just 29 percent of those who want management to select representatives favor an arbitrator resolving disagreements.

Exhibit 7.2 shows the distribution of workers according to their preferences on the two items together. Forty-four percent of workers want an organization that both elects worker members and uses an outside arbitrator to resolve disputes — which we will call a "strongly independent" worker organization. (Had worker preference on these two items been unrelated, the proportion choosing this organization would have been less: 35 percent.) Under current U.S. labor regulations, the only organization that has both of these desires is a trade union. That the percentage of workers who want a strongly independent workplace organization is exactly the same as the 44 percent who said they would vote union in an NLRB election if given the opportunity is an accident, but that the two statistics are of the same magnitude is not. Many more U.S. workers want some independent organization at their workplace than currently have it.

At the opposite end of the spectrum, 7 percent of workers want management to select representatives to any workplace organization and to decide on issues of disagreement. We will label this a "not independent" workplace organization. Most in this group said that they also wanted management to make final decisions when the management-selected representatives disagreed with management, but one-third said they wanted an outside arbitrator to make the final decision.[10] Still, as long as they want management to select worker representatives, they belong in the "not independent" group. An additional 7 percent of workers said that they did not want any organization to either of these items, or to some other question about their preferred organizational form.

Somewhere between these two clearly defined groups are the remaining workers who want something more than to be completely dependent on management and something less than a strongly independent organization.

EXHIBIT 7.2. Proportions of workers favoring a workplace organization with different degrees of independence from management.

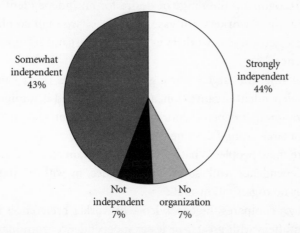

Somewhat independent 43%

Strongly independent 44%

Not independent 7%

No organization 7%

Note: "Strongly independent" means that respondents want elected representatives and arbitration of disagreements; "somewhat independent" refers to all other combinations (volunteer representatives with or without arbitration, elected representatives without arbitration, management-selected representatives with arbitration); "not independent" means that management selects worker representatives and decides issues of disagreement; "no organization" refers to those who want no organization on any item on the WRPS questions that are the source of this pie chart.

Source: Tabulated only for nonmanagers from this WRPS question: (W1.48) "Thinking now about any kind of employee organization, not just unions, how would *you* like it to work? If it was your decision alone to make, and everybody went along with it, would you prefer (W1.48a) An organization that can use an *outside* referee or arbitrator to settle issues? (W1.48b) An organization in which *management* makes the final decisions about issues? (W1.48c) An organization in which the key participants are *volunteers*? (W1.48d) An organization in which the key participants are *elected*? (W1.48e) An organization in which the key participants are *appointed* by management?"

Seventeen percent want an organization in which workers elect representatives but in which management makes final decisions when workers and management disagree. A strongly independent group? Not by our criterion, as they give management the final word. But any organization to which workers elect representatives will have some independent standing at the workplace.

Twenty-six percent of workers want an organization in which worker members are volunteers. Nearly sixty percent of these want disputes with management to go to an outside arbitrator, which would give their ideal organization some independent power to affect decisions at the workplace. The other 40 or so percent want to leave the final decision to management, which makes their organization closer to the "not independent" group.

While recognizing the range of desire for an independent organization among these workers, for ease of analysis, we shall combine them into a single category: as workers who want an organization with "some independence."

Summarizing, the largest single group of workers (by a hair) want a strongly independent organization, as we have defined it, a minority want an organization that depends entirely on management or no organization at all, and a large group fall somewhere in between.

Who are these people? What sort of workers want an organization with strong independence, with some independence, or with no independent standing or no organization at all?

Exhibit 7.3 compares the dependence of worker preferences for workplace committees with greater or lesser independence from management — indeed, for any organization at all according to the characteristics of the worker and his or her workplace. The upper part of the exhibit shows that preferences for different types of organizations varies relatively modestly by workers' personal characteristics. College graduates are less likely to want an independent organization and more likely to want no organization than are persons with high school or less schooling. Black workers are more likely to want an independent organization than are whites. Blue-collar workers have a greater preference for an independent organization than white-collar workers. But there are essentially no differences between men and women or between workers with different levels of pay, and the biggest difference among groups — between blacks and whites — is not all that large.

By contrast, the differences in preferences by the condition of the workplace, shown in the bottom part of the exhibit, are huge. The biggest single factor that determines people's desire for a more independent workplace organization is the quality of labor-management relations. Workers with poor employee-management relations are much more likely to want an independent organization as workers with good employee-management relations. Seventeen percent of employees who report excellent employee-management relations want no organization or one that is highly dependent on management. Unionized workers and nonunion workers who say they would vote union in an NLRB election also greatly favor an organization with independent authority. By contrast, only 37 percent of workers who participate in employee-involvement (EI) committees at their work-

EXHIBIT 7.3. Employee-management relations dominate workers' desire for independence of the employee organization.

| | Percentage of workers who want organization to be | | | |
Worker characteristics	Strongly independent	Somewhat independent	Not independent	No organization
Sex				
Male	42	43	7	8
Female	45	43	7	6
Race				
Black	49	39	7	5
White	43	43	7	7
Education				
College graduate	38	47	7	9
High school or less	44	41	8	6
Occupation				
Professional	41	43	6	10
Other nonmanagerial white collar	39	47	8	7
Blue collar (craft, operatives, service, laborers	49	39	6	6
Level of pay				
Upper quartile of wages	45	43	7	6
Lower quartile of wages	44	41	11	4
Workplace characteristics				
Employee-management relations				
Excellent	37	46	9	8
Good	45	41	6	7
Only fair	53	36	4	7
Poor	65	25	5	5
Union status				
Union member	69	25	2	5
Nonunion employee favorable to union	60	32	5	3
Nonunion employee opposed to union	26	55	9	10
Employee involvement (EI)				
Participant in EI committee	37	46	8	8
Nonparticipant in EI firm	45	43	7	6
Firm has no EI	47	41	6	7

Note: "Strongly independent" means that respondents want elected representatives and arbitration of disagreements; "somewhat independent" means that respondents want any of the following combinations: (volunteer representatives with or without arbitration, elected representatives without arbitration, or management-selected representatives with arbitration); "not independent" means that management selects worker representatives and decides issues of disagreement; "no organization" refers to those who want no organization on any item on the WRPS questions that are the source of this table.
Source: Tabulated from WRPS question as described in Exhibit 7.2; cross-tabulated with other relevant questions. The wage quartile data are based on the wages in the entire sample, including managers.

place want a strongly independent organization. Mr. or Ms. Manager, if you provide your employees with say at their workplace and an excellent labor-relations environment, they see less need for an independent worker organization than otherwise.

The conclusion seems inescapable: The variation in the attributes of the ideal workplace organization that workers want is largely grounded in their diverse experiences on the job.

Choosing a Single Option

Our second way of determining the workplace institution that employees want was to ask workers to choose a single best way to improve their situation at the workplace. Having found that workers wanted more unionization, expanded EI programs, and more legal protection, we asked, "During this interview we've talked about a few different ways to increase employees' say in workplace matters and make sure they are treated fairly. Which *one* of the following three ways do *you* think would be most effective? (1) *Laws* that protect the rights of individual employees, (2) joint employee and management *committees* that *discuss* problems, or (3) unions (employee organizations) that *negotiate* or bargain with management over issues?"

Using the split-question design, we asked half of the sample if they wanted a *union* that "negotiates or bargains" and the other half if they wanted an *employee organization* that "negotiates or bargains." Because an "employee organization that negotiates or bargains" with management over issues is essentially a union, this verbal distinction might seem silly. But one of our union advisors said that if we asked about "unions," we would be biasing responses against organizations that negotiated for workers. He cited AFL-CIO polls that showed that workers respond less favorably to "the U word" than to other nomenclature and respond least favorably to AFL-CIO–affiliated unions. (In fact, the National Education Association, the Association of University Professors, and various police organizations often defeat AFL-CIO affiliates in elections for union representation because these groups are seen as something different from a union, although in fact they bargain collectively just as do AFL-CIO affiliates.)

Exhibit 7.4 shows the results. Twenty-three percent chose a union as their preferred option. This is much greater than the 14 percent in our sample who currently belong to unions. But 31 percent chose an employee organization that negotiates with employers, a union in all but name. Our

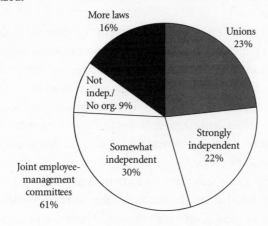

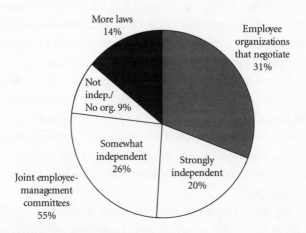

(Not indep./no org. = Not independent/no organization.)
Source: Based on this WRPS question: (W1.58) "During this interview, we've talked about a few different ways to increase employees' say in workplace matters and to make sure they are treated fairly. Which *one* of the following three ways do *you* think would be most effective?: *Laws* that protect the rights of individual employees; Joint employee and management *committees* that *discuss* problems; (FOR FIRST HALVES OF FORMS A AND B) Employee organizations; (FOR SECOND HALVES OF FORMS A AND B) Employee organizations that *negotiate* or bargain with management over issues."

union adviser was right: Simply dropping "the U word" made a big difference in how many workers wanted an organization that would negotiate for them with management. By contrast, only a small proportion of workers selected additional laws as the most effective way to increase their say at the workplace and make sure they are fairly treated. Consistent with the

If Workers Could Choose | 151

findings in Chapter 6, employees prefer workplace-based organizations and arrangements for dealing with workplace problems over additional legal protections.

The majority of workers, roughly 58 percent (the average of the 61 percent in the upper panel and 55 percent in the lower panel of Exhibit 7.4) of the population, want an institutional form that does not effectively exist in the United States: joint employee-management committees that discuss and resolve workplace problems. At least in practice, U.S. labor law nowhere encourages an organization of this form, and many believe that if such an organization discussed issues that fall into the domain of collective bargaining, it would be illegal.[11]

What do workers who seek this new form of organization have in mind? The questions we asked about the attributes that workers would choose in a workplace organization gives us an answer. Thirty-six percent of those who said they favored joint committees and told us about their organizational preferences reported that their ideal organization was one in which workers elected their own representatives and disputes between their representatives and management were resolved by an outside arbitrator — a strongly independent organization. Fifty-six percent of those favoring joint committees wanted an organization in which workers volunteered for the committee (usually with an arbitrator to resolve disputes) or elected representatives but which did not rely on an outside arbitrator to resolve disputes or — a less independent group. Eight percent of those favoring a joint committee wanted an organization with effectively no independence from management.[12]

Combining these responses with the other answers to our "ultimate" question gives the distribution of worker desires for different ways to increase employees' say and make sure they are fairly treated (see Exhibit 7.4). Exhibit 7.4 shows that almost half of American workers want an organization that has considerable independence at the workplace — 45 percent want a union or a strongly independent joint committee; 51 percent want an employee organization that negotiates or a strongly independent joint committee. Between 26 percent and 30 percent of workers want a somewhat independent organization. Nine percent want either no organization or an organization with no independence.[13]

The Consistency of Choices

When we began this study, our labor and management advisors warned us that worker responses to hypothetical questions concerning labor reforms could be unreliable, dependent on the wording and context of questions rather than on more deeply rooted attitudes. If this is a serious problem, we would expect to see little consistency between the objective situation of workers or how they judge existing institutions and their choice of a single most effective way to increase their say in workplace matters and assure fair treatment. Alternatively, if what workers told us about unions, management policies, and government regulations in earlier chapters are closely related to their bottom-line assessment of how to improve workplaces, we can put aside the worry that workers' views of reforms are unreliable.

Exhibit 7.5 shows that, contrary to the fears of our advisors, employees' choices seem well-grounded in their experiences in the job market and fit with their attitudes toward unions and the state of worker-management relations at their firm.

Consider first the responses of workers according to their union status or desire to join a union. Union and nonunion workers who would vote union in an NLRB election are much more likely to say that their first-choice institution is a union or other employee group that negotiates with management than are nonunion workers opposed to unions. More union workers want a union than a joint committee, and nonunion workers favorable to a union are evenly split. A larger proportion of union members want a union than want an employee group that negotiates, perhaps because union members fear that such a group would be weaker than a traditional union. By contrast, a large majority of nonunion workers opposed to a union want joint committees.

Given that workers with experience on EI committees report generally good experiences with them, we would expect those workers to be *more* favorable to joint management-worker committees than other workers. Exhibit 7.5 shows that, faced with the option of a union, laws, or a joint committee, 68 percent of EI participants choose a joint committee, as compared with 61 percent of nonparticipants in firms with EI and 58 percent of workers in firms without EI. The proportion of EI participants favoring a joint committee falls when the option is an employee organization to negotiate with management but remains above the comparable proportions for other workers.

Finally, the exhibit shows that workers who said that they would prefer to go to court or a government agency if their workplace rights had been violated are more likely to view increased laws as the most effective way of improving their situation than workers who said that they would prefer

EXHIBIT 7.5. Percentage of workers who choose different ways to increase workers' say.

	Union option			Employee organization option		
	Union to negotiate	Joint committee	Laws	Employee organization to negotiate	Joint committee	Laws
By union status						
Union member	54	39	7	44	45	11
Nonunion employee favoring union	40	42	18	44	43	13
Nonunion employee opposing union	5	78	17	20	66	14
By employee involvement (EI) status						
Participant in EI committee	19	68	12	30	59	11
Nonparticipant in EI firm	21	61	18	32	55	13
No EI at firm	26	58	17	32	52	16
By attitude toward government solutions to workplace problems						
Prefer to take problems to court/government agency	23	58	19	36	47	16
Prefer arbitration system	24	63	13	29	60	11

Source: Based on WRPS question (W1.58) as described in Exhibit 7.4; cross-tabulated with questions on union status, employee-involvement status, and intention to vote union, and also with question (W1.57), "If you felt your own legal workplace rights had been violated, would you prefer to use this alternative system, or would you prefer to go to court or to a government agency?"

going to an arbitrator to resolve their workplace problem. Even here, however, increased legal protection is the least preferred first option.

Conclusion: Toward Improving U.S. Workplaces

Our central finding in *What Workers Want* is that, given a choice, workers want "more" — more say in the workplace decisions that affect their lives, more employee involvement at their firms, more legal protection at the workplace, and more union representation. Most workers reported that existing institutions — from unions to EI committees to government regulations — are either insufficiently available to them or do not go far enough to provide the workplace voice they want. A substantial number of nonunion workers want the benefits of unionization. An even larger number would like to see some sort of employee-management committee, with varying degrees of independence from management, at their workplace. Irrespective of the workplace organization they desire, however, most workers do not believe that, under current U.S. policies, they can get the additional input into workplace decisions that they want. They believe that management is unwilling to share power or authority with them. And management generally agrees. Left alone, this system promises continued frustration of worker desire for more say.

Perhaps surprisingly, *What Workers Want* has shown that employees can specify with some precision new forms and attributes of workplace organization and ways to enforce regulations. Employee desire for additional voice and input into workplace decisions is not inchoate but well-formed and practical enough that it could readily guide business, union, and political leaders in modernizing our labor-relations system. Workers want a more decentralized and varied system of workplace organization than the one now offered them — a system that admits new institutions as well as extension of current ones. And throughout, they want more cooperative and equal relations with management in making workplace decisions.

The basic message to decision-makers in business, labor, and government is clear: A huge opportunity exists for America to increase the representation and participation of workers at their jobs and thereby to improve the quality of working life. Political leaders will find potential votes for such reforms; unions will find scores of potential members; business will find a better and more loyal workforce. Of course, whether any of these groups take full advantage of this opportunity is their choice. But the right choice for private action and public policy would be to help workers gain the voice and representation in workplace decisions that they so clearly want.

Wave 1 of the WRPS: Structure and Methodology

Wave 1 survey results were based on telephone interviews with a nationally representative sample of 2,408 adults, 18 years of age and older, who were currently working in private companies or nonprofit organizations in the continental United States with 25 or more employees (excluding company owners and their families and upper management). The sample was split in two (Form A and Form B). The interviews were conducted from September 15, 1994, through October 13, 1994.

Sample Design and Response Rate

We used a random-digit sample of telephone numbers selected from exchanges in the continental United States. The sample of telephone numbers was designed to produce a representative sample of continental U.S. telephone households; random-digit sampling assures representation of unlisted or not-yet-listed numbers, and is thus superior to random selection from a frame of listed telephone households. Attempts were made to contact each of the sampled households, and potential respondents were then identified and screened to determine their eligibility for the survey.

At least five attempts were made to complete an interview at every sampled telephone number. The calls were staggered over times of day and days of the week to maximize the chances of making a contact with a potential respondent. All interview breakoffs and refusals were recontacted at least once in order to attempt to convert them to completed interviews.

If contact was made, the respondent was asked several screening questions to determine eligibility. Quotas for completed screening interviews were set by gender and region to match U.S. Census Bureau parameters of worker distribution. Respondents meeting our criteria continued with the full interview.

Interviewers conducted the screening interview with a potential respondent at 58 percent of the sampled residential telephone numbers. In this calculation, we exclude from the base (denominator) of "residential telephone numbers" — those determined to be inoperative, business, or dedicated to fax lines — and three-quarters of those that consistently rang with no answer (according to informal estimates from AT&T, only one-fourth of such numbers are actually assigned to a residence).

Twenty percent of respondents submitting to the screening procedure were determined to be eligible for interviewing, and 88 percent of the respondents who were determined to be eligible went on to complete the entire interview.

Weighting

Nonresponse in telephone-interview surveys produces some known biases in survey-derived estimates because participation tends to vary for different subgroups of the population, and these subgroups are likely to vary also on questions of substantive interest. For example, men are more difficult than women to reach at home by telephone, and people with relatively low educational attainment are less likely than others to agree to participate in telephone surveys. To compensate for these known biases, the sample data are weighted in analysis.

The demographic weighting parameters are derived from a special analysis of the most recently available Census Bureau Annual Demographic File (the March 1993 Current Population Survey). This analysis produced population parameters for the demographic characteristics of workers aged eighteen or older living in telephone households in the continental United States and working in private companies or nonprofit organizations with at least twenty-five employees. (Note that owners and upper-level managers are included in demographic weighting for comparability with the census parameters. These respondents were only asked the screening questions and the demographic questions at the end of the interview. They were not asked the full questionnaire and are not reported on in this report.) These parameters were compared with the sample characteristics to construct sample weights.

The data for this survey were weighted to bring the demographic characteristics of the sample into alignment with the population parameters on age within gender, education within gender, education within age, race, marital status, presence of children under age eighteen in the household, and region. The data were weighted separately by questionnaire form, as different versions of questions were asked of random subsets of respondents.

The weights were derived using an iterative technique that simultaneously balances the distributions of all weighting parameters. After an optimum sample balancing solution was reached, the weights were constrained to fall within the range of 1 to 5. This constraint is useful to ensure that individual respondents do not exert an inordinate effect on the survey's overall results.

Multiple Forms

In some cases, we further split the Form A/Form B sample — for instance, asking a question worded one way to the first half of both forms and worded another to the second half. Throughout, we made full use of computer-assisted interviewing, with various "skips" (moving to different questions depending on the answer to a preceding one) and probes built in for different constituencies.

Wave 1 of the WRPS: Questionnaire

- N = 2,408 workers in private companies/non-profit organizations with 25 or more employees who are not part of upper management
- Interviewing dates: September 15 to October 13, 1994
- Margin of error: ±2 percentage points for total sample; ±3 percentage points for Form A and Form B

Introduction

Hello, I am calling for Princeton Survey Research of Princeton, New Jersey. We're conducting a national public opinion survey. May I please speak with the youngest male, 18 years of age or older, who has a paying job and is now at home? (IF NO MALE, ASK: May I please speak with the oldest female, 18 years of age or older, who has a paying job and is now at home?)

Introduction to Screening Questions

We're calling households across the country for a national research project on work in America. I'd like to ask you some questions about your own work situation. Your responses are completely confidential.

S1. Are you now employed at a paying job? (Yes, Not employed/student/ retired/disabled)

S2. How many paying jobs do you now have, including night jobs, and any part-time work in addition to your main job? (One, Two or more)

S3. (In your main job), are you employed by . . . (a *private for profit* company, a *private non-profit* organization)?

S4. Including all its locations and worksites, not just your own, about how many people are employed by the (company/organization) you work for (in your main job)? Just stop me when I get to the right category. Would you say there are . . . (25 to 99 employees, 100 to 499 employees, 500 to 999 employees, 1000 or more employees)?

S5. How many people are employed at the particular location, worksite or branch office where you are based? (Fewer than 25 employees, 25 to 99 employees, 100 to 499 employees, 500 to 999 employees, 1,000 or more employees)

S6. Do you happen to be either a member of the family that owns your (company/organization), or are you one of the managers of the (company/ organization)? (Yes ownership family, Yes — manager, Yes — both, No — neither manager nor part of owning family)

S7. Would you say you are part of . . . (lower management, middle management, nonmanagers)?

Survey Questions

1. As an official part of your (main) job, do you supervise the work of other employees or tell other employees what to do?

- Yes
- No

2. In your current (main) job, what kind of work do you do?
   - Professional worker — lawyer, doctor, scientist, teacher, engineer, nurse (RN), accountant, programmer, musician
   - Manager — store manager, sales manager, office manager
   - Clerical or office worker — typist, secretary, postal clerk, telephone operator, computer operator, bank clerk, etc.
   - Sales worker — clerk in store, door-to-door salesman
   - Manufacturer's representative — outside salesperson, sales representative
   - Service worker — policeman/woman, fireman, waiter or waitress, maid, nurse's aide, attendant, barber, hairstylist, etc.
   - Skilled tradesman — printer, baker, tailor, electrician, machinist, linesman, plumber, carpenter, mechanic, etc.
   - Semi-skilled worker — operates machine in factory, assembly line worker, truck driver, taxi or bus driver, etc.
   - Laborer — plumber's helper, construction worker, longshoreman, garbage man, or other physical work
   - Other

3. About how many hours do you usually work at your (main) job each week?

4. What kind of business is your (company/organization)? That is, what does it make, or do? (IF COMPANY IS INVOLVED IN MORE THAN ONE BUSINESS, RECORD BELOW AND THEN PROBE: What does it make or do at the location, worksite, or branch office where *you* work?)
   - Agricultural services/forestry/fishing
   - Mining
   - Construction
   - Manufacturing
   - Transportation/public utilities/communication
   - Wholesale trade
   - Retail trade
   - Finance/insurance/real estate
   - Health services
   - Business services/law
   - Educational, social services/membership organizations
   - Other services

5. For how many years have you worked for your (company/organization) — at any location or job?

6. If for some reason you were to leave your current job — say because you were laid off or decided to quit — how confident are you that you could quickly get another job at about the same pay, without having to move? Would you say you are . . .
   - Very confident?
   - Somewhat confident?
   - Not too confident?
   - Not confident at all?

7. Which *one* of the following four statements best describes how you think of your *current* job?
    - A *long-term* job you will stay in
    - An opportunity for *advancement* in this *same* (company/organization)
    - Part of a *career* or profession that will probably take you to *different* companies
    - A job you will probably *leave* that is *not* part of a career
8. On an average day, what best describes your feeling about going to work? Would you say you usually . . .
    - Look forward to it?
    - Wish you didn't have to go?
9a. How much *loyalty* would you say you feel toward your *immediate* supervisor?
    - A lot of loyalty
    - Some loyalty
    - Only a little loyalty
    - No loyalty at all
9b. (TO NONMANAGERS) And how much loyalty would you say you feel toward your fellow employees?
    - A lot of loyalty
    - Some loyalty
    - Only a little loyalty
    - No loyalty at all
9b1. (TO MANAGERS) How much loyalty would you say you feel toward the people you manage?
    - A lot of loyalty
    - Some loyalty
    - Only a little loyalty
    - No loyalty at all
9c. And how much loyalty would you say you feel toward the (company/ organization) you work for as a whole?
    - A lot of loyalty
    - Some loyalty
    - Only a little loyalty
    - No loyalty at all
10a. (BASED ON FORM A) In general, how much do you trust your (company/ organization) to keep its promises to you and other employees? Would you say you trust your (company/organization) . . .
    - A lot?
    - Somewhat?
    - Only a little?
    - Not at all?
10b. (BASED ON FORM B) Overall, how would you rate relations between employees and management at your (company/ organization)? Would you say they are . . .
    - Excellent?
    - Good?

- Only fair?
- Poor?

11. Do you think relations between employees and management at your (company/organization) are . . .
- Better than average?
- Worse than average?
- About the same as in other places?

14_1. (BASED ON FIRST RANDOM HALF OF FORM A) Now I want to ask about your involvement in decisions on the job. Overall, how satisfied are you with the influence you have in company decisions that affect your job or work life? Would you say you are . . .
- Very satisfied?
- Somewhat satisfied?
- Not too satisfied?
- Not satisfied at all?

12a. (BASED ON THE FIRST RANDOM HALF OF FORM A) How much direct involvement and influence do *you* have in . . .

12aa. Deciding *how* to do your job and organize the work?
- A lot
- Some
- Only a little
- No direct involvement and influence at all

12ab. Deciding what *training* is needed for people in your work group or department?
- A lot
- Some
- Only a little
- No direct involvement and influence at all

12ac. Setting work *schedules*, including breaks, overtime and time off?
- A lot
- Some
- Only a little
- No direct involvement and influence at all

12ad. Deciding how much of a *raise* in pay the people in your work group should get?
- A lot
- Some
- Only a little
- No direct involvement and influence at all

12a. (BASED ON THE SECOND RANDOM HALF OF FORM A) How much direct involvement and influence do *you* have in . . .

12ae. Setting *goals* for your work group or department?
- A lot
- Some
- Only a little
- No direct involvement and influence at all

12af. Deciding how to work with new *equipment or software*, if that's ever been needed?
- A lot
- Some
- Only a little
- No direct involvement and influence at all

12ag. Setting *safety* standards and practices?
- A lot
- Some
- Only a little
- No direct involvement and influence at all

12ah. Deciding what kinds of *benefits* are offered to employees?
- A lot
- Some
- Only a little
- No direct involvement and influence at all

13a. (BASED ON THE FIRST RANDOM HALF OF FORM A) Suppose you *could* have *a lot* of influence in all these areas at work — whether you do now or not. As I read each area again, please tell me how important it would be to you to have *a lot* of influence on these decisions.

13aa. Deciding *how* to do your job:
- Very important
- Somewhat important
- Not too important
- Not important at all

13ab. Deciding what *training* is needed:
- Very important
- Somewhat important
- Not too important
- Not important at all

13ac. Setting work *schedules*:
- Very important
- Somewhat important
- Not too important
- Not important at all

13ad. Deciding how much of a *raise* in pay the people in your work group should get:
- Very important
- Somewhat important
- Not too important
- Not important at all

13a. (BASED ON THE SECOND RANDOM HALF OF FORM A) Suppose you *could* have *a lot* of influence in all these areas at work — whether you do now or not. As I read the area again, please tell me how important it would be to you to have *a lot* of influence on these decisions.

13ae. Setting *goals* for your work group:
- Very important
- Somewhat important
- Not too important
- Not important at all

13af. Deciding how to work with new *equipment or software*:
- Very important
- Somewhat important
- Not too important
- Not important at all

13ag. Setting *safety* standards and practices:
- Very important
- Somewhat important
- Not too important
- Not important at all

13ah. Deciding what kinds of *benefits* are offered:
- Very important
- Somewhat important
- Not too important
- Not important at all

14_2. (BASED ON THE SECOND RANDOM HALF OF FORM A) Overall, how satisfied are you with the influence you have in company decisions that affect your job or work life? Would you say you are . . .
- Very satisfied?
- Somewhat satisfied?
- Not too satisfied?
- Not satisfied at all?

14_3. (BASED ON THE SECOND RANDOM HALF OF FORM B) Now I want to ask about your involvement in decisions on the job. Overall, how satisfied are you with the influence you have in company decisions that affect your job or work life? Would you say you are . . .
- Very satisfied?
- Somewhat satisfied?
- Not too satisfied?
- Not satisfied at all?

12b. (BASED ON THE FIRST RANDOM HALF OF FORM A) Now I want to ask about your influence in different decisions on the job. How satisfied are you with the direct involvement and influence *you* have in . . .

12ba. Deciding *how* to do your job and organize the work?
- Very satisfied
- Somewhat satisfied
- Not too satisfied
- Not satisfied at all

12bb. Deciding what *training* is needed for people in your work group or department?

- Very satisfied
- Somewhat satisfied
- Not too satisfied
- Not satisfied at all

12bc. Setting work *schedules*, including breaks, overtime and time off?
- Very satisfied
- Somewhat satisfied
- Not too satisfied
- Not satisfied at all

12bd. Deciding how much of a *raise* in pay the people in your work group should get?
- Very satisfied
- Somewhat satisfied
- Not too satisfied
- Not satisfied at all

12b. (BASED ON THE SECOND RANDOM HALF OF FORM B) How satisfied are you with the direct involvement and influence *you* have in . . .

12be. Setting *goals* for your work group or department?
- Very satisfied
- Somewhat satisfied
- Not too satisfied
- Not satisfied at all

12bf. Deciding how to work with new *equipment or software*, if that's ever been needed?
- Very satisfied
- Somewhat satisfied
- Not too satisfied
- Not satisfied at all

12bg. Setting *safety* standards and practices?
- Very satisfied
- Somewhat satisfied
- Not too satisfied
- Not satisfied at all

12bh. Deciding what kinds of *benefits* are offered to employees?
- Very satisfied
- Somewhat satisfied
- Not too satisfied
- Not satisfied at all

13b. (BASED ON FORM B) If it were *your* decision alone, and everyone went along with it, would you generally like to have *more* influence in these areas, *less* influence, *or* would you want to keep things the way they are now?
- More influence
- Less influence
- Keep things as they are

15b. (BASED ON FORM B RESPONDENTS WHO WANT MORE INFLUENCE AT WORK) The way things are set up now in your (company/organization), how likely is it that you *could* get the influence you want, if you *tried* to get more influence? Would you say it is . . .
- Very likely?
- Somewhat likely?
- Not too likely?
- Not likely at all?

14_4. (BASED ON SECOND RANDOM HALF OF FORM B) Overall, how satisfied are you with the influence you have in company decisions that affect your job or work life? Would you say you are . . .
- Very satisfied?
- Somewhat satisfied?
- Not too satisfied?
- Not satisfied at all?

16. (TO NONMANAGERS) Still thinking about your influence on company decisions that concern you, how much *more* influence do you think you would have if there was a *group* of employees who met regularly with management to discuss workplace issues? Do you think a group like this would give you . . .
- A lot more influence?
- Somewhat more influence?
- Only a little more influence?
- No more influence at all?

16a. (TO MANAGERS) Still thinking about your influence on company decisions that concern you, how much *more* influence do you think you would have if there was a *group* of managers at your level who met regularly with *upper* management to discuss workplace issues? Do you think a group like this would give you. . .
- A lot more influence?
- Somewhat more influence?
- Only a little more influence?
- No more influence at all?

17. (TO NONMANAGERS) How often, if ever, do *you* make suggestions to your supervisor or to management about how to improve quality or productivity? Would you say you make such suggestions . . .
- Often?
- Sometimes?
- Hardly ever?
- Never?

17a. (TO MANAGERS) How often, if ever, do *you* get suggestions from the people you manage about how to improve quality or productivity? Would you say you get such suggestions . . .
- Often?
- Sometimes?
- Hardly ever?
- Never?

18.　(TO NONMANAGERS) When you, or other employees like you, make suggestions about improving quality or productivity, how often does management take them seriously? Would you say management . . .
- Almost always?
- Sometimes?
- Hardly ever?
- Never . . . takes them seriously?

18a.　(TO MANAGERS) How often do you find these suggestions useful?
- Almost always
- Sometimes
- Hardly ever
- Never

19.　At your workplace, would you say *employees* generally *encourage* each other to make an extra effort on the job, *discourage* each other from making an extra effort, or would you say they *don't care* how hard other employees work?
- Encourage
- Discourage
- Don't care

20.　Have you ever *held back* from making a suggestion about how to do work more efficiently because you thought it might cost you or someone else their job?
- Yes
- No

22.　Imagine that *more* decisions about production and operations were made by employees, instead of by managers. How do you think this would affect your (company/organization) in the following areas? (ROTATE ITEMS)

22a.　(BASED ON FORM A) Would your (company/organization) be *stronger* or *weaker* against its competitors?
- Stronger
- Weaker

22b.　(BASED ON FORM B) Would the *quality* of the (company's/organization's) products or services get *better*, or *worse*?
- Better
- Worse

22c.　Would *employees* enjoy their jobs *more*, or *less*?
- More
- Less

23.　Some companies are organizing workplace decision-making in new ways to get employees more involved — using things like self-directed work teams, total quality management, quality circles, or other employee-involvement programs. Is anything like this now being done in your (company/organization)?
- Yes
- No

23a.　Would you *like* to have a program like this at your (company/organization), or not?

- Yes
- No

24. Are you personally involved in any of these programs at work?
    - Yes
    - No

25. (TO THOSE PARTICIPATING IN AN EMPLOYEE-INVOLVEMENT PROGRAM) As part of this program, do you *ever* talk about *wages* and *benefits*, or do you *only* talk about ways to improve productivity or quality?
    - Wages and benefits sometimes
    - Just production issues

26. (TO THOSE PARTICIPATING IN AN EMPLOYEE-INVOLVEMENT PROGRAM) Have you personally benefited from your involvement in the program by getting any of the following?

26a. An increase in pay:
    - Yes
    - No

26b. More influence over how your job is done:
    - Yes
    - No

27. (TO THOSE IN COMPANIES WITH EMPLOYEE-INVOLVEMENT PROGRAMS) How effective would you say these programs have been in improving productivity or quality? Would you say . . .
    - Very effective?
    - Somewhat effective?
    - Not too effective?
    - Not effective at all?

28. (TO THOSE IN COMPANIES WITH EMPLOYEE-INVOLVEMENT PROGRAMS) If employees, as a group, had *more say* in how these programs are run at your (company/organization), do you think they would be *more* effective, or *less* effective?
    - More
    - Less

29. On a different subject, I want to ask how problems involving *individual employees* are solved at your workplace. Which of the following, if any, does your (company/organization) have? (READ AND ROTATE)

29a. A *personnel* or human resources department:
    - Yes
    - No

29b. An *open door* policy so employees can tell upper management about problems with their immediate supervisors:
    - Yes
    - No

29c. A *grievance* procedure that uses an outside referee or arbitrator to settle disputes between an employee and management:

- Yes
- No

32. *Overall,* how effective is your (company's/organization's) system for resolving the problems *individual* employees have at work? Would you say it is . . .
    - Very effective?
    - Somewhat effective?
    - Not too effective?
    - Not effective at all?

33. If employees, as a group, had *more say* in how the workplace problems of individual employees are solved at your (company/organization), do you think this system would be *more* effective, or *less* effective?
    - More
    - Less

34. (TO MANAGERS) When the people you manage have workplace problems, do you feel more comfortable dealing with them individually, or in a group?
    - Individually
    - In a group

34a. (BASED ON FORM A TO NONMANAGERS) Do you agree or disagree with the following statement: "I'd feel more comfortable raising workplace problems through an employee association, rather than as an individual."
    - Agree
    - Disagree

34b. (BASED ON FORM B TO NONMANAGERS) How would *you* prefer to solve a workplace problem of your own? Would you feel more comfortable dealing directly with management *yourself,* or would you feel more comfortable having a *group* of your fellow employees *help* you deal with management?
    - Deal directly
    - Have help of fellow employees

35. (TO THOSE WHO ANSWERED "NO" TO QUESTION 29C) Before, you said your (company/ organization) does not have a grievance procedure using an outside referee or arbitrator to make the final decision in disputes between employees and management. Is this something you would *like* to have in your (company/organization)?
    - Yes
    - No

36. Now let's talk about company policies regarding wages, benefits, and other things affecting employees as a group. Which of the following, if any, does your (company/organization) have to deal with issues that affect employees as a group?

36a. Are there regular "town" meetings with employees, called by management?
    - Yes
    - No

36b. Is there an open door policy for *groups* of employees to raise issues about policies with upper management?

- Yes
- No

36c. Is there a committee of employees that discusses problems with management on a regular basis?
- Yes
- No

36d. Is there a union that negotiates with management on a regular basis?
- Yes
- No

37. (BASED ON ALL WHOSE COMPANY HAS AN ITEM IN QUESTION 36) How effective (has the item/have the items) been in resolving group problems or concerns?

37a. The "town" meetings:
- Very effective
- Somewhat effective
- Not too effective
- Not effective at all

37b. The open door policy:
- Very effective
- Somewhat effective
- Not too effective
- Not effective at all

37c. The employee committee:
- Very effective
- Somewhat effective
- Not too effective
- Not effective at all

37d. The union:
- Very effective
- Somewhat effective
- Not too effective
- Not effective at all

38a. (BASED ON FORM A RESPONDENTS IN COMPANIES WITH NO EMPLOYEE COMMITTEE OR UNION) Imagine *management* selected a committee of employees to discuss the problems employees have as a group with them. Do you think this would be a *more* effective or *less* effective to resolve employees' concerns?
- More effective
- Less effective

38c. (BASED ON FORM B RESPONDENTS IN COMPANIES WITH NO EMPLOYEE COMMITTEE OR UNION) Imagine employees chose their *own* representatives to meet with management and discuss the problems employees have as a group. Do you think this would be a *more* effective or *less* effective to resolve employees' concerns?
- More effective
- Less effective

38e. (BASED ON THOSE IN NONUNION COMPANIES WITH AN EMPLOYEE COMMITTEE) Before, you said your (company/organization) had an employee committee that meets regularly with management. How are employees selected for this committee? Does management pick them, are they volunteers, or do employees elect them?
- Management picks them
- They are volunteers
- Employees elect them

38f. (BASED ON THOSE IN NONUNION COMPANIES WITH AN EMPLOYEE COMMITTEE) If it was your decision alone, and everyone went along with it, what do you think would be the *best* way for committee members to be picked?
- Management should pick them
- They should be volunteers
- Employees should elect them

39_1. (TO MANAGERS IN UNION COMPANIES) In your day-to- day work, does the presence of a union affect how you do your job?
- Yes
- No

39_2. (TO MANAGERS IN UNION COMPANIES REPLYING TO QUESTION 39_1) Is that because you deal directly with union representatives, or because you are bound by the terms of a union contract?
- Deal with representatives
- Am bound by a union contract

39_3. (TO MANAGERS IN UNION COMPANIES) Overall, would you say having a union makes your job *easier* or *harder* to do?
- Easier
- Harder

39_4. (TO MANAGERS IN UNION COMPANIES) How does the union affect your (company's/organization's) performance? Overall, would you say having a union *helps* or *hurts* performance, or does the union have no effect?
- It *helps* or *hurts* performance
- It has no effect

39_5. (TO MANAGERS IN UNION COMPANIES WHO REPLIED "HELPS/ HURTS" TO QUESTION 39_4) Would you say it (helps/hurts) a lot of a little?
- A lot
- A little

39_6. (TO MANAGERS IN UNION COMPANIES) In recent years, have you found the union to be more *cooperative* with your (company/organization), more *confrontational*, or about the same as it's always been?
- More cooperative
- More confrontational
- About the same

39_7. (TO MANAGERS IN UNION COMPANIES) In your view, does the union make the work lives of its members better or worse?

- Better
- Worse

39_8. (TO MANAGERS IN UNION COMPANIES REPLYING TO QUESTION 39_7) Would you say a lot (better/worse) or only a little (better/worse)?
- A lot
- A little

39_9. (TO MANAGERS IN UNION COMPANIES) Overall, would you say your (company's/organization's) management accepts the union as a partner in workplace decisions, or does it wish it could get rid of the union?
- Accepts the union as a partner
- Wishes it could get rid of the union

39a. (TO NONMANAGERS) Are you a member of the union at your company?
- Yes
- No

39b. (TO NONMANAGERS) Have you *ever* been a member of a union?
- Yes
- No

39c. (TO NONMANAGERS IN LIEU OF QUESTION 39b) Before, you said there is no union at your (company/organization). Have you *ever* been a member of a union?
- Was a member at some point
- Have never been a member

40a. (TO CURRENT UNION MEMBERS) How would you describe your personal experience with the union at your (company/ organization)? Has it been . . .
- Very good?
- Good?
- Bad?
- Very bad?
- Neither good nor bad?

40b. (TO NONMANAGERS WHO ARE FORMER UNION MEMBERS) How would you describe your personal experience with unions? Would you say it has been . . .
- Very good?
- Good?
- Bad?
- Very bad?
- Neither good nor bad?

41a. (TO CURRENT UNION MEMBERS) If a new election were held *today* to decide whether to keep the union at your (company/organization), would you vote to keep the union or get rid of it?
- Keep the union
- Get rid of the union

41b. (TO NONMANAGERS WHO ARE NOT CURRENT UNION MEMBERS) If an election were held *today* to decide whether employees like you should be represented by a union, would you vote for the union or against the union?
- For the union
- Against the union

42. (TO NONMANAGERS) How do you think most of your *fellow employees* would vote? Would more than *half* of them vote for the union or would more than *half* of them vote against the union?
    - More than half would vote for the union
    - More than half would vote against the union

43. (TO CURRENT UNION MEMBERS; N = 282) How satisfied are you with the influence you and fellow union members have in union decisions about . . . (ROTATE ITEMS)

43a. Choosing local leaders?
    - Very satisfied
    - Somewhat satisfied
    - Not too satisfied
    - Not satisfied at all

43b. Choosing national leaders of your union?
    - Very satisfied
    - Somewhat satisfied
    - Not too satisfied
    - Not satisfied at all

43c. Bargaining about wages and benefits?
    - Very satisfied
    - Somewhat satisfied
    - Not too satisfied
    - Not satisfied at all

43d. Endorsements of candidates in political campaigns?
    - Very satisfied
    - Somewhat satisfied
    - Not too satisfied
    - Not satisfied at all

43e. Union positions on national political issues?
    - Very satisfied
    - Somewhat satisfied
    - Not too satisfied
    - Not satisfied at all

44. (TO THE TOTAL SAMPLE) Have you ever worked at a (company/ organization) at a time when employees were trying to form a union?
    - Yes
    - No

45. (TO THOSE WHO WORKED AT A COMPANY WHEN WORKERS TRIED TO FORM A UNION) Which best describes how management responded to this effort? Did management . . .
    - Welcome the union?
    - Oppose the union with information only?
    - Oppose the union by threatening or harassing some union supporters?
    - Or, did it do nothing?

46.   (TO MANAGERS IN NONUNION COMPANIES) If a group of employees tried to form a union now at your (company/organization), how would *you* react? Would you welcome the union, oppose it, or not care one way or the other?
  • Welcome
  • Oppose
  • Not care one way or the other

46a. (TO NONMANAGERS IN UNION COMPANIES) If your (company/ organization) didn't already have a union and employees tried to form one, can you imagine how management would react? Do you think they would . . .
  • Welcome the union?
  • Oppose the union with information only?
  • Oppose the union by threatening or harassing some union supporters?
  • Do you think they would do nothing?
  • Don't know/Refuse to answer

46b. (TO NONMANAGERS IN NONUNION COMPANIES) If a group of employees tried to form a union now at your (company/organization), how do you think management would react? Do you think they would . . .
  • Welcome the union?
  • Oppose the union with information only?
  • Oppose the union by threatening or harassing some union supporters?
  • Do you think they would do nothing?
  • Don't know/Refuse to answer

47.   (TO MANAGERS IN NONUNION COMPANIES) If the employees you manage formed a union, would that help or hurt your advancement in your (company/organization)?
  • Help
  • Hurt
  • No effect/neither

47_1. (TO MANAGERS IN NONUNION COMPANIES REPLYING TO QUESTION 47) Would it (help/hurt) a lot, or only a little?
  • A lot
  • A little
  • No effect/neither

47a. (TO NONMANAGERS WHO WOULD VOTE AGAINST A UNION AND THINK MANAGEMENT WOULD OPPOSE ONE) Before, you said you would vote *against* a union. If you thought the management of your (company/ organization) would *not oppose* the union, would you *still* vote against it, or would you now vote *for* it?
  • Still against
  • Change vote to support union

47b. (TO NONMANAGERS WHO WOULD VOTE FOR A UNION AND THINK MANAGEMENT WOULD NOT OPPOSE ONE) Before, you said you would vote *for* a union. If you thought the management of your (company/

organization) would *oppose* the union, would you *still* vote for it, or would you now vote *against* it?

- Still for the union
- Change vote against the union

48. Thinking now about any kind of employee organization, not just unions, how would *you* like it to work? If it was your decision alone to make, and everybody went along with it, would you prefer . . .

48a. An organization that can use an *outside* referee or arbitrator to settle issues, or one where *management* makes the final decisions about issues?

- Outside arbitrator
- Management decides

48b. An organization run by employees, or one run *jointly* by employees and management?

- Employee run
- Run jointly by employees and management

48c. An organization where the key participants are *volunteers*, one where they are *elected*, or one where they are *appointed* by management?

- Volunteers
- Elected by employees
- Appointed by management

48d. An organization that includes *everyone* except upper management, or one that just includes employees doing the *same* kind of work *you* do?

- Everyone except upper management
- Only employees doing same kind of work

48e. An organization that has access to *confidential* information about company performance, or one that only has access to information the company has made *public*?

- Confidential information
- Only public information

48f. An organization that has its *own* budget and staff paid through *employee* contributions, or one that conducts its business with the budget and staff given by the *company*?

- Own budget and staff
- Company budget and staff

48_1. Do you think the employees who participate in an employee organization like this would need legal protection from discrimination and harassment, or would legal protection not be necessary?

- Legal protection needed
- Not necessary

49a. (TO NONMANAGERS) How willing would *you* be to volunteer two or three hours a month to participate in an employee organization to discuss workplace issues with your (company's/ organization's) management? If the organization was set up the way you just described, would you be . . .

- Definitely willing?
- Probably willing?

- Probably not willing?
- Definitely not willing?

49. (TO MANAGERS) How willing would you be to work with such an organization in solving workplace problems? If the organization was set up the way you just described, would you be . . .
    - Definitely willing?
    - Probably willing?
    - Probably not willing?
    - Definitely not willing?

49b. Do you think employee organizations can be effective *even if* management does not cooperate with them, or do you think they can *only* be effective if management cooperates?
    - Can be effective without cooperation
    - Can only be effective if management cooperates

49c. (TO NONMANAGERS) Which *one* of these employee organizations would you prefer? (ROTATE ORDER)
    - One that management cooperated with in discussing issues, but had no power to make decisions
    - One that had more power, but management opposed

50. Federal law guarantees employees certain protections in the workplace. To the best of your knowledge, please tell me if you think it is now legal or not legal for employers to do each of the following.

50a. Fire an employee for no reason:
    - Legal
    - Illegal

50b. Move someone to a job with less pay or responsibility for trying to form a union:
    - Legal
    - Illegal

50c. Refuse family leave so an employee can care for a sick child:
    - Legal
    - Illegal

50d. Fire someone for refusing to do hazardous work:
    - Legal
    - Illegal

50e. Permanently replace someone who goes on strike:
    - Legal
    - Illegal

50f. Avoid hiring blacks or other minorities, if they have good business reasons for doing so:
    - Legal
    - Illegal

51a. (BASED ON THE FIRST RANDOM HALF OF FORM A) In the following areas, do you think current laws give employees *too little* legal protection, or *more protection than is necessary*?

51aa. Job discrimination based on race, sex, or age:
- Too little protection
- More protection than is necessary

51ab. Being fired without cause:
- Too little protection
- More protection than is necessary

51ac. Layoffs and plant closings:
- Too little protection
- More protection than is necessary

51a. (BASED ON THE SECOND RANDOM HALF OF FORM A) In the following areas, do you think current laws give employees *too little* legal protection, or *more protection than is necessary*?

51ad. Use of temporary or part-time employees to replace full-time employees:
- Too little protection
- More protection than is necessary

51ae. Rights to form unions and·employee associations:
- Too little protection
- More protection than is necessary

51af. Conflicts between work responsibilities and family responsibilities:
- Too little protection
- More protection than is necessary

51b. (BASED ON THE FIRST RANDOM HALF OF FORM B) In the following areas, do you think current laws put *too few* legal restrictions on management, or *more* restrictions than are *necessary*?

51ba. Job discrimination based on race, sex, or age:
- Too few restrictions on management
- More restrictions than are necessary

51bb. Being fired without cause:
- Too few restrictions on management
- More restrictions than are necessary

51bc. Layoffs and plant closings:
- Too few restrictions on management
- More restrictions than are necessary

51b. (BASED ON THE SECOND RANDOM HALF OF FORM B) In the following areas, do you think current laws put *too few* legal restrictions on management or *more than are necessary*?

51bd. Use of temporary or part-time employees to replace full-time employees:
- Too few restrictions on management
- More restrictions than are necessary

51be. Rights to form unions and employee associations:
- Too few restrictions on management
- More restrictions than are necessary

51bf. Conflicts between work responsibilities and family responsibilities:
- Too few restrictions on management
- More restrictions than are necessary

52. Have you, or anyone you know personally, ever gone to court or to a government agency because of a possible violation of workplace rights?
    - Yes, myself
    - Yes, someone I know
    - Both self and someone else
    - No, neither

53. (TO THOSE WHO WENT TO COURT OVER WORKPLACE RIGHTS) How satisfied were you with the outcome of your complaint?
    - Very satisfied
    - Somewhat satisfied
    - Not too satisfied
    - Not satisfied at all

54. Have you, or anyone you know personally, ever *thought about* going to court or to a government agency about a possible violation of workplace rights, but decided *not* to go?
    - Yes, myself
    - Yes, someone I know
    - Both self and someone else
    - No, neither

55. (TO THOSE WHO THOUGHT ABOUT GOING TO COURT OVER WORKPLACE RIGHTS BUT DID NOT GO) Why did you decide not to pursue your complaint? (DO NOT READ. RECORD ALL MENTIONS.)
    - Problem wasn't that important/not worth the trouble
    - Couldn't find/afford a lawyer
    - Was afraid of what employer would do
    - Was intimidated by process of making complaint
    - Problem was solved in another way
    - Quit the job
    - Other reason (*Specify.*)

56a. (BASED ON FORM A) Going to court or to a government agency can be expensive and time-consuming. Here is an alternative I'd like your opinion about: In legal disputes between employees and management, *management* would choose an outside referee or arbitrator, from a list approved by the government, to make a decision in the case. How effective would this be in *fairly* resolving disputes over legal rights in your (company/organization)? Would you say . . .
    - Very effective?
    - Somewhat effective?
    - Not too effective?
    - Not effective at all?

56b. (BASED ON FORM B) Going to court or to a government agency can be expensive and time-consuming. Here is an alternative I'd like your opinion about: In legal disputes between employees and management, an *elected* committee of employees and management would *jointly* choose an outside referee or arbitrator, from a list approved by the government, to make a decision in the case. How effective would this be in *fairly* resolving disputes over legal rights in your (company/organization)? Would you say . . .

- Very effective?
- Somewhat effective?
- Not too effective?
- Not effective at all?

57.   If you felt your own legal workplace rights had been violated, would you prefer to use this alternative system or would you prefer to go to court or to a government agency?

- Use the alternative system
- Go to court or government agency

58a.   (BASED ON THE FIRST RANDOM HALF OF FORMS A AND B) During this interview, we've talked about a few different ways to increase employees' say in workplace matters and make sure they are treated fairly. Which *one* of the following three ways do *you* think would be most effective?

- *Laws* that protect the rights of individual employees
- Joint employee and management *committees* that *discuss* problems
- Employee organizations that *negotiate* or bargain with management over issues

58b.   (BASED ON THE SECOND RANDOM HALF OF FORMS A AND B) During this interview, we've talked about a few different ways to increase employees' say in workplace matters and make sure they are treated fairly. Which *one* of the following three ways do *you* think would be most effective?

- *Laws* that protect the rights of individual employees
- Joint employee and management *committees* that *discuss* problems
- Employee organizations that *negotiate* or bargain with management over issues

Background Questions
(ASKED FOR STATISTICAL PURPOSES ONLY)

D1.   Now I have a few background questions that we'll use for statistical purposes only. First, what was your age on your last birthday?

- 18–24
- 25–34
- 35–44
- 45–54
- 55–64
- 65+

D2.   Are you now

- Married?
- Living as married?
- Widowed?

- Divorced?
- Separated?
- Never been married?

D3. Do you have any children *under* the age of 18?
- Yes
- No

D4. What is the age of your *youngest* child?
- Less than 3 years old
- 3 to 4 years old
- 5 to 9 years old
- 10 to 13 years old
- 14 to 17 years old

D5. What is the last grade or class that you completed in school?
- None, or grade 1 to 8
- High school incomplete (Grades 9–11)
- High school graduate (Grade 12)
- Business, technical or vocational school after high school
- Some college, no four-year degree
- College graduate, four-year degree
- Post-graduate or professional schooling, after college

D6. Are you, yourself, of Hispanic or Latino background such as Mexican, Puerto Rican, Cuban, or some other Spanish background?
- Yes
- No

D7. What is your race? Are you white, black, Asian, or some other race?
- White
- Black
- African-American
- Asian American
- Other or mixed race

D8. RECORD RESPONDENT'S SEX.
- Male
- Female

D9. In politics today, do you consider yourself to be
- Republican?
- Democrat?
- Independent?
- Other (VOLUNTEERED)

D10. Thinking back to the 1992 presidential election, when Clinton ran against Bush and Perot, did things come up to keep you from voting, or did you happen to vote?
- Voted
- Didn't vote

D11. Did you vote for Clinton, Bush or Perot?

- Clinton
- Bush
- Perot
- Other (VOLUNTEERED)

D12. Thinking once more about your (main) job, are you
- Salaried?
- Paid by the hour?
- Some other way?

D13. (TO SALARIED WORKERS) What is your current salary, *before* taxes and deductions are taken out?
- Current salary up to $999,997 (PROBE FOR ONE NUMBER)
- $999,998 or more

D13a. (TO SALARIED WORKERS) What is your current salary, *before* taxes and deductions are taken out?
- Per week
- Per two week period
- Per month
- Per year
- Other period (SPECIFY)

D14.1 (TO WORKERS PAID AN HOURLY WAGE) What is your current hourly wage (for your main job)?
- Current hourly rate up to $99.97 (PROBE FOR ONE NUMBER)
- $99.98 or more

D15. (TO NONSALARIED WORKERS) On average, what are your weekly earnings (from your main job)?
- Current earnings up to $9,997 (PROBE FOR ONE NUMBER)
- $9,998 or more

D15a. Do your earnings provide
- Just about all or almost all of your household's income?
- Most of it?
- Less than half of it?
- Very little of it?

D16. On your (main) job, do you
- Receive any bonuses based on profit sharing?
- Receive any bonuses based on meeting workplace goals?
- Participate in an employee stock ownership or ESOP plan?
- Work in an employee-owned (company/organization)?
- Have health insurance available to you that the (company/organization) helps to pay for?
- Have paid vacation time?

D17. We're almost done. There's just one more question. We'd like to mail you some material describing possible changes in the laws about employee-management relations. After you've had a chance to read the material, we'd like to call you back and briefly get your reactions to these new ideas. Again, your responses will be completely confidential, but I'll need your name and mailing address so I can send you the material.

- NAME:
- STREET ADDRESS:
- CITY AND STATE:
- ZIP CODE:

That completes the interview. Thank you *very much* for your cooperation.

Wave 2 of the WRPS: Structure and Methodology

The Wave 2 survey consisted of re-interviews of 801 participants in Wave 1. It was supported by various written materials, sent to all of the roughly 1,400 participants in Wave 1 who there agreed to participate in Wave 2 and read those materials in advance. Telephone re-interviews were conducted between December 6, 1994 and January 24, 1995.

Survey Procedures

The packet of materials mailed included a description of either "Arbitration to Settle Disputes about Employment Rights" or a description of "Committees for Workplace Standards." The packet also included a cover letter that reminded recipients about taking part in the initial survey, described the materials enclosed, and notified recipients they would be contacted in a week or so to complete the follow-up telephone interview. These packets were posted on November 18 and November 21, 1994 via first-class mail.

Potential Wave 2 respondents were randomly divided into four subsets. Two of these received the material on arbitration, with one having its possible advantages listed first and the other having its possible disadvantages listed first. The other two received the material on workplace regulatory committees, again with one getting advantages listed before disadvantages and the other the reverse.

Telephone calls to these respondents were made between December 6, 1994, and January 24, 1995. If the respondent had not received the packet of materials or had misplaced it by the time the interviewer called, a new packet of material was sent via two-day priority mail, and a follow-up telephone call was made a few days later. These "resends" were mailed on a daily basis.

Response Rates

Fifty-six percent of those who agreed in the original survey to be recontacted completed a Wave 2 interview. Seventeen percent were never contacted because (1) the original number obtained for them was not working at the time of the recontact, (2) the number obtained was incorrect, or (3) the packet of materials sent was returned as undeliverable and no telephone contact was attempted (two months had passed between the close of the first survey and the beginning of Wave 2, which might account for the rather substantial number of nonworking or disconnected numbers). Fifteen percent were never contacted despite repeated attempts; some of these might, in fact, have been "refusals" or people avoiding the interview. Twelve percent refused to participate at the time they were recontacted or broke off the interview before completion.

Weighting

Data were weighted to bring the demographic characteristics of the recontacted sample into alignment with the *weighted* demographic characteristics of all Wave 1 respondents on relevant dimensions. This weighting strategy corrects for nonresponse in the initial survey as well as any nonresponse in Wave 2.

Recontact surveys provide the opportunity to evaluate, to some extent, the amount of nonresponse bias present in the data because it is possible to identify nonrespondents in Wave 2 and look at their demographic and substantive information from the Wave 1 interview. Wave 2 respondents can be compared with respondents from Wave 1 who agreed to be recontacted and to the total sample of Wave 1 respondents on key demographic and substantive measures to see if substantial differences existed among the three samples. Our analysis shows little difference between Wave 2 and Wave 1 participants, however; nonresponse appears not to have been a problem.

Wave 2 of the WRPS: Materials

Here is the text of the letter that all potential Wave 2 participants received, and the two basic sets of materials on arbitration and workplace regulatory committees. On the latter, again, one-quarter of the group received the arbitration materials with advantages listed before disadvantages, one the same material with disadvantages listed before advantages, one the material on committees with advantages listed first, and one the same material with advantages listed second—in total, four different "forms" of the materials.

The Letter

Thank you very much for taking part in our telephone opinion survey about work in America. We appreciate the time you gave us, and your thoughtful answers. We also appreciate your willingness to receive information about workplace issues and talk to us again about these issues.

Right now, Congress and a national government commission are working on proposals to change the laws about labor-management relations. It is important for them to learn what people in different kinds of jobs think about these proposals. That is why we have been conducting this independent, scientific study of employee opinion.

One of our goals is to find out what employees think about *new ways to resolve problems in the workplace*. We asked you some questions about this during the telephone interview, but you had only a few moments to think about these ideas before answering. Now, we want to tell you more about some proposals that are being made, and get your reaction.

Enclosed is a description of one proposed new way to handle problems at work. Please read it carefully, and then think about how well this new procedure might work at your own company or organization. You might even want to talk to some of your co-workers about this idea to help you make up your mind.

In the next week or so, one of our interviewers will call you at home to ask you some questions about this idea, along with a few other questions to follow up on the earlier telephone interview.

Thank you again for all your help. We look forward to talking to you again soon.

The Arbitration Materials

(The order of the "advantages"/"disadvantages" sections was switched for Forms 1 and 4.)

Arbitration to Settle Disputes about Employment Rights
What Is Arbitration?

Arbitration is a system in which a neutral person (called an arbitrator, referee, or umpire) makes a decision in cases where individuals disagree. This system is now used in disputes between companies that want to avoid going to court, and is found in nearly all union workplaces to settle the contract disputes of union employees.

One proposal under consideration is *to use arbitrators to resolve disputes between an employer and an employee* who feels his or her *legal workplace rights* have been violated by that employer. Here's how this might work:

- The arbitrator would have no personal connection either to the company or to the employee involved in the case. The arbitrator would be selected from a government-approved list of people who specialize in employment cases.
- Both the company and the employee would have to agree on the person selected to be the arbitrator.
- The employee and the company would then present their cases to the arbitrator, who would make a decision that followed current employment laws. A decision would be made within a short period of time—for example, a few weeks.
- Except in extraordinary cases—where either the employee or the company could prove that the arbitrator's decision was biased or improper—the decision in each case would be final.

What Kinds of Problems Would Be Covered under This Plan?

Employees could use this system any time they think their employer has violated their legal rights at work. For example:

- If an employee feels she was denied a promotion because she refused to date her boss.
- If an employee thinks his employer is treating him more harshly than other employees because he is close to retirement age.
- If an employee is not being paid "time and a half" for the extra hours he works each week beyond 40 hours.
- If an employee feels she was fired illegally.

How Is This Plan Different from the Procedures That Are Used Now?

Employees who feel their legal rights have been violated usually hire a lawyer and sue their employer in court. Or, for some problems, they can take their complaint directly to a government agency, like the Equal Employment Opportunity Commission, to investigate and act on the complaint.

What Are Some Disadvantages of Arbitration over the Current System?

Arbitration of employee rights would turn decisions about legal rights over to *private* decision-makers, who might favor companies over employees in their decisions.

Arbitrators reach decisions with less information than a court. Unlike in court proceedings, persons involved in an arbitration would not have the rights to call and cross-examine witnesses and demand the release of documents as evidence. Unlike judges, arbitrators do not have to make decisions that fit with the way similar cases were decided in the past.

Some also worry that, even though the process is simpler, employees will still need to hire a lawyer or other professional in order to help them win a case in arbitration.

Arbitrators will depend on companies and employees for their business. But companies might need to use an arbitrator in more than one case, while any individual employee will probably only use an arbitrator once. Arbitrators might see companies as their source of "repeat business," and thus might either make decisions in companies' favor or give lighter punishments to companies that violate workplace rights.

Cases decided by arbitration will get less publicity than court cases. Some people worry that if employers are no longer threatened with losing a lot of money on a case, or getting a lot of bad publicity, they might start to ignore employees' rights.

What Are Some Advantages of Arbitration?

Arbitration would be quicker, less expensive and simpler than the current system, and might make it easier for average employees to have their cases heard and resolved.

Now, it often takes years for the courts or regulatory agencies to decide a case. For example, there are over 90,000 cases waiting for a decision from the U.S. Equal Employment Opportunity Commission, and many state agencies are three years behind in their caseload.

Arbitration generally costs less than formal court proceedings. Hiring a lawyer to take a case through the legal system is too expensive for many employees who feel their rights have been violated. As a result, most individual lawsuits are filed by executives rather than by ordinary employees. Under an arbitration system, average employees might be better able to afford making claims.

Even taking a complaint to a government agency requires knowing something about how these agencies operate. Most employees need the help of a professional to do this, but can't afford one. The delay and cost of making a formal legal complaint discourages many employees from making any complaint at all.

Is It Fair to Require Arbitration?

A few companies now *require* their employees to use arbitration rather than go to court or a government agency if they feel their legal employment rights have been violated. These companies will not hire a person unless he or she signs an agreement only to use arbitration in future disputes with the company.

Some say this type of requirement is unfair. They think arbitration is fair only when both parties agree to use it, not when one side is forced into it.

Others think it is reasonable for companies to try to protect themselves against the expense of having to go to court by setting rules like this for employees.

What Do We Want to Know from You?

What do you like about arbitration? What bothers you about it? Would this system work at your own company or organization? Is this new idea for solving employment problems better or worse than the current system? Would you like to see it used in most cases?

The Regulatory Committees Materials

(The order of the "advantages"/"disadvantages" sections was switched for Forms 2 and 3.)

Committees for Workplace Standards

What Is a Committee for Workplace Standards?

A committee for workplace standards is a group of workers and managers within a company that meets regularly to discuss and solve problems with how the company meets government standards and regulations.

A company might have several different committees operating at the same time with responsibility for different types of standards and regulations. For example, there might be one committee for health and safety standards, one for wage and overtime standards, and one for production standards.

The managers on the committee would be appointed by management. The employees on the committee would be elected by their fellow-employees. The company would pay for all committee members to receive training about the regulations and standards for which they are responsible.

The company would set aside time during company hours for the committee to meet, it and would give the committee the support it needs to investigate problems.

In areas of special concern, such as health and safety regulation, members of the committee would be given legal powers by the government—for example, to stop a practice that it thought was harmful to employees' health. When they needed help, committee members could call government inspectors to give advice about difficult problems.

How Is This Different from the Procedures That Are Used Now?

There are many state and national laws that set workplace standards for companies. The government enforces these laws by sending inspectors to companies to make sure they are following the regulations. Sometimes an inspector visits a company because one of the employees has made a complaint about a problem. Sometimes an inspector visits just to check up on things, with no specific complaint to investigate. If an inspector finds a violation, he or she tells the company what it has to do to solve the problem.

What Are Some of the Advantages of Standards Committees over the Current System?

The committees would make sure all companies pay attention to workplace standards. The government does not have enough money or people to make sure all companies are meeting workplace standards, and it is difficult for inspectors to take the time to get to know how any individual company really works.

For example, there are about six million U.S. workplaces but only a few thousand government health and safety inspectors. With committees on site at each company, government inspectors can concentrate on the companies that need the most help meeting standards.

Since committee members work at the company, they are more likely to come up with solutions to problems that fit well with the company's existing procedures. Sometimes the solutions required by government inspectors are very expensive to put in place, or cause too much disruption at the company. The committees would make sure that government standards are met in ways that make the most sense.

Some people say workers would enjoy their jobs more if they had more say over some workplace decisions. If workers and managers cooperate with each other on these committees, there might be better labor-management relations at companies.

What Are Some of the Disadvantages of Standards Committees over the Current System?

The committees would cost companies money to train employees and managers to learn about workplace standards and regulations and to give them time off from their regular jobs to attend committee meetings. It would also cost money to support the committees in their monitoring of standards and investigation of problems.

Some people worry that even with training, members of these committees would not have enough knowledge and skill to make good decisions about enforcement of government regulations. They feel there is no substitute for inspectors and other professionals who specialize in monitoring and enforcing particular types of standards.

Employees on these committees might also feel they are putting their jobs at risk if they point out problems at work. They might feel pressure to overlook problems and hesitate to recommend serious action if they think management might object to it. Employees who think their company might lose money and lay off workers if it were forced to meet government standards might agree to ignore the standards in order to save jobs. In any of these situations, the committees would not be effective in making sure government standards are being met.

What Do We Want to Know from You?

What do you like about these committees? What bothers you about them? Would these committees work at your own company or organization? Is this new idea for solving company problems better or worse than the current system? Would you like to see it used in most companies?

Wave 2 of the WRPS: Questionnaire

- N = 801 workers in private companies/nonprofit organizations with 25 or more employees who are not part of upper management
- Margin of error: ±4 percentage points for total sample; ±5 percentage points for Form 1 and Form 4 (N = 410); ±6 percentage points for Forms 2 and 3 (N = 391)

Preliminary Questions

Hello. I am calling for Princeton Survey Research of Princeton, New Jersey. May I please speak with (NAME OF RESPONDENT FROM WAVE 1 OF THE SURVEY)?

A. In (MONTH) you were kind enough to take part in an opinion survey about work in America. About a week ago we mailed you some material that describes a new way to solve work-related problems in companies. Did you receive this information in the mail?
- Yes
- No

A2. (IN RESPONSE TO THOSE WHO DIDN'T RECEIVE THE MATERIAL) We're sorry the information hasn't reached you yet. We'll mail it out again to you, and then call back in about a week. (TERMINATE CALL AND CONFIRM ADDRESS.)

B. Have you had a chance to read the material yet?
- Yes
- No, don't have the material anymore
- No, but still have material

B2. (IN RESPONSE TO THOSE WHO DON'T HAVE THE MATERIAL) We'll mail it out again to you, and then call back in about a week. (TERMINATE CALL AND CONFIRM ADDRESS.)

B3. (IN RESPONSE TO THOSE WHO HAVEN'T READ THE MATERIAL) I hope you'll be able to look it over soon. I'll call back in a couple of days, so you'll have a chance to read it and think about it. What is a good time for me to call back? (TERMINATE CALL; RESCHEDULE INTERVIEW.)

(ON THE SECOND TRY TO PEOPLE WHO ANSWERED "NO" TO QUESTION 2, IF THEY ANSWER "NO" ON THE CALLBACK, GO TO QUESTION 12 INSTEAD OF TERMINATING.)

(FORMS 1 AND 4 RECEIVED FOLLOW-UP MATERIAL ON "ARBITRATION TO SETTLE DISPUTES ABOUT EMPLOYMENT RIGHTS" AND FORMS 2 AND 3 RECEIVED FOLLOW-UP MATERIAL ON "COMMITTEES FOR WORKPLACE STANDARDS.")

Follow-Up Survey

1. Did you read
- all the material
- most of it

- some of it
- only a little of it

2. How would you rate your own understanding of the description of arbitration to settle legal disputes/committees for workplace standards?
   - Excellent
   - Good
   - Only fair
   - Poor

3. After you read the material, did you talk about this new idea with anyone, such as your co-workers, family, or friends?
   - Yes
   - No

4. (IF "YES" TO QUESTION 3) With whom did you discuss it?
   - Spouse
   - Other family member
   - Friend or neighbor
   - Other

5. Overall, what do you think about using (arbitration to settle legal disputes/committees for workplace standards)? Do you think it is . . .
   - A very good idea?
   - A good idea?
   - A bad idea?
   - A very bad idea?

   (FORMS 2 AND 3 SKIP TO QUESTION 6B.)

6a. Now let's talk in more detail about the plan to use arbitrators. Suppose a system like this was set up in your (company/organization). That is, employees who felt their *legal* rights had been violated would take the case to a neutral arbitrator to be decided, rather than to court. Do you think this system would work well, or not well, at your own (company/organization)?
   - Well
   - Not well

7A. I'd like to know what you think would happen if arbitrators replaced the courts in solving most employee disputes about legal rights. In each of the following areas, please tell me what changes you think would take place. If you think things would stay about the same, just tell me that. (ROTATE ORDER OF CHOICES.)

7aa. Would *more* employees or *fewer* employees bring complaints against their employers?
   - More would bring complaints
   - Fewer would bring complaints
   - Stay the same

7ab. Would disputes be settled *more* fairly or *less* fairly?
   - More fairly
   - Less fairly
   - Stay the same

7ac. Would it be *easier* or *harder* for ordinary workers to get a fair hearing of their complaints?
- Easier for ordinary workers
- Harder
- Stay the same

7ad. Overall, would *workers* be *better off* or *worse off* with this kind of system?
- Workers would be better off
- Worse off
- Stay the same

7ae. Overall, would *management* be *better off* or *worse off* with this kind of system?
- Management would be better off
- Worse off
- Stay the same

(ROTATE THE ORDER OF QUESTIONS 8A AND 9A.)

8A. People who *favor* a system of arbitration argue that it has a number of advantages over using courts or government agencies. How convincing are each of these *positive* arguments to you?

8aa. Arbitration would be *faster*.
- Very convincing
- Somewhat convincing
- Not too convincing
- Not convincing at all

8ab Arbitration would cost less for *companies*.
- Very convincing
- Somewhat convincing
- Not too convincing
- Not convincing at all

8ac. Arbitration would cost less for *employees*.
- Very convincing
- Somewhat convincing
- Not too convincing
- Not convincing at all

8ad. Arbitration would be *easier* for employees to use.
- Very convincing
- Somewhat convincing
- Not too convincing
- Not convincing at all

9A. People who *oppose* a system of arbitration argue that it has a number of *disadvantages* over using courts or government agencies. How convincing are each of these *negative* arguments to you?

9aa. Arbitrators' decisions would be made *less carefully*.
- Very convincing
- Somewhat convincing
- Not too convincing
- Not convincing at all

9ab. Employees would not have *lawyers* to help them win their cases.
- Very convincing
- Somewhat convincing
- Not too convincing
- Not convincing at all

9ac. Arbitrators' decisions would tend to favor *management.*
- Very convincing
- Somewhat convincing
- Not too convincing
- Not convincing at all

9ad. Employees would not be able to have their "*day in court.*"
- Very convincing
- Somewhat convincing
- Not too convincing
- Not convincing at all

10A. Suppose Congress passed a law that encouraged companies to use arbitration to settle employee disputes about legal rights. If it were your decision to make and everyone went along with it, what type of system would you like Congress to encourage? (ROTATE ORDER OF CHOICES.)

10aa. A system where the procedures for using it are set up
- By management alone?
- By employees alone?
- By management and employees together?

10ab. A system that
- Allows employees to take a legal workplace dispute *either* to an arbitrator or to courts?
- Or one that requires employees to use arbitration *only*?

10ac. A system where the expenses are paid
- By *management* alone?
- By management and the individual employee *together*?
- By management and the employee with a contribution from the *government*?

10ad. A system
- That provides expert advice and assistance to all employees in preparing their cases?
- Or one that makes each employee responsible for preparing his or her own case?

10ae. A system
- In which decisions are reviewed by a government agency?
- That operates without government review?

11a. Right now, some companies *require* employees, as a condition of keeping their jobs, to settle any legal disputes with them through arbitration rather than going to court. Do you think it should be *legal* or *illegal* for a company to require employees to sign a contract requiring arbitration?
- Legal
- Not legal, illegal

(FORMS 1 AND 4 SKIP TO QUESTION 12.)

6b.   Let's talk in more detail about the plan to set up committees for workplace standards, such as health and safety. These would be groups of employees and managers meeting together regularly to *discuss and solve* problems in meeting those standards and regulations. How do you think such a system would work at your company?
  • Well
  • Not well

7B.   I'd like to know what you think would happen if workplace committees were given some responsibility for enforcing workplace standards. In each of the following areas, please tell me what changes you think would take place. If you think things would stay about the same, just tell me that. (ROTATE ORDER OF CHOICES.)

7ba. Would standards be enforced *more often* or *less often* than they are now?
  • More often
  • Less often
  • Stay the same

7bb. Would it be *easier* or *harder* for companies to meet standards in a way that fits well with how they operate?
  • Easier
  • Harder
  • Stay the same

7bc. Would enforcement be *more strict* or *less strict*?
  • More strict
  • Less strict
  • Stay the same

7bd. Overall, would *workers* be *better off* or *worse off* with this kind of system?
  • Better off
  • Worse off
  • Stay the same

7be. Overall, would *management* be *better off* or *worse off* with this kind of system?
  • Better off
  • Worse off
  • Stay the same

  (ROTATE THE ORDER OF QUESTIONS 8B AND 9B.)

8B.   People who *favor* committees for workplace standards argue that they have a number of *advantages* over using government inspectors or other outside enforcement. How convincing are each of these *positive* arguments to you?

8ba. Committees would get more companies to *follow* government standards.
  • Very convincing
  • Somewhat convincing
  • Not too convincing
  • Not convincing at all .

8bb. Committees would give companies more *choices* about how standards are met.
  • Very convincing
  • Somewhat convincing

- Not too convincing
- Not convincing at all

8bc. Committees would give workers more *say* in workplace decisions.
- Very convincing
- Somewhat convincing
- Not too convincing
- Not convincing at all

9B. People who *oppose* committees for workplace standards argue that they have a number of *disadvantages* over using government inspectors or other outside enforcement. How convincing are each of these *negative* arguments to you?

9ba. It costs *money* to train committee members and give them time off to attend meetings.
- Very convincing
- Somewhat convincing
- Not too convincing
- Not convincing at all

9bb. Committee members would be *less skilled* and knowledgeable, even after training, than government inspectors.
- Very convincing
- Somewhat convincing
- Not too convincing
- Not convincing at all

9bc. Committees would not enforce standards as *carefully* as government inspectors.
- Very convincing
- Somewhat convincing
- Not too convincing
- Not convincing at all

10B. Suppose Congress passed a law encouraging companies to set up workplace standards committees. If it were your decision to make and everyone went along with it, what type of committee would you like Congress to encourage?

10ba. Committees with employee members who are *elected* by employees, or those committees with members who are *chosen* by management?
- Elected by employees
- Chosen by management

10bb. Committees that are responsible for *all* types of workplace standards or those that are responsible for only a *few*?
- Covers all standards
- Only a few standards

10bc. Committees that can get advice and help from outside experts or those that operate on their own?
- Can get help
- Operate on their own

10bd. Committees that have power to *enforce* regulations directly or those that only give *advice* to management about how to meet regulations?

- Can enforce
- Can give only advice

I'd now like to ask you a few general questions about your company.

12. Would you describe your (company's/organization's) business as
    - very successful?
    - Somewhat successful?
    - Not too successful?
    - Not successful at all?

13. Over the past five years or so, has the number of employees at your (company/organization)
    - Increased?
    - Decreased?
    - Stayed about the same?

14. (TO THOSE WHO ANSWERED "INCREASED" OR "DECREASED" TO QUESTION 13) Over the past five years, has the number of employees increased or decreased
    - A lot?
    - Only a little?

15. Over the past five years or so, has your (company/organization) made any changes in its structure or the way it operates so that a lot of employees had to take on new jobs or tasks in the company?
    - Yes
    - No

(ROTATE THE ORDER OF QUESTIONS 16A AND 16B.)

16A. If you were to rate the performance of management in your company on a scale similar to school grades — A for excellent, B for good, C for Fair, D for Poor, and F for failure — what grade would you give *management* in the following areas? (ROTATE ORDER OF CHOICES.)

16aa. Overall company leadership

16ab. Concern for employees

16ac. Giving fair pay increases and benefits

16ad. Understanding and knowledge of the business

16ae. Willingness to share power and authority

16B. If you were to rate the performance of employees in your company on a scale similar to school grades — A for excellent, B for good, C for fair, D for poor, and F for failure — what grade would you give *employees* in the following areas? (ROTATE ORDER OF CHOICES.)

16ba. Willingness to work hard

16bb. Concern for the success of the company

16bc. Willingness to take on new responsibilities

17. If there was some company policy that you *spoke up against* in your (company/organization), how would that affect your chances for advancement in the (company/organization)? Would it *help* or *hurt* you in getting ahead?
    - Help
    - Hurt

18. (TO THOSE WHO ANSWERED "HELP" OR "HURT" TO QUESTION 17)
Would it (help/hurt) your chances of advancement a lot or only a little?
- Lot
- Little

(ASK QUESTIONS 21–28 ONLY IF RESPONDENTS TO WAVE 1 QUESTION 24
ANSWERED "YES"; OTHERWISE, GO TO QUESTION 29.)

21. The last time we spoke you said you were part of an employee involvement
program at your (company/organization), either a work team, a quality
program, or something else like that. Is this correct?
- Yes
- No

22. We'd like to know a little more about this program. First, does it use
- Teams or committees set up for *short* periods of time to discuss particular
problems?
- *Long-term* teams or committees that discuss different problems over a long
period of time?
- Both?

23. (TO THOSE WHO ANSWERED THE FIRST OR THIRD OPTION TO
QUESTION 22) What kinds of problems do the short-term committees discuss?
(OPEN QUESTION. PROBE FOR FULL RESPONSE. PROBE FOR ANY
OTHER PROBLEMS.)

24. (TO THOSE WHO ANSWERED THE SECOND OR THIRD OPTION TO
QUESTION 22) What kinds of problems do the long-term committees discuss?
(OPEN QUESTION. PROBE FOR FULL RESPONSE. PROBE FOR ANY
OTHER PROBLEMS.)

25. As part of this program, do you *ever* talk about *wages* and *benefits*, or do you
only talk about ways to improve productivity or quality?
- Wages and benefits sometimes
- Just production issues

26a. (TO THOSE WHO ANSWERED "WAGES AND BENEFITS SOMETIMES" TO
QUESTION 25) For this program to be a success, how important is it to
continue talking about wages and benefits? Is it . . .
- Very important?
- Somewhat important?
- Not too important?
- Not at all important?

26b. (TO THOSE WHO ANSWERED "JUST PRODUCTION ISSUES" TO
QUESTION 25) Do you think this program would work better if you also talked
about wages and benefits, or not?
- Yes
- No

26c. (TO THOSE WHO ANSWERED "YES" TO QUESTION 26b) Do you think it
would work
- A lot better?
- Only a little better?

27. As far as you know, how dedicated is the upper management of your (company/organization) to continuing this kind of program?
    - Completely dedicated
    - Mostly dedicated
    - Not too dedicated
    - Not dedicated at all

28. Imagine your (company/organization) was taken over tomorrow by new managers who did not want to continue the employee-involvement program. If your (company/organization) got rid of these teams or committees, how would it affect you personally? Would it be . . .
    - Very good?
    - Good?
    - Bad?
    - Very bad?
    - Wouldn't care one way or the other/neither good nor bad?

(ASK QUESTIONS 29–33 ONLY TO THOSE WHO ANSWERED "YES" TO WAVE 1 QUESTION 36b; OTHERWISE, GO TO QUESTION 34.)

29. Last time we spoke you said your company had a open-door policy for groups of employees to raise issues about policies with upper management. Is this correct?
    - Yes
    - No

30. Have *you* ever used this open-door policy?
    - Yes
    - No

31. In the past twelve months, about how many times have you used it?
    - Not at all
    - Once
    - Twice
    - Three or more times

32. The *last time* you used the open-door policy, what kind of problem did you discuss with management? (DO NOT READ. RECORD ALL MENTIONS.)
    - Wages
    - Benefits
    - Working conditions
    - Problem with supervisor
    - Problem with coworker
    - Production/procedures/operation
    - Other

33. (TO RESPONDENTS WHO ANSWERED OTHER THAN "DON'T KNOW" IN QUESTION 32) How effective was your use of the open-door policy in dealing with this problem?
    - Very effective
    - Somewhat effective
    - Not too effective
    - Not effective at all

(ASK QUESTIONS 34 AND 35 ONLY TO RESPONDENTS WHO ANSWERED WAVE 1 QUESTION 22a AS "STRONGER" OR QUESTION 22b AS "BETTER"; OTHERWISE, GO TO QUESTION 36.)

34. When we interviewed you last time, you told us you thought your firm would be stronger or better if *more* decisions were made by employees instead of by managers. Is this *mainly* because you think. . .
   - Employees have better *ideas* about how to make improvements?
   - Employees will work *harder* if they have more say over their jobs?
   - Or is it some other reason? (SPECIFY.)

35. Why do you think your (company's/organization's) management does not let employees make more workplace decisions themselves? Is this mainly because you think . . .
   - Management doesn't want to give up power?
   - Management doesn't think employees are able to make good decisions?
   - Is it some other reason? (SPECIFY.)

36. On a different subject, I want to ask how you prefer to deal with any complaints you might have about something at work. For each of the following problems, please tell me whether you would prefer to deal directly with management *yourself* or would prefer to have a *group* of your co-workers *help* you deal with management. (ROTATE ITEMS) First, if *you* had a problem with (ITEM)— would you prefer to deal with management yourself, or with a group of employees?

36a. Sexual harassment

36b. Workplace health and safety

36c. Training

36d. The (company's/organization's) benefits

36e. Unfair treatment by a supervisor

37. Now I have a few questions about *unions*. What is the *most* important thing a union does for its members? Is it that they get members . . . (READ; ROTATE FIRST THREE CATEGORIES)
   - More respect and fair treatment on the job?
   - More say in workplace decisions?
   - Better pay and working conditions?
   - Is it something else? (SPECIFY.)

38. (TO RESPONDENTS WHO CITED ANY OF THE FOUR OPTIONS OF QUESTION 37) And what is the *second* most important thing unions do for their members? Is it that they get members . . . (READ; CATEGORIZE IF NECESSARY; DROP CATEGORY SELECTED IN QUESTION 37.)
   - More respect and fair treatment on the job?
   - More say in workplace decisions?
   - Better pay and working conditions?
   - Is it something else? (SPECIFY.)

39. (ASK ONLY IF RESPONDENTS TO WAVE 1 QUESTION 42 ANSWERED "MORE THAN HALF WOULD VOTE AGAINST THE UNION") When we interviewed you last time, you told us a majority of employees at your

(company/organization) would vote *against* a union if an election were held at your (company/organization) today. What is the *main* reason you think they feel this way? Is it because . . .

- They prefer to take care of workplace problems best *on their own*?
- They don't like the way unions *operate*?
- They think that having a union would create too much *tension* in the (company/organization)?
- They think unions are too *weak* to help workers?
- Is it some other reason? (SPECIFY.)

40.   (ASK ONLY IF RESPONDENTS TO WAVE 1 QUESTION 42 ANSWERED "MORE THAN HALF WOULD VOTE FOR THE UNION") When we interviewed you last time, you told us a majority of employees at your (company/organization) would vote *for* a union if an election were held at your (company/organization) today. Why do you think there is no union coverage now for employee like you at your (company/organization)? Is it *mainly* because . . .(READ; ROTATE THE FIRST TWO OPTIONS.)

- Management opposes unions?
- No union is interested in organizing employees like ours?
- Is it some other reason? (SPECIFY.)

40a. (ASK ONLY IF RESPONDENTS TO WAVE 1 QUESTION 36d ANSWERED "NO") As far as you know, have any employees at your (company/organization) ever talked about forming a union?

- Yes
- No

41.   Thinking now about any kind of employee organization, not just union, where employees and management discuss workplace issues together, how would *you* like it to work? If it was your decision alone to make, and everybody went along with it, would you prefer . . .

41a. An organization in which *either* management or employees can raise problems for discussion at meetings, or one in which *management* decides the problems that should be discussed?

- Either can raise problems for discussion
- Management decides what should be discussed

41b. An organization in which the employees in the group sometimes meet *on their own* to discuss workplace problems before meeting with management, or one in which all the meetings are held with employees and management *together*?

- Employees meet on their own.
- Employees meet only with management.

41c. An organization in which *management* makes the final decisions about issues or ones in which employees and management have to *agree* on decisions?

- Management makes final decision
- Employees and management have to agree

42.   Many employees told us they want management to *cooperate* with them in discussing workplace issues. What do you think *employees* get when management is cooperative? Do they mainly get. . .

- A chance to *give* their opinions and ideas?
- Some *power* to influence company decision?

43. If a company always *listens* to what employees have to say but doesn't *follow* their advice, is management being cooperative or uncooperative in dealing with employees?
   - Cooperative
   - Uncooperative

46. In general, what do you think American workers *most* need? Is it . . .
   - More power to *make decisions* about how their companies operate?
   - More opportunities to give *advice* to management about how to improve their companies?
   - Better pay and benefits?
   - Something else? (SPECIFY.)

47. (IF ANY OF THE FOUR OPTIONS OF QUESTION 46 IS SELECTED) What is the *second* most important thing you think American workers need? (REREAD OPTIONS IF NECESSARY; USING SAME ROTATION AS IN QUESTION 46 AND DROPPING OPTIONS 1, 2, OR 3 IF SELECTED FOR QUESTION 46.)
   - More power to *make* decisions about how their companies operate
   - More opportunities to give *advice* to management about how to improve their companies
   - Better pay and benefits
   - Something else (SPECIFY.)

(THANK ALL) That's the last question I have. Thank you so much for being a part of this survey. We really appreciate the time you took to look over the material we sent and to answer these additional questions.

(IF THE RESPONDENT WANTS MORE INFORMATION) Princeton Survey Research is conducting this survey for researchers at Harvard University and the University of Wisconsin. They are going to share the results with the Dunlop Commission[1], a national commission set up to study labor-management relations in the United States and to make recommendations to Congress about changing the labor laws. You'll probably see some mention of the survey results in newspapers or on television sometime early in December.

[1]The Commission on the Future of Worker-Management Relations was often referred to as the Dunlop Commission.

CHAPTER 1

1. Contrast this with another leading capitalist power, Germany, where 29 percent of the labor force is unionized but where 95 percent are covered by a collective agreement — through the process of "extension" of collective-bargaining terms from the union to the nonunion sector; or with France, where just 9 percent of workers are organized but where 95 percent are also covered. See OECD, *Employment Outlook*, July 1997 (Paris: OECD, 1997), Table 3.3.

2. Several books and articles address the disconnect between the U.S. labor-relations system to fit the modern economy. Among the major studies are Richard B. Freeman and Joel Rogers, "Who Speaks for Us? Employee Representation in a Non-Union Labor Market," in *Employee Representation: Alternatives and Future Directions*, ed. Bruce Kaufman and Morris Kleiner (Madison, Wis.: Industrial Relations Research Association, 1993); William B. Gould IV, *Agenda for Reform: The Future of Employment Relationships and the Law* (Cambridge, Mass.: MIT Press, 1993); Bruce Kaufman, "Company Unions: Sham Organizations or Victims of the New Deal?" *Industrial Relations Research Annual* (1997):166–80; Thomas Kochan, "Principles for a Post-New Deal Employment Policy," in *Labor Economics and Industrial Relations: Markets and Institutions*, ed. Clark Kerr and Paul Staudohar (Cambridge, Mass.: Harvard University Press, 1994), 646–71; Joel Rogers, "Reforming U.S. Labor Relations," in *The Legal Future of Employee Representation*, ed. Matthew W. Finkin (Ithaca, N.Y.: ILR Press, 1994), 95–125; David Levine, *Reinventing the Workplace: How Business and Employees Can Both Win* (Washington D.C.: Brookings Institute, 1995); Miles Raymond, "A New Industrial Relations System for the 21st Century," *California Management Review* 21 (Winter 1989): 9-28; Kim Moody, *Workers in a Lean World* (London: Verso, 1997); Michael Piore, "The Future of Unions," in *The State of the Unions*, ed. George Strauss, Daniel Gallagher, and Jack Fiorito (Madison, Wis.: Industrial Relations Research Association, 1991), 386–410; Joseph Reid, "Future Unions," *Industrial Relations* 31, no. 1 (1992): 122–36; George Strauss, "Is the New Deal System Collapsing? With What Might It Be Replaced?" *Industrial Relations* 34, no. 3 (1995): 329–49; Lowell Turner, *Democracy at Work: Changing World Markets and the Future of Labor Unions* (Ithaca, N.Y.: Cornell University Press, 1991); Paul C. Weiler, *Governing the Workplace: The Future of Labor and Employment* (Cambridge, Mass.: Harvard University Press, 1990); and Charles C. Heckscher, *The New Unionism: Employee Involvement in the Changing Corporation* (Ithaca, N.Y.: ILR Press, 1996).

3. The benchmark is the Quality of Employment Survey, conducted by the Department of Labor in 1977. Since then many opinion polls have been conducted on this or that aspect of worker attitudes, but none that focuses on workers' desires for participation or representation across a wide variety of forms or institutions.

4. The WRPS was limited to private-sector workers in firms or organizations with

twenty-five or more employees. It excluded public-sector workers and workers in small firms who face different workplace governance issues than those in larger private firms. Since completing the WRPS, we have surveyed workers in Canada and in some parts of the U.S. public sector using essentially the same survey instrument. Other researchers have applied a version of our survey to workers in the United Kingdom, and others are using it in analyses in Australia and Japan.

5. All the data are available for further inspection at the NBER Web site listing for on-line data: http://www.nber.org/data_index.html

6. For discussions of the commission, see Thomas Kochan, "Using the Dunlop Report to Achieve Mutual Gains," *Industrial Relations* 34, no. 3 (1995); and John T. Addison, "The Dunlop Report: European Links and Other Odd Connections," *Journal of Labor Research* 17, no. 1 (Winter 1996): 77–99.

7. In the WRPS, the rate of unionization was 16 percent. This exceeds the national average for the private sector because we excluded workers from small firms who are less likely to be unionized than those in larger firms. If workers in small firms were included in the survey, the rate of unionization that workers want would probably be lower, but it would still be three or more times the national average for private-sector workers of around 10 percent to 11 percent in the late 1990s. The WRPS covered roughly three-fourths of the American workforce.

8. William Bridges, "The End of the Job," excerpt from "JobShift," *Fortune*, September 1994, 62–66.

9. Studies based on the standard monthly survey of American households — the Current Population Survey — as well as studies based on data sets that follow given groups of workers for many years of their lives, such as the Michigan Panel Survey of Income Dynamics, show that Americans stay with their firm for long periods. See Henry Farber, "Are Lifetime Jobs Disappearing? Job Duration in the United States," *NBER Working Paper No.* 5014, 1 February 1995; Francis X. Diebold, David Neumark, and Daniel Polsky, "Job Stability in the United States," *NBER Working Paper No.* 4859, 1 September 1994; David Neumark, Daniel Polsky, and Daniel Hansen, "Has Job Stability Declined Yet? New Evidence for the 1990's," *NBER Working Paper No.* 6330, 1 December 1997. It is true that Americans are more mobile than workers in most advanced countries, and that they also spend fewer years with the same firm than, say, the Japanese or Germans (Organization for Economic Cooperation and Development, *Employment Outlook, July* 1993 [Paris: OECD, 1993]). But the main reason for this is that Americans frequently shift jobs early in life as they search for the right match. And while years with a firm fell modestly for men in the 1990s, average employment duration has risen for women. Most important, the men whose tenure declined the most were younger and less educated. The phenomenon of lower male job tenure is thus best understood as part of the more general story of a worsened market for the less skilled, not as evidence of a sweeping trend away from traditional employee-employer relations.

10. In analyzing duration data, completed spells of tenure are roughly twice as long as incomplete spells.

11. These figures are from Exhibit 3.3.

12. Workers who leave have little or no incentive to tell employers what really both-

ers them, because if they complain, the employer might hold it against them and not give them a good recommendation for another job. Some firms have "exit" interviews to try to discover why workers are leaving, but these interviews often are noninformative. There is no benefit to giving your gripes when you are out the door.

13. Richard Freeman and James Medoff, *What Do Unions Do?* (New York: Basic Books, 1984). The importance of voice in society has been stressed by Albert Hirschman in his classic *Exit, Voice, and Loyalty* (Cambridge, Mass.: Harvard University Press, 1971).

14. This argument can be put formally. Let V be the total value of the relationship and let λ be Party I's share in that value. Then let W_I be what Party I gets from breaking the relationship and W_{II} be what Party II gets from breaking the relationship. Party I will stay with the relationship when $\lambda V > W_I$ and Party II will stay when $(1 - \lambda)V > W_{II}$. As long as $V > W_I + W_{II}$, it pays the two parties to resolve disagreements through bargaining rather than splitting. If $\lambda V < W_I$ it behooves them to increase Party I's share of the benefits, and conversely if $(1 - \lambda)V < W_{II}$. If $V < W_I + W_{II}$, no value of λ can make the relationship work for both parties.

15. This also can be demonstrated formally. See Richard B. Freeman and Edward P. Lazear, "An Economic Analysis of Works Councils," in *Works Councils*, ed. Joel Rogers and Wolfgang Streeck (Chicago: University of Chicago Press for NBER, 1995).

16. Many analysts have documented these facts. See, for example, Richard B. Freeman, *When Earnings Diverge: Causes, Consequences, and Cures for the New Inequality in the U.S.*, National Policy Association Report #284 (Washington, D.C.: NPA, 1997); U.S. Department of Labor, *Report on the American Workforce* (Washington, D.C.: U.S. Government Printing Office, 1994); Lawrence Mishel, Jared Bernstein, and John Schmitt, *State of Working America* (Washington, D.C.: Economic Policy Institute, 1997).

17. Calculated from data in OECD, 1993.

18. The data on family incomes are taken from U.S. Bureau of the Census, *Historical Income Tables: Families*, Tables F-6 and F-3, U.S. Bureau of the Census Web site. The GDP figures are from *Economic Report of the President, February* 1998 (Washington, D.C.: U.S. Government Printing Office, 1998), Table B-2, adjusted for 1996 prices on the basis of Table B-3. The poverty rates are from Table B-33.

CHAPTER 2

1. Studs Terkel, *Working* (New York: Avon, 1975).

2. The reference is to Dennis Rivera, head of the hospital workers union in New York City.

3. The sample for the survey was a random-digit sample of telephone numbers selected from telephone exchanges in the continental United States. Many of the numbers called were not in service or were fax or business numbers, and some numbers called were never answered or picked up by an answering machine. A survey of this kind offers several possible ways to report response rates. Many households who talked with the interviewers did not have an eligible member. We identified 2,751 households with an eligible member and obtained a completed interview with 2,408 of these, an 88

percent response rate. But 3,423 households refused to answer our screening questions. If, conservatively, we assume that these households are divided between eligibles and noneligibles in the same proportion as households who did answer our survey, 20.5 percent (or 701 households) were in the group we were seeking to interview. This gives a response rate from our desired population of 70 percent. See Princeton Survey Research Associates, *Worker Representation and Participation Survey: Report on the Findings*, (Princeton, N.J.: PSRA, 1994), technical appendix.

4. This group should be distinguished from the Commission on the Future of Worker-Management Relations, which dealt with private-sector workers.

5. Richard Freeman discusses the public-sector survey results in "The Evolving Environment of Public Sector Labor Relations," in *Public Sector Employment in a Time of Transition*, ed. Dale Belman, Morley Gunderson, and Douglas Hyatt (Madison, Wis.: Industrial Relations Research Association, 1997).

CHAPTER 3

1. If you have problems that we have not considered or alternative interpretations you want to explore, contact us via e-mail or download the WRPS from our Web site (see Chapter 1, note 5) and perform your own analysis.

2. We use several questions to illuminate attitudes in an area, because all questions on a survey invariably have shortcomings. They could be phrased differently, located in different places, and so on. To find out what workers want at the workplace, we chose a particular set of questions. Someone else might choose a different set. We would choose a different set today. The best way to view particular items is as *indicators* of underlying attitudes or tendencies that subsume any single item. Technically, this underlying attitude/tendency is called "the latent variable." Various statistical models measure latent variables, essentially by identifying the common pattern or factor among particular items addressed to the same issue.

3. In this exhibit and throughout the book, we report tabulations that use the sample weights developed by Princeton Survey Research Associates for the study. But because the WRPS sample had such a good response rate, results that do not use the sample weights give virtually identical figures to those based on the sample weights in almost all cases.

4. Sixty-seven percent of workers with 10 or more years of tenure said that they wanted more influence, as compared with 52 percent of workers with less than one year of tenure; 67 percent of those working more than 45 hours wanted more influence, as compared with 55 percent of those working less than 35 hours; 66 percent of those with a bachelor's or higher degree wanted more influence, as compared with 61 percent of those with no college education. The relationship between skill and position in the firm with the desire for more influence does not, however, hold for all groups, as some highly committed workers already have considerable influence.

5. This is shown in two questions, the first regarding the problems of individuals and the second regarding the problems of groups. The first question was, "If employees as a group had *more say* in how the workplace problems of individual employees are

solved at your company/organization, do you think this system would be *more* effective or *less* effective?" Seventy-six percent said more; 10 percent said less; 4 percent said the same; and 4 percent did not answer. The second question was asked of respondents in companies with no employee committee or union: "Imagine that *management* selected a committee of employees to discuss the problems employees have as a group with them. Do you think this would be *more* effective or *less* effective to resolve employees' concerns?" Seventy-three percent said more effective; 21 percent said less effective; 2 percent said the same; and 4 percent hadn't a clue.

6. The issue here is fundamental in economics, relating to the possible effect of the distribution of output on the level of output. If one side in a working arrangement (such as management) gives more decision-making power to the other side, such as workers, will the first side benefit or lose? If devolving authority raises the total value of the working arrangement, it is at least possible that both sides gain, although the workers' side might use its power to increase its share of total output.

7. The specific proportions who do not look forward to work: 39 percent for those earning between $200 and $599 a week; 43 percent among high school dropouts; 42 percent among black workers; and 42 percent among manufacturing workers.

8. Individual responses produces a bigger estimate of the proportion of workers whose trust of their employers falls short of their loyalty than the averages give, because the averages mix these workers with those whose trust exceeds their loyalty. We used the same four-point scale and wording to make it easier to compare the differences in responses.

9. Richard B. Freeman, "Evolving Institutions for Employee Voice," in *Exit and Voice in the Actual Working of the Economies*, ed. Luca Meldolosi (unpublished manuscript, 1998).

10. To see how the compression loses information, consider two workers who want a lot of influence. One reports that he has some influence on workplace decisions; the other says she has no influence. The latter is a more serious problem, but our measure does not distinguish between them. There are ways to check the seriousness of this problem, ranging from eyeballing cross-tabulations to computing separate item response variables for the importance of influence and for having influence, and examining the difference between those scales. Such analyses show that the summary statistic does not distort anything in the text.

11. To take an extreme case, if 60 percent of people wanted a lot of influence but had no influence and 40 percent had a lot of influence but did not want a lot of influence, 60 percent of workers would lack their desired influence, whereas our aggregate gap would be just 20 percent. Similarly, if someone wants a lot of influence on, say, workplace safety issues and has no influence, but has a lot of influence on training, which she does not want, the aggregate measure would show no representation/participation gap, when in fact such a gap exists in the safety area.

12. The average in this column does not give the percentage of workers who report that they have less influence than they want on *any* issue. The majority (83 percent) report some area in which they feel their influence falls short of what they want.

13. We performed a similar analysis using Rasch scaling and obtained comparable results.

14. Freeman, "Evolving Institutions for Employee Voice."

15. This was the view of some 80 percent of workers.

16. This group constituted 24 percent of our sample.

17. Forty-three percent said management opposed the union with information only; 23 percent said the firm threatened or harassed union supporters.

18. Thirty-six percent said they would certainly be willing to do so; 47 percent said that they were probably willing to do so.

19. In fact, this is not the whole story. Many U.S. managers set up EI committees, workplace teams, and other worker groups and delegate important decisions to those groups. But American labor institutions and laws make it difficult for nonunion firms to build on their interest in increasing employee voice. And the country's labor system provides no vehicle for workers to develop an organization to represent them at workplaces, short of a majority union. But these are not issues that we raised with workers.

20. The classic analysis of the interrelation between exit and voice is Albert Hirschman, *Exit, Voice, and Loyalty* (Cambridge, Mass: Harvard University Press, 1972).

CHAPTER 4

1. See Richard B. Freeman and Joel Rogers, "Who Speaks for Us," and Henry Farber and Alan Krueger, "Union Membership in the U.S.: The Decline Continues," in *Employee Representation: Alternatives and Future Directions*, ed. Bruce Kaufman and Morris Kleiner (Madison, Wis.: Industrial Relations Research Association, 1993).

2. A 1993 Employment Policy Foundation survey did ask this question. They reported that 62 percent of private-sector union members would support the union; 15 percent (to whom the question must have been confusing) said they had a union; and 18 percent said they would vote against the union. If we sum the 62 percent and 15 percent we get 78 percent presumably supporting the union, as compared with 18 percent against it. The level of union support by union members is massive, although less than the 90 percent support found by the WRPS. Larger samples of union members are needed to pin down the proportion of supporters with certainty, but whether it is 62 percent or 78 percent or 90 percent for unions and 8 percent or 18 percent against, the qualitative story is the same: Union members support their union.

3. This question used a five-point scale, giving workers an option to provide a neutral (neither good nor bad) answer.

4. This is not true of the public sector, in which unions have organized many highly educated and skilled workers, such as teachers, nurses, police officers and firefighters, as well as the blue-collar workers they largely organize in the private sector.

5. Note also that because we do not have evidence on workers' desires for say or preference for dealing with workplace problems as a group prior to their current work experience, this calculation overstates the extent to which differences in views explain the differing intentions to vote for or against unions if, as seems likely, the union experience itself increases worker demands for say or their belief in the value of collective activity.

6. A linear probability regression of intention to vote union on dummy variables for gender, race, age groups, and education groups gave a significant positive coefficient of

0.095, with a standard error of 0.029 on former union members, implying that 9.5 percent more of them were likely to vote union. Adding the log of weekly pay reduced the coefficient to 0.065, with a standard error of 0.033. But the coefficient on former union members falls to an insignificant 0.024 with the addition of measures for employee-management relations. Thus, former members are always more likely to vote union than nonmembers, but the effect varies depending on the situation at their nonunion workplace.

7. Daniel Kahneman, Jack L. Knetsch, and Richard H. Thaler, "The Endowment Effect, Loss Aversion, and Status Quo Bias: Anomolies," *Journal of Economic Perspectives* 5, no. 1 (Winter 1991): 193–206; Daniel Kahneman, Jack L. Knetsch, and Richard Thaler, "Fairness as a Constraint on Profit-Seeking: Entitlements in the Market," *American Economic Review* 76, no. 4 (September 1986): 728–41. For a different analysis, see Tom Langford, "Involvement with Unions, Union Belief Perspectives, and Desires for Union Membership," *Journal of Labor Research* 15, no. 3 (summer 1994): 257–70.

8. Tom Kochan, "How American Workers View Labor Unions," *Monthly Labor Review* 102 (April 1979): 15–22. For a study of how local unions function, see Tove Hammer and David L. Wazeter, "Dimensions of Local Union Effectiveness," *Industrial and Labor Relations Review* 46, no. 2 (1993): 302–19.

9. See Wilson Center for Public Research, *Workers' Views of the Value of Unions* (May 1992).

10. We could do better by simply assigning to each worker the outcome vote against a union. Because two-thirds of nonunion workers vote against the union, this would give us, on average, a two-thirds correct classification. But this is obviously a cop out. It is equivalent to predicting that there will never be a stock market collapse or a hurricane or any other rare event, and then claiming success because these are rare events. The flaw in the cop-out prediction approach is that there is a big payoff to predicting the rare event correctly, only a small cost to predicting it incorrectly, and little payoff to predicting the normal event.

11. For earlier comparisons of how workers view unions, and the characteristics of workers that lead them to favor or oppose unionization for their workplace, see Karen E. Boroff and David Lewin, "Loyalty, Voice, and Intent to Exit a Union Firm: A Conceptual and Empirical Analysis," *Industrial and Labor Relations Review* 51, no. 1 (1997): 50–63; Gary Chaison and Dileep G. Dhavale, "The Choice between Union Membership and Free-Rider Status," *Journal of Labor Research* 13, no. 4 (1992); Gregory Defreitas, "Unionization among Racial and Ethnic Minorities," *Industrial and Labor Relations Review* 46, no. 2 (1993): 284–301; Richard B. Freeman and James Medoff, *What Do Unions Do?* (New York: Basic Books, 1984); Daniel S. Hamermesh and Albert Rees, *The Economics of Work and Pay* (New York: Harper & Row, 1988); Henry Farber and Daniel Saks, "Why Workers Want Unions: The Role of Relative Wages and Job Characteristics," *Journal of Political Economy* 88 (1980): 349–69; Henry Farber, "The Determination of the Union Status of Workers," *Econometrica* 51 (1983): 1417–37; Duane Leigh, "The Determinants of the Workers' Union Status: Evidence from the National Longitudinal Surveys," *Journal of Human Resources* 20 (1985): 555–66; Barry Hirsch, "The Determinants of Unionization: An Analysis of Interarea Differences," *Industrial and Labor Rela-*

tions Review 33 (1980): 158; William Dickens and Jonathan Leonard, "Accounting for the Decline in Union Membership, 1950–1980," *Industrial and Labor Relations Review* 38 (1985): 323–34; George Neumann and Ellen Rissman, "Where Have All the Union Members Gone?" *Journal of Labor Economics* 2 (1984): 175–92; Robert Flanagan, "NLRA Litigation and Union Representation," *Stanford Law Review* 38, no. 4 (1986): 957–89; Rebecca Demsetz, "Voting Behavior in Union Representation Elections: The Influence of Skill Homogeneity and Skill Group Size," *Industrial and Labor Relations Review* 47, no. 1 (1993): 99–113; John S. Heywood, "Who Queues for a Union Job?" *Industrial Relations* 29, no. 1 (1990): 119–27; Steve Hills, "The Attitudes of Union and Non-Union Male Workers toward Representation," *Industrial and Labor Relations Review* 38 (July 1985); Lisa Schur and Douglas L. Kruse, "Gender Differences in Attitudes toward Unions," *Industrial and Labor Relations Review* 46, no. 1 (1992): 89–102.

12. In addition to the models reported in the exhibit, we examined the effect of other measures of workplace conditions on workers' voting for a union. These measures–the state of employee-management relations at the workplace, the number of employees, the influence gap — gave similar results to those in the exhibit. This is because workers who report good or bad relations with their firm on one question give similar responses on others.

13. Henry Farber, "Trends in Worker Demand for Unionization," *American Economic Review* 79, no. 2 (1989): 166–71; Henry Farber, "The Decline of Unionization in the United States: What Can Be Learned from Recent Experience," *Journal of Labor Economics* 8, no. 1, part 2 (1990): S75–105; Henry Farber and Alan Krueger, "Union Membership in the United States: The Decline Continues," *NBER Working Paper No.* 4216 (1992). The predominant view that management resistance is critical to union success or failure is given by Paul Weiler, "Striking a New Balance: Freedom of Contract and the Prospects for Union Representation," *Harvard Law Review* 98 (1984): 351–420; Paul Weiler, "Promises to Keep: Securing Workers' Rights to Self-Organization Under the NLRA," *Harvard Law Review* 96 (1984): 1769–1827; Richard B. Freeman, "Why Are Unions Faring Poorly in NLRB Representation Elections?" in *Challenges and Choices Facing American Labor*, ed. Tom Kochan (Cambridge, Mass.: MIT Press, 1985); Freeman and Medoff, *What Do Unions Do?* The literature on union-organizing efforts is also voluminous: Stephen Bronars and Donald R. Deere, "Union Organizing Activity, Form Growth, and the Business Cycle," *American Economic Review* 83, no. 1 (1993): 203–20; Marion Crane, "Gender and Union Organizing," *Industrial and Labor Relations Review* 47, no. 2 (1994): 227–48; Gary Chaison and Dileep Dhavale, "The Changing Scope of Union Organizing," *Journal of Labor Research* 11, no. 3 (1990): 307–22; Gary Chaison and Dileep Dhavale, "A Note on the Severity of the Decline in Union Organizing Activity," *Industrial and Labor Relations Review* 43, no. 4 (1990): 366–73; William Dickens, "The Effect of Company Campaigns on Certification Elections: Law and Reality Once Again," *Industrial and Labor Relations Review* 36, no. 4 (July 1983): 560–75; Richard B. Freeman and Morris M. Kleiner, "Employer Behavior in the Face of Union Organizing Drives," *Industrial and Labor Relations Review* 43, no. 4 (April 1990): 351–65; Thomas Lee and Barbara Finnegan, "Strategies and Tactics in Union Organizing Campaigns," *Industrial Relations* 31, no. 2 (1992): 370–81; Terry Leap et al., "Discrimination

against Pro-Union Job Applicants," *Industrial Relations* 29, no. 3 (1990): 469–78; Monty Lynn and Jozell Brister, "Trends in Union Organizing Issues and Tactics," *Industrial Relations* 28, no. 1 (1989): 104–13; Joseph B. Rose and Gary N. Chaison, "New Measures of Union Organizing Effectiveness," *Industrial Relations* 29, no. 3 (1990): 457–68; Donna Stockwell and John Thomas Delaney, "Union Organizing and the Reagan NLRB," *Contemporary Policy Issues* 5, no. 4 (1987): 28–45.

14. Employment Policy Foundation, *Fact and Fallacy: Updating the reasons for Union Decline*, May 1998.

15. This is a correct perception. In a study of NLRB elections in the Kansas City and Boston NLRB districts, Freeman and Kleiner found that on the order of one in five managers in firms that voted union were fired.

16. Nineteen percent said "a lot" better, and 45 percent said "a little" better.

17. Thirty-one percent said relations were more cooperative, as compared with 16 percent who said they were more confrontational and 42 percent who reported no change. For studies that examine how management views union efforts to be more cooperative, see Martin M. Perline and Edwin A. Sexton, "Managerial Perceptions of Labor-Management Cooperation," *Industrial Relations* 33, no. 3 (1994): 377–85.

18. The specifics are 66 percent, "no difference"; 23 percent, "makes job harder"; and 7 percent, "makes job easier."

CHAPTER 5

1. In the 1980s, when Japanese management practices were in vogue, two different publishers brought out copies of Miyamoto Mushashi's Samurai classic, *A Book of Five Rings*: Overlook Press (Woodstock, N.Y., 1982) and Viking Press (New York, 1982). A more recent edition was published by Random House (New York, 1993). *The Leadership Secrets of Attila the Hun*, by Wess Roberts (NY: Warner Books, 1991) was a big seller in the 1990s.

2. Among the many books in this vein are Jeffrey Pfeffer, *Competitive Advantage through People: Unleashing the Power of the Workforce* (Boston: Harvard Business School Press, 1994), and Thomas A. Kochan and Paul Osterman, *The Mutual Gains Enterprise* (Boston: Harvard Business School Press, 1994).

3. These percentages exceed the proportion of workers in firms with employee stock-ownership plans (ESOPs) that fall under the ESOP regulations or are counted by the National Council on Employee Ownership as employee-owned, largely because the WRPS did not probe workers about the specifics of their stock plan. Many companies have 401K and other retirement plans that hold company shares. This does not make them employee-owned, but workers may not have made the distinction.

4. Two other major studies have sought to identify the prevalence of advanced human-resource practices: Paul Osterman, "How Common Is Workplace Transformation and Who Adopts It?" *Industrial and Labor Relations Review* 47, no. 2 (January 1994): 173–88, and Edward Lawler, Susan Mohrman, and Gerald Ledford, *Employee Involvement and Total Quality Management: Practices and Results in Fortune 1000 Com-*

panies (San Francisco: Jossey-Bass, 1992). Both pose questions about various practices to managers, as opposed to workers. Osterman's study is based on a sample of establishments from Dun and Bradstreet. The work by Lawler, Mohrman, and Ledford is based on a sample of Fortune 1000 firms. The general picture that they find on the breadth of practices is similar to what workers reported to us.

5. For instance, 84 percent of workers in large firms say their firm has a personnel/human-resource department; 77 percent of workers in manufacturing also report this. This exceeds the 68 percent in the table.

6. When data fit the Guttman model perfectly, they can be arrayed in a triangular matrix, so that the individual who has the lowest total score answers correctly only the easiest items; the individual with the next lowest score answers those items plus the next easiest, and so on:

Items (X = "correct" response)

	1	2	3	4
Individual 1	X	o	o	o
Individual 2	X	X	o	o
Individual 3	X	X	X	o
Individual 4	X	X	X	X

7. The key statistical assumption is that individual responses to an item follow a logistic probability distribution. David Bartholemew, *The Statistical Approach to Social Measurement* (San Diego: Academic Press, 1996), shows that the sufficiency principle for conditional distributions of latent variables yields the Rasch logistic model on the assumption that individuals and items can be located on a single continuum. Gerhard H. Fischer and Ivo W. Molenaar, *Rasch Models: Foundations, Recent Developments, and Applications* (New York: Springer-Verlag TELOS, 1995), give alternative algorithms for estimating Rasch models.

8. We had ready access to a survey of establishments conducted by Paul Osterman of MIT (Osterman, 1996), and a survey of firms conducted by Cheri Ostroff. See Richard B. Freeman, Morris M. Kleiner, and Cheri Ostroff, "The Anatomy and Effects of Employee Involvement," mimeo, 16 July 1997. University of Minnesota, 1998. In both cases, we found that the number or scope of practices fit well a single latent scale, and that as we looked at more practices, the bell curve gave a more valid summary of the data than the alternative hypothesis that the distribution was sharply bifurcated between good and bad firms.

9. This is the case for the practices covered in the WRPS but not true of all practices. Osterman reports that some advanced practices are less likely to be found in the union setting.

10. The absence of small firms from the WRPS does not mean that we have no information on small establishments or workplaces. Many workers in large firms work in small establishments or workplaces. Citibank is a big fish in the banking industry, but the typical Citibank branch has a manager and five to ten employees.

11. Specifically, 21 percent used the system three or more times in the previous 12 months versus 24 percent who used it once or twice.

12. Specifically, 61 percent of managers and 58 percent of college graduates used the policy in the past year.

13. Specifically, 46 percent of 18- to 24-year-olds; 47 percent of those 55 and older; 47 percent of the semi-skilled; and 42 percent of laborers.

14. These figures are from Wave 2 of the survey, which had a special module on open-door policies. We also compared the reported effectiveness of EI on Wave 1 with reported use on Wave 2 and obtained similar results. In this case, 50 percent of the workers who said that their system was "very effective" used it three or more times in the past year, as compared with 35 percent of other workers.

15. Thirty-eight percent reported using it to deal with production/procedures/operations, and 22 percent reported using it to deal with general working conditions, giving a 60 percent use for these areas.

16. Specifically, 8 percent raised problems with a supervisor, 11 percent raised problems with wages or benefits; 18 percent of managers and 17 percent of union members raised problems about wages or benefits.

17. Nearly one-third (32 percent) of workers who used the open door for wage or benefit problems reported that it was ineffective, whereas just 12 percent of workers who used it to deal with production problems reported that it was ineffective. Twenty-two percent of workers said the open door was ineffective for dealing with a problem of working conditions.

18. See Charles J. Morris, "A Dialogue with the Chairman of the Labor Board: Challenging Conventional Wisdom on the Impact of Current Law on Alternative Forms of Employee Representation," *Hofstra Labor & Employment Law Journal* 15 (1998): 319–44, and "Alternative Labor Organizations under the National Labor Relations Act: a How-To Manual for Employees Councils, American Style (unpublished manuscript, 1998).

19. The WRPS asked both workers and managers about the frequency of suggestions and management's response to suggestions. The exhibit combines the information about which workers should have the most accurate knowledge — the frequency of their suggestions — and the information about which managers should have the most accurate knowledge — how useful they find suggestions. Alternatively, one can examine the perceptions of workers and managers separately. Here also EI appears to increase the frequency and value of suggestions, although workers report a greater difference between EI and non-EI settings than do managers.

20. Here are the percentages who supervise others: EI participants, 48 percent; non-participants in firms with EI, 28 percent; employees in other firms, 32 percent.

21. Specifically, 32 percent found it "very effective"; 55 percent, "somewhat effective"; 11 percent, "not too effective" or "not effective at all."

22. Exhibit 5.5 also shows that workers in a firm with EI who do not participate in the program have a less positive view of its effectiveness. Proportionately more of them rate the program as "not too effective" or "not at all effective" than rate it as "very effective." Whether this difference is due to nonparticipants' unfamiliarity with the program's effects or to participants' excessively favorable view of the virtues of something in which they were involved (a kind of endowment effect) is anyone's guess.

23. See, for example, Harry Katz, Thomas Kochan, and Jeffrey Keefe, "Industrial

Relations and Productivity in the U.S. Automobile Industry," *Brookings Papers on Economic Activity* 3 (1987): 685–728.

24. For a general review of studies through the mid-1980s, see the various chapters in Alan Blinder, ed., *Paying for Productivity* (Washington, D.C.: Brookings Institution, 1990). Other studies include Joel Cutcher Gershenfeld, "The Impact on Economic Performance of a Transformation in Workplace Practices," *Industrial and Labor Relations Review* 44 (January 1991): 241–60; John Paul MacDuffie and John F. Krafcik, "Integrating Technology and Human Resources for High-Performance Manufacturing: Evidence from the International Motor Vehicle Research Program," in *Transforming Organizations*, Thomas A. Kochan and Michael Useem (New York: Oxford University Press, 1992), 209–26; Casey Ichniowski, Kathryn Shaw, and Giovanna Prennushi, "The Effects of Human Resource Management Practices on Productivity: A Study of Steel Finishing Lines," *American Economic Review* 87, no. 3 (June 1997): 291–313. For articles on the effects of EI programs, see Paul S. Aidler, Barbara Goldoftas, and David I. Levine, "Ergonomics, Employee Involvement, and the Toyota Production System: A Case Study of NUUMI's 1993 Model Introduction," *Industrial and Labor Relations Review* 50, no. 3 (1997): 416–37; Rosemary Batt and Eileen Appelbaum, "Worker Participation in Diverse Settings: Does the Form Affect the Outcome, and If So, Who Benefits?" *British Journal of Industrial Relations* 33, no. 3 (1995); 353–78; Avner Ben-Ner and Derek C. Jones, "Employee Participation, Ownership, and Productivity: A Theoretical Framework," *Industrial Relations* 34, no. 4 (1995): 532–54; Peter Berg, Eileen Appelbaum, Thomas Baily, and Arne Kolleberg, "The Performance Effects of Modular Production in the Apparel Industry," *Industrial Relations* 35, no. 3 (1996): 356–73; Denis Collins, "Self-Interests and Group-Interests in Employee-Involvement Programs: A Case Study," *Journal of Labor Research* 16, no. 1 (1995): Edward M. Shephard III, "Profit Sharing and Productivity: Further Evidence from the Chemicals Industry," *Industrial Relations* 33, no. 4 (1994): 452–66; Mark Huselid, "The Impact of Human Resource Management Practices on Turnover, Productivity, and Corporate Financial Performance," *Academy of Management Journal* (June 1995): n.p.; Casey Ichniowski and Katherine Shaw, "Old Dogs and New Tricks: Determinants of the Adoption of Productivity-Enhancing Work Practices," *Brookings Paper on Economic Activity: Microeconomics* (1995): 1–65; Casey Ichniowski et al., "What Works at Work: Overview and Assessment," Industrial Relations 35, no. 3 (1996): 299–333; Ichniowski, Prennushi, and Shaw, "The Effects of Human Resource Management Practices on Productivity."

25. The change in output by 3 percent raises profits by four times that amount (12 percent) because profits are only one-fourth of output.

26. Lisa M. Lynch and Sandra E. Black, "How to Compete: The Impact of Workplace Practices and Information," *NBER Working Paper Series No. 6120*, 1 August 1997; Mary Ellen Kelley and Bennett Harrison, "Unions, Technology, and Labor-Management Cooperation," in *Unions and Economic Competitiveness*, ed. Lawrence Mishel and Paula B. Voos (NY: M.E. Sharpe, 1992). For articles on the union role in EI programs, see William Cooke, "Employee Participation Programs, Group-Led Incentives, and Company Performance: A Union-Nonunion Comparison," *Industrial and Labor Relations Review* 47, no. 4 (1994): 594–609; Adrienne E. Eaton, "The Survival of Employee Participation in Unionized Settings," *Industrial and Labor Relations Review* 47, no. 2 (1994): 173–88; Charles Hecksher and

Sue Schurman, "Can Labor-Management Cooperation Deliver Jobs and Justice?" *Industrial Relations Journal* 28, no. 4 (1997): 323–30; Tom Juravich, Howard Harris, and Andrea Brooks, "Mutual gains? Labor and Management Evaluate Their Employee Involvement Programs," *Journal of Labor Research* 14, no. 2 (spring 1993): 165–85; Maryellen R. Kelley, "Participatory Bureaucracy and Productivity in the Machined Products Sector," *Industrial Relations* 35, no. 3 (1996): 374–99; Maryellen R. Kelley and Bennett Harrison, "Unions, Technology, and Labor-Management Cooperation," in Lawrence Mishel and Paula Voos, eds., *Unions and Economic Competitiveness* (New York: M. E. Sharpe, 1992), 247–86; John Paul Macduffie, "Human Resource Bundles and Manufacturing Performance: Organizational Logic and Flexible Production Systems in the World Auto Industry," *Industrial and Labor Relations Review* 48, no. 2 (1995): 197–221; Paul Osterman, "How Common Is Workplace Transformation and Who Adopts It?" *Industrial and Labor Relations Review* 47, no. 2 (1994): 173–88.

27. See Ralph T. King Jr., "Infighting Rises, Productivity Falls, Employees Miss Piecework System," *Wall Street Journal*, 20 May 1998, 1.

28. "Vast majority" in this case means 79 percent.

29. Forty-four percent said the management was "completely dedicated" to the program; 47 percent said it was "mostly dedicated"; and just 9 percent said it was "not too dedicated" or "not at all dedicated."

30. Recall that the gap is the difference between the share of workers who said it was very important to them to have a lot of influence in decisions and the proportion who reported a lot of direct involvement in those decisions.

31. Consistent with this, some 17 percent of employees in firms with EI who said they had worked in a company at a time when employees were forming a union reported that the company had harassed or threatened union supporters, while 32 percent of employees in firms without EI said the company had harassed or threatened union supporters. As the question on the union drive did not ask whether the drive occurred at the employee's current firm or some other firm, this result might not relate to the current firm. It could be that the drive occurred at the current firm. It could also be that current EI participants have work histories that have disproportionately put them in more worker-friendly firms. Or it could be that their favorable attitudes toward their current management retrospectively colors their judgment of previous ones.

32. See United States Department of Labor. Commission on the Future of Worker-Management Relations, *Fact-Finding Report, Commission on the Future of Worker-Management Relations* (Washington, D.C.: U.S. Department of Labor: U.S. Department of Commerce, 1994).

33. Kelley and Harrison, "Unions, Technology, and Labor-Management Cooperation"; Lynch and Black, "How to Compete: The Impact of Workplace Practices and Information."

CHAPTER 6

1. The major legislation of the 1960s included the Equal Pay Act (1963), the Civil Rights Act (1964), and the Age Discrimination in Employment Act (1967). Legislation

of the 1970s included the Equal Opportunity Act (1972), the Rehabilitation Act (1973), the Occupational Health and Safety Act (1970), the Federal Mine Safety and Health Act (1977), and the Employee Retirement Income Security Act (1974), as well as Executive Order 11246, which established affirmative action for federal contractors. Legislation of the 1980s included the Immigration Reform and Control Act (1986), the Employee Polygraph Protection Act (1988), and the Worker Adjustment and Retraining Notification Act (1988). The 1990s saw the Americans with Disabilities Act (1990), the Civil Rights Act (1991), and the Family and Medical Leave Act (1993).

2. Because we used a split-question design, half of the sample was asked about three of the items in the exhibit, and the other half about three other items. If people had simply guessed on the three items they were presented, 12.5 percent would have gotten all items correct. In fact, only 9 percent of employees got all three items correct; 51 percent got one question wrong, 35 percent answered two wrong, and 5 percent answered all three wrong.

3. This doctrine has been challenged in some courts. In 1987 Montana enacted a Wrongful Discharge from Employment Act that gives all nonunion employees broad legal protections from arbitrary dismissals. The National Conference of Commissioners on Uniform State Laws agreed on a model Employment Termination Act in 1991, but no state has adopted this act.

4. The 400,000 is the yearly average of 6 million visits to courts/agencies over 15 years. It is an underestimate of the actual number of individual complaints, as some persons might complain several times. Still, it is a ballpark figure.

5. Between 1971 and 1991, the number of federal district court cases on labor and employment law increased from 6,800 to 25,000 (Commission on the Future of Worker-Management Relations, *Fact-Finding Report, May* 1994 [Washington, D.C.: U.S. Department of Labor, 1994], Exhibit IV-3). By 1996, American workers brought 23,000 lawsuits against their employers on discrimination grounds alone. From 1983 to 1993, complaints to OSHA increased from 15,601 to 32,359. Figures for other agencies show a similar pattern of rise. See U.S. Department of Labor, *Tables on Staffing, Workload, and Backlog: Five Agencies,* 3 March 1995.

6. State administrative agencies and courts in Wisconsin estimate at *least* 5,000 disputes (court cases, administrative complains, special hearings, whatever) in the enforcement annually. Simply extrapolating from Wisconsin's 5 million population to the rest of the United States would suggest a universe of state-based formal claims on the order of at least 250,000 annually. As Wisconsin is noted for its "progressive" traditions and strong state bureaucracy, it might have more legal disputes than other states, so in the text we used a 200,000 estimate.

7. Stephen Overall, "Court Out on Discrimination Law," *Financial Times,* 16 July 1997, 11.

8. Consider, for example, what happens when a worker goes to the National Labor Relations Board (NLRB) with the claim that an employer illegally fired him or her for union activity. Say the NLRB and perhaps later a court rules in the worker's favor, which entitles him or her to reinstatement and back pay one or two years later. Many workers will take a new job in the interim and choose to remain there rather than return to the firm that illegally discriminated against them in the first place. Back-pay settle-

ments under the NLRA are modest. They are the difference between what the worker would have made at the firm that committed the unfair practice and what the worker earned elsewhere while waiting for the resolution of the problem.

9. A low-paid worker without the money to hire a lawyer probably cannot so threaten the firm, but a high-paid worker (often an older white male) might be able to so threaten the firm. U.S. labor law forbids firing for reasons of discrimination but generally permits firing for no reason.

10. As we did not ask workers whether their complaint was against their current employer or a previous employer, these data probably understate the true relationship between workplace problems and complaints to government regulators. Some workers who brought a case because management was treating them poorly surely moved to a different and better employment situation, weakening the still-noticeable pattern.

11. Consistent with the notion that access to resources increases the use of going to court/an agency, proportionately fewer unionized and high-paid workers (who have such access) than nonunion or low-paid workers report that they had thought about going to court or an agency but did not do so.

12. Specifically, 19 percent said they were afraid of employer reprisal, and 13 percent said they were intimidated. But many workers decided not to go to court for other reasons as well. More than one-third (36 percent) of workers who had thought about but decided against taking a problem to court said that the problem wasn't that important or worth the trouble; 13 percent said the problem got resolved in some other way; and 4 percent resolved the problem by quitting their job.

13. The average of the 61 percent in the upper panel and 55 percent in the lower panel of Exhibit 7.4. Note also that the question offered respondents only two choices, as if they were in a voting situation. Some respondents, however, volunteered that they thought current laws in particular areas offered the right amount of protection or restrictions, and we recorded those responses as well.

14. Specifically, 13 percent said "not too effective"; 8 percent said "not effective at all."

15. Twenty-five percent of persons who had never brought a complaint to court or an agency said arbitration would be "very effective" if management appointed the arbitrator, and 26 percent said it would be "very effective" if workers and management together appointed the arbitrator. By contrast, 17 percent of persons who had brought a complaint to a court/an agency said arbitration would be "very effective" if management appointed the arbitrator, whereas 35 percent said it would be "very effective" if workers and management together appointed the arbitrator.

16. Specifically, 22 percent had an excellent understanding; 55 percent has a good understanding.

17. Literature on the effectiveness (or the lack thereof) of current programs to increase health and safety in the workplace is extensive. Some analysts consider what might happen if workers had more authority in this area. See John F. Burton and James R. Chelius, "Workplace Safety and Health Regulations: Rationale and Results," in *Government Regulation of the Employment Relationship*, ed. Bruce E. Kaufman (Madison, Wis.: Industrial Relations Research Association, 1997), 253–93; Greg LaBar, "What If

Your Workers Had the Right to Act?" *Occupational Hazards* 52, no. 2 (1990): 49–54; David Levine, "They Should Solve Their Own Problems: Reinventing Workplace Regulation," in *Government Regulation of the Employment Relationship*, 475–97; and Robert S. Smith, "Have OSHA and Workers' Compensation Made the Workplace Safer?" in *Research Frontiers in Industrial Relations and Human Resources*, ed. David Lewin, Olivia S. Mitchell, and Peter D. Sherer (Madison, Wis.: Industrial Relations Research Association, 1992), 557–86.

18. Commission on the Future of Worker-Management Relations (1994), 121–22.

19. Why are workers so divided on the decision-making power to give to a committee? We speculate that some workers feared that some regulatory issues would involve substantial capital investments with repercussions for the financial well-being of the entire firm, whereas others were thinking of standards that would be less expensive to attain.

CHAPTER 7

1. By choosing some attributes and not others, we have obviously limited what we can find out about worker preferences. In this sense, we have guided the discussion of workplace organizations. Our statement of the options are, however, as neutral as we could make them — factual with no adjectives or accompanying description that might prejudice workers one way or the other.

2. The percentages given in the text are percentages for the entire sample. We did not ask workers who said they did not want an organization if they would give time to the organization. They are included in the estimated 23 percent who reject a workplace organization.

3. Fifty-four percent of managers in firms with unions favor elected representatives versus 45 percent of managers in nonunion firms. Forty-three percent of managers in the union firms favor arbitration to resolve disputes, as compared with 37 percent of managers in nonunion firms. In both of these tabulations we included managers who said they want no organization or who refused to answer as valid responses.

4. Specifically, of the managers who favored employees electing representatives, 24 percent were "very satisfied" with their influence on workplace decisions, while 16 percent were "not very satisfied" or "not at all satisfied," giving an 8-point edge to being "very satisfied." By contrast, 35 percent of other managers were "very satisfied" with their influence, and just 11 percent "not very satisfied" or "not at all satisfied," giving a 24-point edge to being "very satisfied." Thirty-nine percent of managers who wanted employees to elect representatives trusted their firm a lot, as compared with 54 percent of other managers.

5. Twenty percent of the managers favoring elected employee representatives rated labor-management relations at their firm as fair or poor, as compared with 16 percent of other managers; 8 percent thought their firm's labor relations were worse than average, as compared with 4 percent of other managers.

6. To give an extreme example, assume the following distribution of preferences for two items with attributes A or B: AA, 20 percent; AB, 40 percent; BA, 40 percent; BB, 0

percent. Sixty percent choose attribute A for the first item. Sixty percent choose A in the second item. But only 20 percent want AA.

7. Specifically, of workers who favor electing representatives, 56 percent are for company funding; for workers who do not want elected representatives, 66 percent are for company funding. Conversely, of those who want company funding for a workplace organization, just 60 percent favor elected representatives, as compared with 69 percent of workers who want the organization to have its own funding and staff. We have excluded all "don't knows" and "want no organization" responses from this calculation.

8. There are 2^5 or 32 configurations for five features for which there are two choices. Multiplying this by 3 for the one feature where we have three choices gives 96.

9. These tabulations are based on the sample of respondents who answered all six items.

10. The specific proportion was 36 percent.

11. See Chapter 5, note 18.

12. These figures are for the entire sample. There are slight differences for those who were asked about the union option and those who were asked about the employee organization that negotiates option.

13. The estimated 9 percent are made up of workers who responded that they wanted a joint committee and a weak organization or who refused to answer the question about the type of organization they wanted. A small number of workers said they wanted more laws or a union or an employee organization that negotiates but also did not answer the question about organizational attributes. We count them according to their answer as favoring laws, unions, or a negotiating organization.

INDEX

AFL-CIO. *See* American Federation of Labor–Congress of Industrial Organizations

Alternative dispute-resolution system. *See* Arbitration; Workplace committees

American Federation of Labor–Congress of Industrial Organizations (AFL-CIO), 27, 31–32, 150

Arbitration, 7, 113, 132–36, 217n15
features of system, 135–36
management cooperation and, 135
organizational preference and, 142, 143, 144, 147–48
selection of arbitrator, 133
in Wave 2 follow-up survey materials, 185–87

Art of War (Sun Tze), 90, 211n1

Benefits
employee involvement (EI) programs and, 107–8, 112
influence and, 42, 48, 51
of unions, 79

British version of WRPS, 36, 37

Business considerations
effects on participation, 21
worker involvement improves performance, 42, 103–5

Canada, 35, 36, 37, 66, 136

Clinton administration, 36, 39

Colasanto, Diane, 17, 28

Coleman, John, 15

Collective bargaining, 66
See also Unions

Collective voice, 5, 53–56, 72

Commission on the Future of Worker-Management Relations, 2, 4, 39, 90–91, 115, 201

Company unions, 102

Confidential information, access to by workplace organization, 142, 143, 144

Contingent work, 9–10

Cooperation, 5, 34–35, 56–60, 63, 64

Corporate culture, 107

Criticism, anticipated, of WRPS, 16–17

"Death of the job" objection, 8, 9–11

Decision-making, 5
areas of influence, 47–50
employee involvement (EI) programs and, 110–13

Dunlop Commission, 4, 201

Dunlop, John, 4, 91

Economy, 9, 12–14, 105–6

Education factors, 52, 71, 98, 149, 206n4

EI. *See* Employee involvement (EI) programs

Employee committees, 54, 58, 91, 92, 93
See also Employee involvement (EI) programs; Joint organizations; Workplace committees

Employee involvement (EI) programs, 6, 27, 43
benefits to workers, 107–8, 112
economy and, 105–6
implementation, 106–7
influence and, 52, 110
job satisfaction and, 108–14
management cooperation and, 114–16
non-EI firms, 103, 104, 108–10, 113, 114
organizational preferences and, 148–50, 153
participants vs. nonparticipants, 103, 104, 108–10, 113, 114, 213n22
productivity and, 103–5
representation/participation gap and, 101, 110–13
suggestions of, 103, 104, 213n19
types of, 101–2
union support and, 83, 114, 115, 215n31
wage discussions and, 102, 107, 121
U.S. labor law limits on, 102, 107, 121
worker attitude and, 107–10, 113
workplace decisions and, 110–13
See also Influence, worker

Employees. *See* Workers
Employment-at-will doctrine, 120, 216n3
Employment Policy Foundation (EPF), 86,
   127–28, 208n
Endowment effect, 75–77
Europe, works councils, 53–54, 136
Exit option, 8, 11–12, 63–64
Expertise in labor relations, 14

Family Leave Act, 120
"Father knows best" objection, 9, 14
Firms, 9–10, 21
   arbitration systems, 135–36
   high-performance, 93–97
   lawsuits and, 123
   See also Employee involvement (EI) pro-
     grams; Management
Focus groups, 2, 17–20, 37, 100
   composition of, 18–20
   critical attitudes and, 40–41
   diversity of, 22–23
   group facilitator in, 18–19
   lack of knowledge in, 19–20
   occupation and, 19–20
   outcomes of, 20–24
   specific issues and problems, 23–24
   See also Workers
Follow-up survey. *See* Wave 2 follow-up survey
Fortune, 8, 10

General Motors, 66
Goals, 48, 112
Government agencies, 153–54
   assessing reforms, 121–22
   factors in complaint decision, 126–27,
     216–17n8, 217n12
   number of complaints, 122–24, 216nn5, 6
   satisfaction rate, 124–26
   workplace committees and, 136–39
   See also Labor laws; Legal protection
Grievance mechanisms, 53, 91, 92
Gross domestic product (GDP), 13
Group decision-making and problem solv-
   ing, 5, 53–56, 72, 113
Guttman scaling technique, 94, 95, 212n6

Harvard University, union of clerical and
   technical workers, 76

High-performance workplaces, 90–91, 93–97
Human-resource practices
   distribution of, 95–97
   effectiveness of, 93, 100
   and employee committees, 91, 92, 93
   and grievance mechanisms, 53, 91, 92
   groups and, 5, 53–56
   in high-performance workplaces, 90–91,
     93–97
   individuals and, 5, 53–56, 93, 100–101
   job satisfaction and, 97, 99
   and open-door policies, 91, 92, 100–101,
     213n17
   and personnel or human-resources de-
     partment, 91, 92
   prevalence of, 90–92
   and town meetings, 91, 92, 93
   unions and, 93, 98
   wages and, 91–92, 98, 211n3
   and worker characteristics, 97, 98

Income inequality, 13–14, 63
   See also Wages
Independence of worker organizations, 5,
   7, 56–60, 138, 142–43
   organizational preferences and, 146–49
Individuals
   human-resource practices and, 5, 53–56,
     93, 100–101
   influence and, 53–56, 72
Influence, worker, 12, 21, 40–43
   benefits of, 42, 48, 51
   collective vs. individual voice, 5, 53–56,
     72, 206–7n5
   differences in the influence gap, 51–53
   employee involvement (EI) programs
     and, 52, 110
   gap in, 51–53
   importance of, 50
   job satisfaction and, 45–48
   joint organization and, 58–59
   labor market and, 63–64
   less than desired, 63
   management cooperation and, 58–59
   management resistance to, 60–63
   productivity and, 103–5
   representation/participation gap, 4,
     47–51

unions and, 72, 78–82
See also Employee involvement (EI) programs
"It's the economy, stupid" objection, 9, 12–14

Job satisfaction, 43–44
employee involvement (EI) programs and, 108–13
human-resource practices and, 97, 99
influence and, 45–48
union support and, 77–82
Job security, 22–23, 35
Job tenure, 9–11, 204n9, 206n4
Joint organizations, 5, 7, 39, 58–59, 152, 153
See also Organizational preferences; Workplace committees

Knowledge workers, 22, 24

Labor laws
assessing reforms, 121–22
decline of unions and, 67–68
elections and, 87
employment-at-will doctrine, 120, 216n3
knowledge of
by management, 120–21
by workers, 19–20, 118–22
See also Government agencies; National Labor Relations Act; Workplace committees
Labor market, 15–16, 63–64
Least-skilled workers, 22–23, 24, 43–44
Legal protection, 5, 6, 118–22, 151–52
areas of, 130
demographics, 131–32
worker preference for, 129–32
Legislation, 39, 117, 215–16n1
Levi Strauss, 107
Living standards, 12–14
Loyalty, of worker to firm, 11, 45, 46, 108, 109, 207n8

Management
cooperative relations with, 5, 8, 34–35, 56–60, 115
distrust of, 21

and employees, cooperative and conflictual relationships, 63
influence of workers and, 42–43
misperceptions of labor law, 120–21
organizational preferences, 56, 57, 144–45, 218nn3, 4, 5
resistance of, 86–88
to worker independence, 5
to sharing power and authority, 60–63
trust of firm, 144–45
in union firms, 88
view of unions, 62, 81, 85–89, 211n17
worker ratings of, 21, 44–45, 60–62, 81–82, 148
WRPS involvement of, 3–4, 7–8, 25–30, 39, 77
See also Firms; Joint organizations; Management cooperation
Management cooperation, 5, 8, 34–35, 56–60, 141–42
arbitration and, 135
employee associations and, 58
employee involvement (EI) programs in, 114–16
workplace committees and, 138
Managerial workers, 29–30
loyalty to firm, 11
management resistance and, 62–63
organizational preferences, 56, 57
Methodology, 15–17, 25, 28, 30–31
Guttman scaling technique, 94, 95, 212n6
latent variables, 206n2
linear probability model, 72, 81–83, 208–9n6
normal distribution, 95–97, 212n8
Rasch scale, 95, 212n7
split-sample design, 28, 37, 40–42, 51, 129, 150, 216n2
summary statistics, 50, 207nn10, 11
summated rating, 51–53, 94–95
workplace choices and, 140–41
See also Worker Representation and Participation Survey
Motorola, 107

National Labor Relations Act (NLRA), 20, 66, 67, 87–88, 102, 121
Section 8(a)(2), 102, 121

National Labor Relations Board (NLRB), 68, 76, 86, 87, 123, 146, 216n8
Noncareer positions, 10–11
Nonmanagerial workers
  independence and, 59, 60
  organizational preferences, 56, 57, 59, 142
  supervisory activity by, 10, 105
Nonunion workers
  demographics, 71–72
  endowment effect and, 76
  human-resource practices and, 93
  influence and, 52
  lack of union support, 84–87
  organizational preferences, 153
  union support, 68–69, 76, 81–84
  See also Union workers

Occupational factors, 19–20, 52, 71, 149
Occupational Safety and Health Administration (OSHA), 22
OECD (Organization for Economic Cooperation and Development), 13
Omnibus survey, 33, 37
Open-door policies, 91, 92, 100–101, 213n17
Organizational preferences, 6–7, 21, 30, 31
  arbitration and, 142, 143, 144, 147–48
  company funding of, 145, 218n7
  consistency of choices of, 152–54
  demographic factors of, 148, 149
  desired attributes of, 141–43
  election of workers to, 142–43, 144
  employee involvement (EI) programs and, 148–50, 153
  labor-management relations and, 147–48
  management preferences and, 56, 57, 144–45
  nonmanagerial workers and, 56, 57, 59, 142
  nonunion workers and, 153
  rejection of any workplace organization, 143–44
  single option selection, 150–52
  union members and, 142, 143, 148, 149
  variation in, 145–50
  volunteer members in, 147
  See also Independence of worker organization; Joint organizations; Unions

Organization for Economic Cooperation and Development (OECD), 13
OSHA (Occupational Safety and Health Administration), 22

Poverty rates, 13–14
Princeton Survey Research Associates (PSRA), 17, 20, 32, 33, 128
Productivity, 103–6
Public-sector survey, 35–36, 37

Quality of Work Survey (1977), 79

Race factors, and workplace preferences, 52, 71, 83, 98, 149
Rasch scale, 95, 212n7
Representation/participation gap, 4, 21, 24, 47–53, 101, 110–13, 207n11
  differences in, 51–53
  employee involvement (EI) programs and, 101, 110–13
  See also Influence, worker

Safety considerations, 48, 112
Secretary of Labor's Task Force on Excellence in State and Local Government through Labor-Management Cooperation, 36
Section 8 (a)(2) (NLRA), 102, 121
Sex difference factors, and workplace preferences, 52, 71, 98, 149
Short-term contracts, 9–10
Specific issues and problems in the workplace, 23–24, 34
Split-sample design, 28, 37, 40–42, 51, 129, 216n2
Starbucks, and wage increase, 66
Summary statistics, 50, 207nn10, 11
Summated rating, 51–53, 94–95
Sun Tze (*Art of War*), 90, 211n1
Supervisory activity, 10, 105
Survey research firms, 17
Surveys
  context, 30–31
  design of, 30–31
  omnibus, 33, 37
  public-sector, 35–36, 37
  Quality of Work Survey (1977), 79

See also Wave 1 telephone survey; Wave 2 follow-up survey

"Take this job and shove it" objection, 8, 11–12, 63–64
Teamwork bills, 102
Technology, worker influence and, 48, 112
Telephone surveys. *See* Wave 1 telephone survey; Wave 2 follow-up survey
Terkel, Studs (*Working*), 15
Town meetings, 91, 92, 93
Training, 48, 51, 112
Trust, 21, 45, 46, 47, 82, 144–45, 207n8
    employee involvement (EI) programs and, 108, 109

Unions
    company, 102
    decline of, 1–2, 35, 66–68
    effectiveness of, 93
    employee involvement (EI) programs in, 83, 114–16, 215n31
    human-resource practices and, 93
    influence of workers and, 72, 78–81, 82
    management view of, 62, 81, 86–89, 211n17
    political candidates and, 78–79
    public-sector, 35–36, 208n4
    satisfaction with, 77–81
    WRPS involvement, 3–4, 25–29, 32–33
    See also organizational preferences
Union support, 6, 204n7
    current union status and, 70, 74–75
    demographic factors and, 71–72, 81, 83
    employee involvement (EI) programs and, 83, 114, 115
    endowment effect and, 75–77
    job satisfaction and, 82
    nonunion workers and, 68–69, 76, 81–84
    organizational preferences and, 56, 57, 59, 142, 153, 154
    sorting argument, 72–74
    workplace conditions and, 81–84, 210n12
    See also Organizational preferences
Union workers
    attitude toward union, 70, 74–75
    human-resource practices and, 98
    independence and, 143

influence and, 52
    organizational preferences, 142, 143, 148, 149
    See also Nonunion workers
United Automobile Workers (UAW), 66
U.S. labor law, and limits on wage discussion, 102, 107, 121
U.S. Society of Human Resource Management, 123

Voice. *See* Influence, worker

Wages
    employee involvement (EI) programs and, 102, 107, 121
    human-resource practices and, 91–92, 98, 211n3
    income inequality, 13–14, 63
    influence and, 48, 51, 52
    organizational preferences and, 149
    union support and, 71
Wave 1 telephone survey, 31–32, 37, 132, 159–82
Wave 2 follow-up survey, 2, 33–34, 37, 58, 100, 183–84
    arbitration materials, 133, 185–87
    questionnaire, 190–201
Worker-management relations, 21
    framework, 1–2
    open-door policies and, 100, 213n17
    organizational preferences and, 147–48
    union support and, 81–84, 210n12
    worker ratings of, 21, 44–45, 60–62, 81–82, 148
    See also Employee involvement (EI) programs; Influence, worker
Worker Representation and Participation Survey (WRPS)
    background, 2–4
    basic findings, 3–8
    British version, 36, 37
    Canadian survey, 35, 36, 37
    criticism of, 16–17
    final design of, 36–38
    and management and labor advisors, 3–4, 7–8, 25–30, 39, 77, 152–53
    omnibus survey, 33, 37
    public-sector survey, 35–36, 37

WRPS (*continued*)
    redesign of, 27–29
    representativeness of, 34–36
    scaling of variables in, 32–33
    student coding, 25
    union involvement, 3, 32–33, 39
    Web site, 204n5
    See also Focus groups; Methodology;
        Surveys; Wave 1 telephone survey;
        Wave 2 follow-up survey
Workers
    diversity of, 22–23
    importance of concerns of, 8–9
    institutions preferred by, 6–7
    and labor law, knowledge of, 19–20,
        118–22
    knowledge, 22, 24
    least-skilled, 22–23, 24, 43–44
    ratings of worker-management relations,
        21, 44–45, 60–62, 81–82, 148

See also Focus groups; Managerial work-
    ers; Nonmanagerial workers;
    Nonunion workers; Union worker
Working (Terkel), 15
Workplace characteristics
    legal protection and, 131–32
    organizational preferences and, 149
Workplace committees, 136–39
    features of, 138–39
    Wave 2 follow-up survey materials,
        187–89
    See also Employee committees
Work schedule, worker influence and, 48,
    51, 112
Works councils, 53–54, 136
Wright, Erik, 29
WRPS. *See* Worker Representation and
    Participation Survey

Xerox, 107